Endangered Animals

VOLUME 9

Skink, Pygmy Blue-Tongued – **Tragopan,** Temminck's

Published 2002 by Grolier Educational, Danbury, CT 06816

This edition published exclusively for the school and library market

Produced by Andromeda Oxford Limited
11–13 The Vineyard, Abingdon,
Oxon OX14 3PX, U.K.
www.andromeda.co.uk

Copyright © Andromeda Oxford Limited 2002

All rights reserved. No part of this publication may be reproduced, stored in a retrieval system, or transmitted in any form or by any means electronic, mechanical, photocopying, recording, or otherwise, without the permission of the copyright holder.

Principal Contributors: *Amy-Jane Beer, Andrew Campbell, Robert and Valerie Davies, John Dawes, Jonathan Elphick, Tim Halliday, Pat Morris. Further contributions by David Capper and John Woodward*

Project Director: *Graham Bateman*
Managing Editors: *Shaun Barrington, Jo Newson*
Editor: *Penelope Mathias*
Art Editor and Designer: *Steve McCurdy*
Cartographic Editor: *Tim Williams*
Editorial Assistant: *Marian Dreier*
Picture Manager: *Claire Turner*
Production: *Clive Sparling*
Indexers: *Indexing Specialists, Hove, East Sussex*

Reproduction by A. T. Color, Milan
Printing by H & Y Printing Ltd., Hong Kong

Set ISBN 0-7172-5584-0

Library of Congress Cataloging-in-Publication Data

Endangered animals.
    p. cm.
    Contents: v. 1. What is an endangered animal? -- v. 2. Addax - blackbuck -- v. 3. Boa, Jamaican - danio, barred -- v. 4. Darter, Watercress - frog, gastric brooding -- v. 5. Frog, green and golden bell - kestrel, lesser -- v. 6. Kestrel, Mauritius - Mulgara -- v. 7. Murrelet, Japanese - Pupfish, Devil's Hole -- v. 8. Pygmy-possum, mountain - Siskin, red -- v. 9. Skink, pygmy blue-tongued - tragopan, Temminck's -- v. 10. Tree-kangaroo, Goodfellow's - zebra, mountain.
    ISBN 0-7172-5584-0 (set : alk. paper) -- ISBN 0-7172-5585-9 (v. 1 : alk. paper) -- ISBN 0-7172-5586-7 (v. 2 : alk. paper) -- ISBN 0-7172-5587-5 (v. 3 : alk. paper) – ISBN 0-7172-5588-3 (v. 4 : alk. paper) -- ISBN 0-7172-5589-1 (v. 5 : alk. paper) – ISBN 0-7172-5590-5 (v. 6 : alk. paper) -- ISBN 0-7172-5591-3 (v. 7 : alk. paper) – ISBN 0-7172-5592-1 (v. 8 : alk. paper) -- ISBN 0-7172-5593-X (v. 9 : alk. paper) – ISBN 0-7172-5594-8 (v. 10 : alk. paper)
    1. Endangered species--Juvenile literature. [1. Endangered species.] I. Grolier Educational (Firm)

QL83 .E54 2001
333.95'42--dc21

Contents

Skink, Pygmy Blue-Tongued	4	**Sucker,** Razorback	38	**Toad,** Mallorcan Midwife	72
Sloth, Maned	6	**Sunfish,** Spring Pygmy	40	**Toad,** Natterjack	74
Snail, *Partula*	8	**Swallow,** Blue	42	**Toad,** Western	76
Snake, Eastern Indigo	10	**Swan,** Trumpeter	44	**Toadlet,** Corroboree	78
Snake, Leopard	12	**Tahr,** Nilgiri	46	**Toothcarp,** Valencia	80
Snake, San Francisco Garter	14	**Takahe**	48	**Tortoise,** Desert	82
Solenodon, Cuban	16	**Takin**	50	**Tortoise,** Egyptian	84
Souslik, European	18	**Tamarin,** Golden Lion	52	**Tortoise,** Galápagos Giant	86
Spatuletail, Marvelous	20	**Tanager,** Seven-Colored	54	**Tortoise,** Geometric	88
Spider, Great Raft	22	**Tapir,** Central American	56	**Tortoise,** Plowshare	90
Spider, Kauai Cave Wolf	24	**Tapir,** Malayan	58	**Totoaba**	92
Spoonbill, Black-Faced	26	**Tarantula,** Red-Kneed	60	**Tragopan,** Temminck's	94
Squirrel, Eurasian Red	28	**Teal,** Baikal	62	Glossary	96
Starling, Bali	30	**Tenrec,** Aquatic	64	Further Reading and Websites	99
Stilt, Black	32	**Thylacine**	66	List of Animals by Group	100
Stork, Greater Adjutant	34	**Tiger**	68	Set Index	102
Sturgeon, Common	36	**Toad,** Golden	70	Picture Credits and Acknowledgments	112

About This Set

Endangered Animals is a 10-volume set that highlights and explains the threats to animal species across the world. Habitat loss is one major threat; another is the introduction of species into areas where they do not normally live.

Examples of different animals facing a range of problems have been chosen to include all the major animal groups. Fish, reptiles, amphibians, and insects and invertebrates are included as well as mammals and birds. Some species may have very large populations, but they nevertheless face problems. Some are already extinct.

Volume 1—What Is an Endangered Animal?—explains how scientists classify animals, the reasons why they are endangered, and what conservationists are doing about it. Cross-references in the text (volume number followed by page number) show relevant pages in the set.

Volumes 2 to 10 contain individual species entries arranged in alphabetical order. Each entry is a double-page spread with a data panel summarizing key facts and a locator map showing its range.

Look for a particular species by its common name, listed in alphabetical order on the Contents page of each book. (Page references for both common and scientific names are in the full set index at the back of each book.) When you have found the species that interests you, you can find related entries by looking first in the data panel. If an animal listed under Related endangered species has an asterisk (*) next to its name, it has its own separate entry. You can also check the cross-references at the bottom of the left-hand page, which refer to entries in other volumes. (For example, "Finch, Gouldian **4:** 74" means that the two-page entry about the Gouldian finch starts on page 74 of Volume 4.) The cross-reference is usually made to an animal that is in the same genus or family as the species you are reading about; but a species may appear here because it is from the same part of the world or faces the same threats.

Each book ends with a glossary of terms, lists of useful publications and websites, and a full set index.

Skink, Pygmy Blue-Tongued

Tiliqua adelaidensis

The pygmy blue-tongued skink—once a common lizard—was presumed to be extinct, since there had been no sightings after 1959. In 1992, however, one was found inside the body of a dead snake. Surveys carried out in the surrounding region—the grasslands of South Australia's Mount Lofty Ranges—revealed a dozen small sites containing pygmy blue-tongued skinks.

Although less than half the size of the larger blue-tongued skinks familiar to many reptile keepers, the pygmy blue-tongued skink is otherwise similar in appearance. Its common name comes from the blue tongue displayed by most lizards of the genus *Tiliqua*. However, while the pygmy skink's mouth lining is pinkish-blue, its tongue is actually pink. The dramatic color combination provides a startling effect that deters attackers.

The lizard is found in the Mount Lofty Ranges north of Adelaide in South Australia. Unfortunately, the animal's preferred habitat is also highly suitable for farming. The climate is ideal, and the native grassland can be easily plowed. Pasture improvement—a process of replacing native plant species with agricultural species such as hay grasses and crops like alfalfa and clover—has further altered the plant diversity in favor of nonnative species.

Habitat Destruction

At the time when the lizards are most active—during the warm months—the soil is too hard for them to dig their own burrows. As a result, they often live in empty spider burrows dug by the spiders during the winter and early spring, when the soil is moist and soft. Plowing of the land is likely to be particularly destructive to the skink's survival, depriving them of shelter and leaving them exposed to snakes, birds, and other predators.

Before Europeans settled in South Australia, much of the area was native grassland supporting other reptile species, as well as birds and plants. Now only about 2 percent of the original grassland is left. All pygmy blue-tongued sites are found in the few unplowed areas. The undisturbed patches also support rare orchids and other plants, butterflies, and an endangered bird: the plains wanderer. Conserving the remaining grasslands will benefit the pygmy blue-tongues as well as the other rare fauna and flora.

Conservation Projects

The discovery of an extinct species was exciting, and various government bodies, museums, zoos, and universities cooperated in the search for new habitat sites. A recovery plan was devised; its first task was to study skinks in the wild and in captivity.

DATA PANEL

Pygmy blue-tongued skink
Tiliqua adelaidensis

Family: Scincidae (subfamily Lygosominae)

World population: About 5,500

Distribution: North Mount Lofty Ranges, southern South Australia

Habitat: Grassland with tussocks and open areas; open woodland

Size: Length: 7 in (18 cm); males often slightly smaller than females

Form: Heavy body with relatively short limbs; scales small and smooth. Male has larger head than female. Color varies from gray-brown to orange-brown with darker flecks along back

Diet: Insects and some plant material

Breeding: Gives birth to 1–4 live young per year

Related endangered species: No close relatives, but more than 40 other skink species are listed by IUCN

Status: IUCN EN; not listed by CITES

See also: Biomes 1: 18; Dragon, Southeastern Lined Earless 4: 38

A group of pygmy blue-tongued skinks was taken to Adelaide Zoo to be studied. Specimens were also displayed to increase public awareness of the lizard's plight. After seven years in captivity the colony had not bred. It was decided to set up another group in private, free from disturbance by the public. Little was known about the animal's behavior and requirements, but captive breeding for possible release into the wild was an important part of the recovery plan.

Pygmy blue-tongues are listed under the Endangered Species Protection Act and the South Australia National Parks and Wildlife Act. An important task has been to persuade landowners to protect known skink habitat sites on their land. There are also several laws that could be enforced to prevent habitat destruction. Law enforcement is perhaps the most important task, since the habitat is fragile and small in area. Recently owners of land enclosing three habitat sites signed a 10-year agreement to run their properties as wildlife sanctuaries. Other landowners are eager to sign up, but legal problems over grazing rights have caused some delay. Two previously unknown sites have also been discovered, although they are at some distance from the existing sites.

By early 2000 the situation for the pygmy blue-tongued skink had improved. An area of native grassland—unpopulated by the species but close to its other habitats—was made into a conservation park in the hope that it will be suitable for translocations. The park could be the first secure home for the animals.

The pygmy blue-tongued skink *has a heavy body with relatively short limbs and a fairly short tail, and its scales are small and smooth. Despite its name, the skink's tongue is, in fact, mainly pink.*

The total number of blue-tongues is difficult to estimate because of their patchy distribution, but it may be about 5,500. However, the figure is still too low to justify changing the lizard's Endangered status to Vulnerable. Although relatively few populations are unprotected now, the lizard will keep its status until larger populations exist in secure habitats.

One project to increase numbers involves the provision of artificial burrows. They are made from wooden tubes that are the same length and diameter as the favored spider hole, but less easily destroyed. Advising landowners on habitat management, such as weed clearance, grazing, and the use of pesticides, is also an important part of the program. Community involvement is a high priority, and a local school has been involved in studies as part of the plan. Despite such efforts, the outlook for the pygmy blue-tongued skink is by no means certain, since funds for wildlife conservation are limited.

Sloth, Maned

Bradypus torquatus

The leaf-eating maned sloth of Brazil depends on good-quality rain forest for its survival. Now that so much of its habitat has been destroyed, the animal is just about surviving in a few parks and protected areas.

The tree-dwelling sloths are legendary for their slowness. They cannot walk on the ground but must drag themselves along using their claws. Neither are they fast movers in the trees, where they cling to branches or hang upside down.

There are six species of sloth living in tropical America, including the three- and two-toed sloths. At one time the ground sloth's range extended into North America, but that species is now extinct.

Sloths are nocturnal, solitary creatures. Females give birth to a single young after a gestation period of about six months, and the baby clings to the mother's fur until it is about six weeks old.

Sloths feed almost entirely on leaves, which are difficult to digest in large quantities. In order to take advantage of what little nutritional value there is in their diet, the sloths have an enormous intestine and an extra stomach compartment containing bacteria that help break down the cellulose contained in the leaves. A meal of leaves may spend three or four weeks in the sloth's digestive system. There is little room for other body organs, and sloths have much less muscle than one would expect for an animal of such a size. A sloth's diet gives it the energy it needs with little to spare, and its body operates at a reduced metabolic rate—less than half that of other mammals of comparable size.

Masters of Disguise

Rapid movement may be out of the question for a sloth, but speed is not really necessary. Sloths do not have to chase prey; and although they are virtually incapable of defending themselves, predators rarely reach the lofty heights of the forest canopy.

Sloths do not make a lot of noise like some of their treetop neighbors; and even if a jaguar is tempted to climb high into the branches, sloths are well camouflaged. They have evolved a special adaptation to help them blend into the background. During the rainy season green algae grow in grooves that run along the length of each hair shaft, giving the sloth's fur a green tint.

Isolated Communities

The maned sloth is just as well adapted to its gentle, arboreal way of life as its more abundant cousins, so there is no natural reason why it should be more

DATA PANEL

Maned sloth

Bradypus torquatus

Family: Bradypodidae

World population: Unknown; perhaps only a few hundred

Distribution: Atlantic coastal regions of Brazil

Habitat: Rain forest

Size: Length: 17–20 in (45–50 cm). Weight: 7.7–9.4 lb (3.5–4.5 kg)

Form: Long-limbed animal with 3 toes on front and back feet; limbs used to hang from tree branches; fur brown and shaggy, darker on head and neck, often tinged with green all over; head small; rudimentary tail

Diet: Leaves of specific types of tree

Breeding: Single young born after 6-month gestation; fully weaned at 6 weeks; independent at 6 months; mature at 3 years. May live up to 12 years in the wild

Related endangered species: Linné's two-toed sloth (*Choloepus didactylus*) DD; Hoffmann's two-toed sloth (*C. hoffmanni*) DD

Status: IUCN EN; not listed by CITES

See also: Specialization 1: 28; Anteater, Giant 2: 24; Armadillo, Giant 2: 30

threatened with extinction than they are. However, it lives in the most heavily exploited rain forests in South America, where its tree habitat is being systematically cut down. Today the animals are restricted to a few patches of Brazilian coastal rain forest that have remained intact. Some patches are protected as nature reserves or national parks, but few are large enough to make secure homes for a healthy population of sloths. The maned sloth's inability to move around on the ground means that it cannot travel from one patch of forest to another. As a result, populations are increasingly isolated in small areas of forest that do not contain the variety of trees needed to support their diet.

Tree to Tree

It was once thought that the maned sloth spent its entire life in one tree. However, the animal usually moves from one tree to another every couple of days. It can cross from the branches of one tree to another directly or by inching its way along connecting liana vines. One sloth may regularly visit trees over an area of up to 16 acres (6.5 ha). They need a large range because each individual only eats the leaves of a particular type of tree—usually the hog plum or the trumpet tree. The preference seems to depend on which tree the mother and her offspring were in when the baby sloth took its first taste of leaves.

Maned sloths, *like other species of sloth, cling to tree branches or hang upside down. They are usually silent but can produce a shrill cry.*

Snail, Partula

Partula spp.

Snail species of the genus Partula *inhabit islands in the Pacific Ocean. In the absence of natural predators they have become well-adapted to their conditions. However, the snails have been unable to cope with predator snails introduced by people (ironically, to curb the effects of other snail pests). A rescue plan has now helped ensure the* Partula *snail's survival.*

Many people are familiar with the story of the Galápagos Islands in the Pacific Ocean; each of the islands in the remote archipelago (island group) has its own characteristic animal life adapted to the individual conditions. On other islands of the South Pacific a similar situation exists, this time for small, relatively inconspicuous snails of the genus *Partula*. The environmental conditions on each island are slightly different, and in the absence of most natural predators such as amphibians, reptiles, and mammals the snails have evolved to become well adapted to the conditions on their island. With the passage of time distinct species of *Partula* became established on the different islands. However, the snails were not adapted to cope with the changes to their habitat brought about by the activities of people.

Specialist Snails

Snails and slugs are gastropods, the largest group in the phylum Mollusca. They live in freshwater or marine habitats or on the ground. Terrestrial snails and slugs have evolved to breathe air and feed mostly on land plants. They are so successful as herbivores that they often come to our attention as agricultural or garden pests. Unlike other plant eaters, snails can release enzymes into their gut that are capable of digesting the cellulose in the cell walls of plants. Other herbivores, such as rabbits, cows, and sheep, have to use microscopic organisms to do this, and their intestines have adapted places to accommodate the microorganisms. *Partula* snails are terrestrial. They rely for their food on the rotting stems of hibiscus plants. Such a specialized diet makes them more vulnerable to threats than some other species.

DATA PANEL

Partula snail

Partula spp.

Family: Partulacea

World population: Unknown

Distribution: Islands of French Polynesia, Micronesia, and South Pacific Ocean

Habitat: Trees of natural rain forest

Size: Length: up to 1.2 in (3 cm)

Form: Small but typical snail. Most species have pointed shell; a few have rounded shells; 2 pairs of retractile tentacles, the rear pair bearing eyes

Diet: Rotting vegetation, especially hibiscus plants

Breeding: Hermaphrodites (both male and female sex organs are present) and livebearers: give birth to single, shelled young measuring 0.1 in (3 mm)

Related endangered species: About 15 species of *Partula* are extinct

Status: Seventy-nine *Partula* species are listed by the IUCN. Many are classified as Extinct, while some are classed as Critically Endangered; not listed by CITES

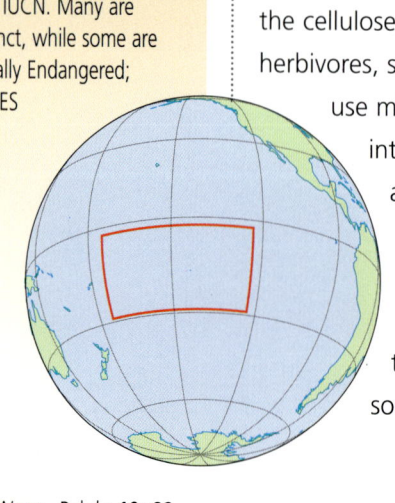

See also: Speciation **1:** 26; Introductions **1:** 54; Worm, Palolo **10:** 82

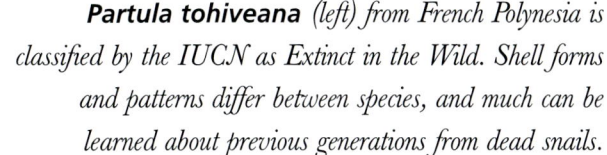

Partula tohiveana *(left) from French Polynesia is classified by the IUCN as Extinct in the Wild. Shell forms and patterns differ between species, and much can be learned about previous generations from dead snails.*

Partula snails are also slow breeding; each adult snail usually produces only one snail at a time. As a result, population growth can never be rapid, and this fact makes them vulnerable to increases in pressure from predators.

Introduced Predators

In the 1960s the giant African land snail was brought to some of the islands by farmers and bred to provide food. Immigrant snails escaped from the snail farms and quickly established themselves in the wild. Soon these populations were out of control. With no natural predators existing on the islands, the snail became a pest, devouring crops and other valuable plants.

In order to bring the giant African land snails under control, a second species of immigrant snail, this time the carnivore *Englandia rosea*, was brought to the islands to prey on it. However, instead of attacking the giant snails, it turned its attention on the native *Partula* snails. The results were devastating for the native snails, who were no match for the predators. In just 10 years many *Partula* snails were extinct.

A conservation program led by the London Zoo in Britain has done much to ensure the survival of some *Partula* snails in the region. By collecting some of the surviving snails and taking them back to London Zoo, the scientists have been able to raise snails in captivity. Now many of the snails bred in the zoo have been reintroduced to their native islands. Special reserves have been created where the snails can reestablish themselves free from competition and predators, and more are being planned.

A Success Story

Island habitats, with their limited but often unique local diversity, are ideal nurseries for new specialized species. However, as the story of the *Partula* snail shows, it can be dangerous to introduce foreign species, even those brought in for biological pest control. Zoos regularly make contributions to conservation programs, and relatively humble animals like snails can benefit from their expertise as much as the endangered birds and mammals that just catch the public imagination.

Snake, Eastern Indigo

Drymarchon corais couperi

The eastern indigo snake has long been a popular subject for research and has frequently been taken from the wild for the pet trade. Collection and habitat loss have brought numbers in the wild to a dangerously low level.

The eastern indigo snake was listed on the federal register as Endangered in 1978 when it became apparent that its numbers were dwindling in the wild. Its former distribution was southeastern Georgia, peninsular Florida and lower Keys, western Florida, and southern Alabama. Today it is largely restricted to Florida and possibly the coastal plains of Georgia.

The indigo eats a variety of small mammals, birds, frogs, and other snakes, including cottonmouths and rattlesnakes. It does not constrict its prey but seizes it in the mouth, presses it against the ground, and then swallows it whole.

When indigo snakes are cornered, they may hiss, flatten their necks vertically, and vibrate their tail tips to produce a rattling sound. However, they rarely bite when caught. Their relatively docile nature and attractive iridescent blue-black coloration make them popular as pets. Young specimens are especially amenable to handling and may become very tame.

Many areas of the indigo's original territory have been lost, fragmented, or otherwise degraded by urban development, forestry, and farming. Field studies using radio tracking have shown that indigo snakes need large areas of undeveloped land to thrive. In one study of indigo den sites, around three-quarters of those studied were sharing gopher tortoise burrows in sandhills. Other types of habitat used by indigos include the longleaf pine forest, much of which has been cut down. Pesticides, pet-collecting, and human ignorance have caused further decline. Road kills, which are sometimes deliberate, have also taken their toll on the snakes.

Indigo snakes are still kept and sold by private breeders, but possession and trade are controlled by a licensing system.

DATA PANEL

Eastern indigo snake

Drymarchon corais couperi

Family: Colubridae

World population: Unknown

Distribution: Now largely restricted to Florida

Habitat: Mainly upland, sandy, well-drained areas

Size: Length: about 8 ft (2.4 m)

Form: Black body with some red or orange-brown on the chin and sides of the head; young specimens have more red and light speckling on the body

Diet: Small mammals, birds, frogs, and other snakes, including cottonmouths and rattlesnakes

Breeding: One clutch of 8–9 eggs laid per year; incubated for 2 months

Related endangered species: None

Status: Not listed by IUCN; not listed by CITES

See also: Organizations 1: 10; Snake, San Francisco Garter 9: 14; Racer, Antiguan 8: 16

Transporting them across state lines without a permit is a punishable offense.

Ensuring a Future

Various conservation measures are being taken to ensure the snake's future. Captive breeding has been studied at Aubun University; protected sites have been designated, including a national wildlife refuge within the Kennedy Space Center. Fifty-six refuges were set up in Florida in 1999 to protect and improve the habitat. Other measures include law enforcement, population monitoring, nest site protection, and control of predators.

Captive propagation has been increased, but releasing or translocating indigos is difficult in view of their territorial instincts and their ability to travel long distances to return home. They are also known to fight over territory—another problem when releases are being considered in a limited area.

In 1998 the Wildlife Habitat Incentives Program was set up to restore wildlife habitat in upland areas frequented by indigo snakes. Under this plan the Natural Resources Conservation Service, various federal agencies, state and local bodies, and the private sector are pooling resources and expertise to develop the conservation of these areas. Information from a radio-tracking study in Brevard County, Florida, carried out by researchers from the Dynamac Corporation (Rockville, MD), is also helping develop a management strategy for this species.

The eastern indigo snake *is the largest nonvenomous snake in North America. Its glossy blue-black color and smooth scales distinguish it from other species.*

Snake, Leopard

Elaphe situla

The leopard snake is generally regarded as Europe's most attractive snake. Its coloration, pattern, small size, and docile nature have made it a target for private and commercial collectors, and its numbers have been further reduced by the loss of large areas of its habitat.

The genus *Elaphe* contains over 50 species, all of which are nonvenomous. Many of them are referred to as ratsnakes. Several species have been (and still are) popular vivarium subjects, frequently kept and commonly bred in captivity. Some of the familiar species are the cornsnake, Baird's ratsnake, Texas ratsnake, and yellow ratsnake. All are constrictors, preying mainly on small mammals and occasionally birds. The leopard snake, particularly when young, is said to favor lizards, although breeders have experienced no difficulty in feeding young mice to hatchlings.

Current distribution of the leopard snake is thought to be southern Italy, Yugoslavia, Bulgaria, Turkey, Sicily, Malta, and Greece, including some of the Greek islands. Its occurrence in the Crimea and the Caucasus is questionable—if it exists there, then it is very rare. Although apparently widespread, much of its habitat is fragmented, and it has evidently disappeared or its numbers have been reduced in many of its former locations.

Before being designated a protected species under the Berne Convention, leopard snakes regularly appeared on dealers' lists. Although once widely kept in Europe, their popularity has waned, possibly due to the availability of more exotic species and partly because of their reputation for not doing well in captivity. Captive-bred specimens are occasionally available, but their authenticity has to be proved if they are to be legally sold. Although collecting is less common today than it was, it almost certainly occurs in some areas.

The leopard snake's common name comes from the row of spots or rather blotches on its body. Coloration and pattern are variable, but there are two basic forms: spotted and striped, both on a brown to light-gray background. According to breeding accounts, both spotted and striped young can hatch from a clutch, irrespective of whether parents are striped or spotted. The young are particularly brightly colored, and unlike some *Elaphe* species, the pattern and colors are retained, apart from a slight fading, into adulthood.

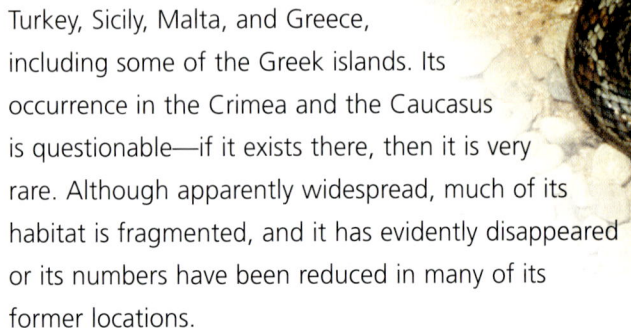

DATA PANEL

Leopard snake

Elaphe situla

Family: Colubridae

World population: Unknown

Distribution: Europe into Turkey

Habitat: Mainly dry, rocky areas and stone walls; human habitations

Size: Length: 30–35 in (75–88 cm)

Form: Two basic forms: spotted and striped. Background color varies from brown to light gray. The blotches or stripes are red to brown with a dark surround. The head typically has a dark bar between the eyes; there is another bar from each eye to the upper jaw on both sides of the head. An "arrowhead" mark of brown or red is present on top of the head. The dorsal blotches (on the back) are often in 2 rows, sometimes connected to form "saddles"

Diet: Small mammals, lizards, and birds, killed by constriction or suffocation

Breeding: One clutch of 3–5 eggs

Related endangered species: None

Status: IUCN DD; not listed by CITES

See also: Categories of Threat 1: 14; Tourism 1: 42; Snake, Eastern Indigo 9: 10; Viper, Milos 10: 30

Leopard snakes, *so called because of the spots on their back, often inhabit rocky areas.*

Leopard snakes are mainly diurnal ground-dwellers, occasionally climbing in bushes or on walls. They are susceptible to high temperatures, seeking shadier quarters in the summer heat. Mainly found below 1,600 feet (500 m), the snakes' habitat includes dry stone walls, rocky areas, and field edges. They can also be found close to human habitation, possibly attracted by the rodents there. In some parts of Greece they were encouraged in residential areas since they were thought to bring good luck and to reduce mouse and rat populations.

When disturbed, the leopard snake rapidly vibrates its tail tip. This is a bluff meant to scare attackers, and not a sign that it is venomous. The same display in rattlesnakes often precedes a poisonous strike.

Harmful Developments

Many of the countries inhabited by leopard snakes have traditionally had a high level of poverty, resulting in the rapid growth of industry to boost employment. Intensification of agriculture has also threatened the snake's survival with clearing of lowland forest and scrubland to make way for livestock and crops. Several of the countries have a pleasant Mediterranean climate, which attracts thousands of tourists every year. The construction of tourist facilities—including roads—has had a devastating impact on natural habitats. In addition, many people have an ingrained fear of snakes and cannot be convinced that they are harmless. In tourist areas leopard snakes, like other snakes and lizards, are often eradicated.

The leopard snake is listed by the IUCN as Data Deficient, which means that there is not enough information on numbers or distribution to assess its vulnerability. Certainly, populations are declining as its habitat is reduced in much of its former range. Further field studies on its distribution, population size, and ecology are needed, but financial and political considerations are likely to prevent or delay them. For a declining species its low reproductive rate is a disadvantage to recovery. Any captive-breeding programs are in the hands of private individuals, and as yet there is no organized recovery program.

Snake, San Francisco Garter

Thamnophis sirtalis tetrataenia

Often regarded as one of North America's most attractive snakes, the San Francisco garter snake is now increasingly rare. It was the first animal nominated for listing under the Federal Endangered Species Act, which became law in 1973. Despite legislation, numbers are still declining.

Owing to its attractive coloration, the San Francisco garter snake is highly prized by private collectors and the pet trade. Overcollection may have contributed to their declining numbers, and illegal collection still occurs in spite of prosecutions. However, the major threat is from habitat destruction.

San Francisco garters are nonvenomous and perfectly harmless to humans, although when caught, they release a foul-smelling secretion from their anal glands. Their prey is found in or near water; the snakes readily take to water to hunt or to escape potential predators. The red-legged frog is the main food, but habitat destruction has reduced numbers, which in turn has reduced snake populations. In recent times bullfrogs have been introduced into the area. Bullfrogs have voracious appetites, eating anything small enough to fit in their mouth, including frogs and young snakes.

Fragmented Habitat

Urban development in the San Francisco Peninsula has taken over much of the snake's former range. As towns expand, people are brought into contact with previously undisturbed countryside, resulting in destruction of vegetation and predation by rats, domestic dogs and cats. Water extraction, land drainage, and pollution from industrial effluent and domestic waste have also destroyed many of the marshlands and ponds that formerly supported garter snakes and red-legged frogs. Over the years grazing cattle have also altered the waterside vegetation, and much land has been taken for agriculture. As a result of such activities the San Francisco garter snake has been squeezed into several small, scattered areas in San Mateo County and the northern tip of Santa Cruz County. Four areas are designated reserves, but such habitats are still declining and fragmenting; a fifth population near San Francisco airport was threatened by construction work when the Bay Area Rapid Transport (BART) scheme

DATA PANEL

San Francisco garter snake

Thamnophis sirtalis tetrataenia

Family: Colubridae

World population: About 2,000

Distribution: Restricted areas on western half of San Francisco Peninsula

Habitat: Marshland; near ponds, ditches, and streams with nearby plant cover and open spaces for basking

Size: Length: up to 4.2 ft (1.3 m)

Form: Several color forms but similar basic pattern: wide dorsal stripe of greenish yellow edged with black; red stripe along each side of the body, followed by black stripe; top of head red, belly bluish green. Females have thicker bodies than males

Diet: Frogs, tadpoles, and occasionally fish; young snakes will eat earthworms and other small invertebrates

Breeding: Mating takes place in fall or spring; female gives birth to 12–24 live young in July or August

Related endangered species: Giant garter snake *(Thamnophis gigas)* VU; two-striped garter snake *(T. hammondi)* DD

Status: Not listed by IUCN; not listed by CITES; Endangered status under American federal law prevents trade

See also: Drainage and Irrigation **1:** 40; Snake, Eastern Indigo **9:** 10; Snake, Leopard **9:** 12

The San Francisco garter snake *has been popular with collectors because of its particularly colorful skin. It favors wetland vegetation but seeks open spaces for basking.*

began. Snakes from the construction site were taken to California State University in Hayward. Once the work is complete, the snakes will be released into the restored habitat, which is hoped to be as near normal as possible.

Conservation and the Future

In 1995 the U.S. Fish and Wildlife Service (USFWS) announced that only five of the 26 populations recorded in 1978 still remained. The Department of the Interior responded with a recovery plan for the snakes and their habitat. Under the plan six sites were to be made secure to allow snake populations to recover. On state-managed land the snakes are more secure than those inhabiting privately owned sites, where further development is a constant threat. However, there have been claims that little in the way of conservation has taken place, and that despite state and federal listing, habitat is still being destroyed.

Captive breeding would seem to be the answer to the snake's plight. Of the huge numbers of snakes collected in the past it is not known how many have survived and bred; few private keepers will admit to owning specimens since it is illegal to do so. A handful of American zoos and three in Europe have breeding groups, but inbreeding is giving rise to problems. A possible solution would be for wild-caught specimens to be introduced into the groups to produce greater genetic diversity, but at the moment such introductions are not allowed. The USFWS is said to be drawing up a comprehensive conservation plan for the San Francisco Bay National Wildlife Refuge Complex, its aim being to restore and protect wetland habitat. Despite such plans, the human population continues to expand, and more land is needed to accommodate greater numbers of people. It is estimated that each year 10,000 acres (4,000 ha) of wild habitat will be lost to urban and other development.

Solenodon, Cuban

Solenodon cubanus

The Cuban solenodon is a primitive animal. Always scarce, its numbers were drastically reduced by the activities of European settlers and exposure to new predators such as dogs.

Solenodons are ancient creatures. They resemble some of earth's earliest mammals, those that evolved millions of years ago. Their closest relatives are now mostly extinct, but the modern solenodon has managed to carve out an existence on the island of Cuba. A similar species is found on the neighboring island of Hispaniola (now divided between Haiti and the Dominican Republic). The Haitian species is also Endangered.

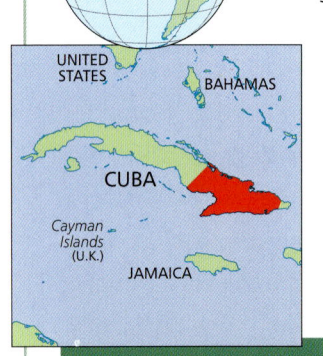

The animals are mainly nocturnal. They feed by rooting around in leaf litter and turning over stones and rotting wood with their long, probing snout. They extract grubs and worms by tearing open rotting wood with the sharp claws on their forefeet.

Solenodons live alone, passing the day in a den among logs or rocks. They particularly favor areas of coraline limestone where there are many nooks and crannies in which to hide. An added attraction are the snails and beetles that congregate in the rocks to avoid the hot, dry conditions in the open.

Like its relatives, the Cuban solenodon is a relatively slow-moving animal that seems to walk with a drunken stagger. Although it can climb well, it is not able to jump, so it is easy game for predators.

Habitat Invasion

Solenodons breed slowly, having only a few young at a time, with long intervals in between. As a result, solenodon populations are not able to withstand heavy losses. The main problem for the Cuban solenodon has been the colonization of its island home by European settlers. The settlers introduced cats and dogs, and later mongoose, to control rats in the sugar plantations. Such predators were previously absent from the island, so the species had evolved

DATA PANEL

Cuban solenodon

Solenodon cubanus

Family: Solenodontidae

World population: Unknown; probably low hundreds

Distribution: Eastern Cuba

Habitat: Dense, damp jungles; also thick scrub and around plantations

Size: Length head/body: 11–13 in (28–32 cm); tail: 7–10 in (17–25 cm). Weight: about 1.5–2.2 lb (0.7–1 kg)

Form: Resembles giant shrew with long, pointed snout and long, bare tail. Usually dark brown or blackish. Five toes on each foot; prominent claws on toes. Grooved lower incisor tooth carries toxic saliva to prey when bitten

Diet: Mainly insects and small animals (lizards and spiders for example); also plant material

Breeding: One or 2 young per litter; young stay with mother for several months (a long time for an insectivore). May live up to 6 years

Related endangered species: Haitian solenodon *(Solenodon paradoxus)* EN

Status: IUCN EN; not listed by CITES

See also: Introductions 1: 54; The History of Mammals 1: 60; Desman, Russian 4: 14; Gymnure, Hainan 5: 48; Tenrec, Aquatic 9: 64

SOLENODON, CUBAN

safely without them. Needless to say, the solenodons' small teeth were no match for a cat or large dog, and specimens were caught in large numbers by the new predators.

Moreover, all the islands in the Caribbean have been under pressure from development, involving clearance of huge areas of subtropical forest. Much forested land has been converted into farms and sugar plantations. Farming activity has deprived the solenodons of their main habitat and feeding places. In addition, the open terrain created by farmland makes solenodons more vulnerable to predation, since they have nowhere to hide. As a result, solenodons have become extremely rare. In fact, by the 1960s the Cuban species was believed to be extinct, since none had been reported since 1890.

Legal Protection

The plight of the solenodon was not as drastic as had been supposed, however. Surveys in the 1970s located some living specimens, and it was concluded that although the animals were rare, they were probably widely distributed in several parts of Oriente Province in eastern Cuba. Although Oriente Province takes up only a small part of the island, the human population is comparatively low, so the solenodon is less at risk from habitat disturbance and predation by domestic animals. Another advantage for the Cuban solenodon is that it is not considered to be of economic or medicinal importance. As a result, there has been little pressure on its numbers from activities such as hunting or trapping. In addition, humans do not eat solenodons, perhaps because of the distasteful smell that they secrete from glands in their skin. The Cuban solenodon has full legal protection. It is hoped that the species will benefit from protected areas in the highlands that have been specially set aside for the conservation of Cuban wildlife.

Solenodons *resemble giant shrews. However, despite their size, they are poorly equipped to defend themselves against introduced predators such as cats and dogs.*

Souslik, European

Spermophilus citellus

Sousliks live in colonies underground. Their extensive tunnel systems are vulnerable to destruction by the modern agricultural machines that are replacing horse-drawn plows in eastern Europe.

Sousliks are the European equivalent of American prairie dogs. Both are ground squirrels that live in underground tunnel systems. While prairie dogs live in social groups called coteries that make up "towns" of interconnected burrows, sousliks live singly within colonies. Each animal has a separate burrow, usually with at least two entrances, but the burrows are close together and cover large areas of ground. The best souslik habitat has short, grassy turf growing over a deep, lime-rich soil that is easy to excavate. In some parts of Yugoslavia, where the habitat is particularly suitable, souslik colonies support up to 20 animals per acre (48 per ha.)

Like prairie dogs, European sousliks sit upright at their burrow entrances, keeping watch for threats to their colony, especially from birds of prey cruising overhead. If danger is spotted, a souslik will let out a loud whistle to warn its neighbors. Foxes, cats, and dogs are also a threat, but rarely get close without being detected.

Sousliks like to eat fresh green vegetation, but they also pick up seeds and insects. They are normally active in the day and are vulnerable to predators out on the short grassland where they live. To reduce the dangers of feeding at the surface, they gather food quickly above ground and stuff it into their cheek pouches. They then scurry into their burrows to eat their meal in safety. Often the food is stowed away in special underground chambers.

Once the breeding season is over, usually by late June, the sousliks begin to build up their nutritional

DATA PANEL

European souslik (European ground squirrel)

Spermophilus citellus

Family: Sciuridae

World population: Unknown, but probably many thousands

Distribution: Southeastern Europe from Hungary to the Black Sea coast

Habitat: Open plains, fields, meadows up to 6,500 ft (2,200 m)

Size: Length head/body: 7.5–8.5 in (19–22 cm); tail: 2–3 in (5.5–7.5 cm). Weight: 8.4–10 oz (240–340 g)

Form: Squirrel with mottled brown fur, short tail, large eyes, and small ears

Diet: Fresh plant material gathered above ground; also seeds, insects, and roots

Breeding: One litter of 5–8 young per year, born April–June after gestation period of 3–6 weeks. Life span up to about 5 years

Related endangered species: Idaho ground squirrel *(Spermophilus brunneus)* EN; Mohave ground squirrel *(S. mohavensis)* VU; European spotted souslik *(S. suslicus)* VU; Washington ground squirrel *(S. washingtoni)* VU

Status: IUCN VU; not listed by CITES

See also: Climate Change 1: 53; Mole-Rat, Balkans 6: 82; Prairie Dog, Black-Tailed 7: 92

reserves for winter. Large amounts of fat accumulate under the skin and around the intestines. The fat provides a store of energy to keep the animal alive while it is dormant. They start to hibernate in October, remaining cold and inactive underground until March. Hibernation enables them to escape the intense cold of continental winters and also helps them avoid the problem of seasonal food shortages as the plants die back during the winter months. Yet it also makes the animals vulnerable, since any form of disturbance can cause them to wake up. Emergence from torpor consumes energy reserves at about 10 times the rate used when staying in hibernation. Animals that are unable to fatten up sufficiently before hibernation and are woken in midwinter may end up starving to death.

Threats from Modern Farming

Sousliks are facing a problem like that confronting prairie dogs and mole-rats: changing farming methods. The switch from horse-drawn plows to tractors in eastern Europe has had a significant impact on the species. It has reduced the need for horses, so there is now much less land set aside on farms for grazing. Grass that would once have been cropped by the horses is left to grow tall and is cut for hay. Tall grass is an unsuitable habitat for sousliks.

Worse still, much former grazing land is now being plowed and used for growing arable crops, again an unsuitable environment for the animals. While the traditional horse-drawn plows only scraped the surface of the soil, powerful modern tractors pull implements that dig deep into the earth over extensive areas, destroying souslik colonies in the subsoil—a particular danger if cultivation takes place in early spring, while the animals are still hibernating. Heavy tractors also crush the burrows.

Already sousliks have become extinct in many parts of the central European plain, especially in Germany and southern Poland. As the agricultural nations of eastern Europe join the European Union, and benefit from increased prosperity and investment in more efficient farming methods, the sousliks will be driven out of more of their strongholds.

The European souslik *spends much of its time sitting upright on its haunches and keeping watch for predators such as foxes and birds of prey. Sousliks generally have large eyes and sharp eyesight.*

Spatuletail, Marvelous

Loddigesia mirabilis

One of the most stunning of all hummingbirds, the marvelous spatuletail has recently been recorded at only two sites in the Peruvian Andes, where it is threatened by habitat destruction and hunting.

Many members of the large hummingbird family have names inspired by their beauty: Examples include the purple-crowned woodnymph, the shining sunbeam, the peacock coquette, and the royal sunangel. The spatuletail is no exception; the word "marvelous" in its title does no more than justice to the male's tail, one of the most extraordinary of any bird species. Unlike all other hummingbirds, which have 10 feathers in their tails, the spatuletail has only four, and the outer two are rudimentary. The other two—actually not part of the tail proper but rather modified tail coverts—are long and pointed, and they support a pair of bare, wirelike, elongated central tail feathers that curve back behind the body to cross one another. Each of these "wires" is tipped with a "racket," the whole suggesting the shape of a flexible, whiplike spatula. These remarkable appendages make up about three-quarters of the bird's overall length; the needlelike bill takes up another 0.5 inches (1.3 cm). In contrast, the tiny head and body are only about 1.1 inches (2.7 cm) long.

As in the case of many rare bird species with limited ranges in little-visited parts of the world, much remains to be learned about the spatuletail. It is restricted to the eastern slopes of the Utcubamba River valley in the Cordillera del Colán mountain range in northern Peru's Amazonas province. In the past three separate populations were known to exist within a 60-mile (100-km) stretch of the region; one lived in the Chachapoyas area, another to the north and east of Leimebamba, and the third around the village of Florida. In recent years, however, the bird has only been seen around Florida, the sole exception being a single sighting some way to the east that was reported in 1987.

Since it was first described scientifically in 1847, the marvelous spatuletail seems always to have been uncommon. There have been only a small number of sightings in recent years, and very few of them have been of the magnificent adult males. The surviving population at Florida appears to be dwindling.

The marvelous spatuletail is a shrubland-dweller, usually living at altitudes between 6,900 and 9,500 feet (2,100 and 2,900 m). It has been seen in open country, at forest

DATA PANEL

Marvelous spatuletail

Loddigesia mirabilis

Family: Trochilidae

World population: Estimated at 250–1,000 birds

Distribution: Only 2 locations on the eastern slopes of the Andes in northern Peru

Habitat: Edge of primary rain forest, second-growth forest, and scrub on valley slopes

Size: Length: male 6–7 in (15–17 cm), of which 4–5 in (11–13 cm) is taken up by tail; female 4 in (10 cm), including tail of 2.5 in (6 cm). Weight: about 0.1 oz (3 g)

Form: Tiny bird with an extraordinary tail in male; 2 elongated coverts support very long outer feathers that end in large, rounded, purplish-black "rackets." Female has much less blue on crown than male or none; white underparts lack black band; tail much shorter, with small drop-shaped rackets

Diet: Mainly nectar from flowering plants

Breeding: Probably late October to early May

Related endangered species: Twenty-eight other hummingbird species are threatened, including the Juan Fernández firecrown (*Sephanoides fernandensis*)* CR; black-breasted puffleg (*Eriocnemis nigrivestis*) CR; Bogotá sunangel (*Heliangelus zusii*) CR; royal sunangel (*H. regalis*) EN. black inca (*Coeligena prunellei*) EN. In addition, 2 species of the Bahamas are extinct

Status: IUCN EN; CITES II

See also: CITES 1: 12; Firecrown, Juan Fernández 4: 78; Hummingbird, Bee 5: 62

The marvelous spatuletail owes its name to its extraordinary tail appendages, which play an important part in the males' courtship rituals.

edges, among areas of mountain scrub, and especially in isolated alder-tree woodlots containing impenetrable, thorny thickets of *Rubus*. Here the birds feed on nectar from at least five species of flowering plants, including *Rubus* itself, although the preferred species seems to be a red-flowered lily called *Alstroemeria formosissima*.

During the breeding season mature males gather together at special communal display sites (leks), where they show off their amazing tails in a bid to impress watching females. Observers have noticed that even at these gatherings males are outnumbered greatly by females and immature males.

Continuing Threats

Like all too many birds of the tropical forest, the spatuletail is threatened by habitat destruction. Over the past 20 years or so much of the forest and shrubland on the mountain slopes of the Cordillera del Colán has been destroyed or degraded by local people, mainly because of the demand for firewood, the spread of slash-and-burn agriculture, and the damage caused by grazing cattle.

The habitat that remains still faces the threat of being cleared for the planting of cash crops such as coffee and marijuana. With luck such clearance need not mean the end for the hummingbirds. They seem to prefer living along the forest edge and among isolated woodlots on steep slopes, so they may not suffer as much as is feared.

Another problem is that the birds are sometimes killed for human consumption. Only the males are hunted—with slingshots—and only for their hearts, which are sought after for their supposed aphrodisiac qualities. Mortality from this practice may even be the cause of the puzzlingly skewed sex ratio in the species. In the past hummingbirds used also to be hunted to supply collectors with skins and stuffed specimens, but it is not clear how many spatuletails were accounted for in this way.

The spatuletail is listed in CITES Appendix II, but otherwise receives no other legal protection. Conservationists have now set themselves urgent targets with a view to saving the bird. Priority tasks include conducting surveys to find possible new sites where the birds could live; estimating the size of the known Florida population; involving local people in an attempt to reduce or prevent hunting; and protecting the birds' habitat from further degradation.

Spider, Great Raft

Dolomedes plantarius

Increasing demand for water to sustain expanding populations has made the great raft spider one of Europe's most threatened invertebrate species. Land-reclamation projects have also damaged its habitats by changing the drainage of wetland soils.

The great raft spider is brown or black in color, and strikingly marked with cream or white stripes. It is one of Europe's larger spiders: Its body is nearly 1 inch (2.5 cm) in length, and the span of its furry legs would almost cover the palm of an adult's hand.

The great raft spider is so named because of the way it climbs onto a plant stem and leans over the water to rest its front legs on the surface. By doing this, it is able to detect vibrations generated in the water by prey such as small pondskaters or very small fish. The hairy surface of the spider's body is water repellent, so it does not get wet.

The great raft spider has the characteristic body form of spiders. It is made up of a joined head and thorax (prosoma, or cephalothorax) and abdomen (opisthosoma). The first pair of appendages on the prosoma bears the chelicerae: pincerlike mouthparts or fangs that end in sharp, hollow spikes. They are used to stab prey, subduing it by injecting it with venom.

Wetland Destruction

The main problem for the great raft spider is destruction of its wetland habitat. In the past farmers used to keep the ground fairly clear and in so doing encouraged the growth of smaller plants. The practice was in keeping with the needs of a rural economy. Sedges and reeds, which grew naturally in wetland habitats, were of economic importance and were cut down for use in making thatched roofs. Grass was cut for hay for feeding cattle during the winter.

Below the surface of the soil vegetable matter decomposing in the water formed layers of peat. Peat contains a lot of carbon and is useful for fuel if it is dug out and dried. Digging peat for fuel created many small flooded peat pools that provided habitats for a variety of aquatic plants and animals and hunting grounds for the great raft spider. Keeping the trees under control by cutting them down for brushwood (branches and twigs) for fires also helped keep the ground clear.

Today many of these rural practices have changed. In addition, more wetland is being reclaimed for

DATA PANEL

Great raft spider

Dolomedes plantarius

Family: Asauridae

World population: Unknown

Distribution: Northern Europe

Habitat: Wetlands with peat soil

Size: Length (body): up to 1 in (2.5 cm); leg span: up to 3.1 in (8 cm)

Form: Typical spider with 8 legs and 2 main body parts: prosoma, or cephalothorax (joined head and thorax) and pisthosoma (abdomen); 8 eyes; 2 chelicerae (segmented, pincerlike mouthparts) at front of prosoma, ending in fangs connected to venom gland. Spinnarets (fingerlike structures at rear end of opisthosoma) produce silk for webs

Diet: Aquatic insects and very small fish

Breeding: Female lays eggs after mating with male; spiderlings emerge

Related endangered species: No close relatives, but IUCN lists 6 other species in Araneae order as Vulnerable and 6 as Data Deficient, plus the Kauai Cave wolf spider (*Adelocosa anops*)* as Endangered

Status: IUCN VU; not listed by CITES

See also: Drainage and Irrigation **1:** 40; Spider, Kauai Cave Wolf **9:** 24; Tarantula, Red-Kneed **9:** 60

human use, including the channeling of water to service new developments. The extraction of water for human use from underground aquifers (deposits or rocks such as sandstone containing water) has depleted the supply to the surface. Many of the pools that the spider depended on have also dried up.

Land reclamation projects encourage the growth of more dense vegetation, obliterating the spider's preferred habitat and placing even more pressure on water supplies. However, some of the spider's last refuges have been saved and the damage reversed because commercial water companies need to hold millions of gallons of water in reserve. What was left of the former wetland areas turned out to be suitable

A great raft spider *straddles small pieces of floating vegetation as it rests its front walking legs on the water's surface while trying to detect movements of prey.*

for large-scale water storage. At the same time, the water companies were able to help conserve the great raft spider by protecting its habitat. Such activities, together with the efforts of volunteers, have now had a beneficial effect on great raft spider populations. By removing peat and creating irrigation networks, volunteers have been able to ensure the return of water to the spiders' breeding pools. Water plants such as sedges have become reestablished in the pools, often surviving well on the poor soil.

Spider, Kauai Cave Wolf

Adelocosa anops

The Kauai cave wolf spider is both rare and unusual. Found only in three caves on Kauai Island, Hawaii, the species is blind—unlike other wolf spiders that are known to hunt using their keen eyesight. Endangered from habitat degradation, it is also thought to be at risk from the pesticide residues seeping into its cave dwelling.

Wolf spiders get their name from their habits as hunters. They are swift runners; instead of snaring their victims in silken webs like most other spiders, they rely on speed to chase their prey and run it down, although they may use silk to set up ambushes or "trip wires." They stalk their prey, watching every movement. Once it is trapped, they bite the victim and inject poison through their fang-tipped chelicerae—the first pair of head appendages, which look like miniature elephant tusks when seen through a lens. The venom paralyzes the prey and also digests its tissues, reducing it to a liquid, which the spider can suck out and swallow through its small mouth; they feed particularly on insects such as beetles and ants. There are many species of wolf spider: over 100 in North America and about 50 in Europe. The best-known wolf spider is probably the Mediterranean tarantula. The wolf spider's enemies are wasps, birds, and people. The spiders occur on all continents apart from Antarctica and on many islands, too: Spiders are often among the leading colonizers of volcanic islands.

Wolf spiders are not large and rarely exceed 1 inch (2.5 cm) in length. Their bodies are covered in short hair or bristles, and in the main they are brown or drab in color. As well as the fangs, the head carries a pair of pedipalps (small leglike appendages located in front of the first pair of long walking legs) and (usually) eyes arranged in three rows.

Usually a favorite habitat is leaf litter on forest floors. The spiders excavate shallow burrows and line them with silk spun by the spinnerets on the abdomen. In some species the burrow has a projecting silk entrance tube. The Kauai cave wolf spider, however, is an exception among wolf spiders. It is restricted in its distribution, being found only at three underground locations on the island of Kauai. The caves in which it lives were formed by ancient volcanic lava flows.

Eyes Wide Shut

Although the eyes of most wolf spiders are fairly simple (they have four large and four small eyes), they generally have

DATA PANEL

Kauai cave wolf spider

Adelocosa anops

Family: Lycosidae

World population: Unknown. Surveys of the 3 remaining populations could only find 30 members of each at any one time

Distribution: Kauai Island, Hawaii

Habitat: Dark, moist areas of Kauai cave system, formed from a lava flow and covering about 4 square miles (10 sq. km). About 75% of former habitat has been lost to human activity

Size: Length: 0.5–0.7 in (1.3–1.9 cm); legs: 1 in (2.5 cm)

Form: Head lacks eyes. Reddish-brown carapace (hard, outer covering); pale abdomen and bright-orange legs. Back part of chelicera (pair of fang-tipped appendages on head) has 3 large teeth

Diet: Small, cave-dwelling crustaceans

Breeding: Female lays up to 30 eggs after mating with male. Spiderlings hatch and ride on their mother's back

Related endangered species: Glacier Bay wolf spider (*Pardosa diuturna*) VU; Lake Placid funnel wolf spider (*Sosippus placidus*) VU; rosemary wolf spider (*Lycosa ericeticola*) DD

Status: IUCN EN; not listed by CITES

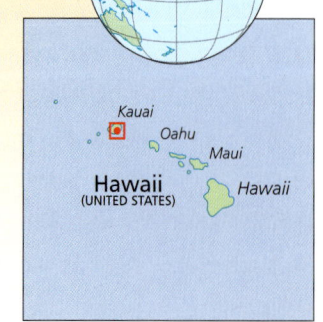

See also: Organizations **1:** 10; Habitat Loss **1:** 38; Spider, Great Raft **9:** 22

Kauai cave wolf spiders *have no eyes (below). More common wolf spiders (right) rely on sight for hunting and courtship rituals. (The male spider on the right is presenting the female with a gift.)*

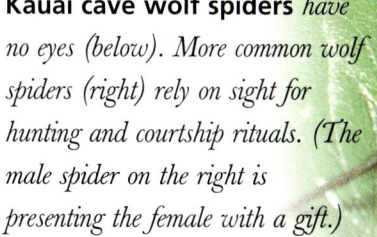

good eyesight. This is important, since many hunt in poor light conditions. The Kauai cave wolf spider, like many cave-dwelling species, is blind. More unusually, it is eyeless—many cave dwellers cannot see but have vestigial eyes. This makes the species unique. It almost certainly detects the presence of potential prey by touch and smell, and is able to stalk its prey by following their scent trails. Hunting has not been observed, but this species probably feeds primarily on the Kauai cave amphipod, a type of crustacean that is also Endangered. Other species of arthropod that enter the caves from time to time may serve as food for the Kauai cave wolf spider.

Eyesight is usually an important tool in courtship and mating behavior for wolf spiders. How the Kauai cave wolf spider copes is unknown. After mating, the female Kauai cave wolf spider lays eggs—up to 30 at a time. They are laid in a round or oval silk cocoon made by the mother. She fastens it to the tip of her abdomen and carries it everywhere with her until the spiderlings hatch. The young climb onto the mother's back and are carried by her until they are old enough to fend for themselves.

At Risk

As a result of its restricted distribution, the Kauai cave wolf spider is highly endangered. Habitat destruction has occurred through soil filling, quarrying, and other activities associated with development and agriculture. The seepage of pesticide residues into the caves is also thought to be a source of risk. In the delicately balanced environment such problems also affect the Kauai cave amphipod, the spider's main prey. The amphipod feeds on rotting tree roots that work their way into the cave system. If the roots dry out or do not enter the cave, both species are affected.

The Kauai cave wolf spider was added to the IUCN Red List in January 2000. Of the 15 spider species considered to be at risk, six are cave spiders: The tooth cave spider of Texas, for example, was listed as Endangered under the United States Endangered Species Act in 1988. It is the limitation of their habitat that makes wolf spiders especially threatened.

Spoonbill, Black-Faced

Platalea minor

Facing an array of threats ranging from human impact on its environment to direct persecution, the black-faced spoonbill—an already rare bird—will suffer further declines unless urgent action is taken.

The black-faced spoonbill is the least known and rarest of the world's six species of spoonbill. It was once apparently common over much of its range along the coasts of eastern Asia. Today it is reduced to a small breeding population in the Far East.

Until recently its only known breeding grounds were on four small, rocky islets off the west coast of the Korean peninsula. In June 1999 a Chinese professor visited the Changshan Islands in Korea Bay, northeastern China. There he saw three pairs of black-faced spoonbills. On a return visit he found a nest containing three chicks. Eggs from two other nests had been taken by fishermen, but the birds were incubating second broods.

Although the other spoonbills are well researched, ornithologists know very little about the black-faced spoonbill's precise ecology. It is known to roost communally and, if prey is abundant enough, to feed in small flocks—up to 25 birds have been recorded feeding together during winter in Hong Kong.

The spoonbill's feeding behavior is distinctive. Wading into the shallows with the long spatulate bill partly open, the bird holds it almost vertically in the water or fine silt and sweeps it from side to side. It locates prey with the help of touch receptors in the tip of the bill; it snaps up small fish, aquatic insects and their larvae, crustaceans, and other small animals.

Breeding Sites

Black-faced spoonbills are migratory. In the fall, after rearing their young, the birds leave the breeding grounds (in temperate regions) to fly to subtropical parts of Asia for winter. Satellite tracking has shown that birds wintering in Hong Kong and Taiwan migrate along China's east coast, then cross the Yellow Sea to the Korean peninsula. Tracking has also identified several important stopover sites in China.

In 1999 seven of 12 birds fitted with transmitters at two different wintering sites (one in Hong Kong, one in Taiwan) returned to islets off the Korean coast. This demonstrated the importance of the main breeding sites for the survival of the species.

DATA PANEL

Black-faced spoonbill (lesser spoonbill)

Platalea minor

Family: Threskiornithidae

World population: About 700 birds

Distribution: Breeds on islets off west coasts of North and South Korea and on one of the Changshan Islands off the coast of southeastern Liaoning Province, China. Winters as far away as Japan, the Philippines, and Russia, but mainly on Tsengwen estuary, Taiwan, Inner Deep Bay, Hong Kong, China, and Red River delta, Vietnam

Habitat: Breeds on offshore islets; migrates south to winter on marshes, mangroves, flooded rice fields, fish ponds, tidal mudflats, and estuaries

Size: Length: 23.5–31 in (60–78.5 cm)

Form: Medium-sized waterbird with spatula-shaped, black-tipped gray bill; long black legs. Plumage white with area of bare black skin on face and throat; yellowish band from base of neck and longer crest on nape in breeding adults; immatures similar to nonbreeding adults but with pinkish-gray bill and darker wingtip feathers

Diet: Mainly fish and aquatic mollusks; also insects and crustaceans, including shrimps and crabs

Breeding: Breeds in small colonies of 2–3 pairs; both sexes build nest of twigs on cliff ledge; 4–6 eggs laid

Related endangered species: Nine species of ibis in the family Threskiornithidae, including the northern bald ibis (*Geronticus eremita*)* CR and crested ibis (*Nipponia nippon*) EN

Status: IUCN EN; not listed by CITES

See also: Pollution 1: 50; Ibis, Northern Bald 5: 72

Although birds have been seen at the Tumen estuary in Russia, there is no evidence that they breed there.

Four of the breeding islets in North Korea are protected as seabird sanctuaries, as are a number of wintering sites in Hong Kong, Vietnam, and Japan. The species is legally protected in China (including Hong Kong), North Korea, South Korea, and Japan.

Threatened by Industry

Despite such protection, the black-faced spoonbill faces a variety of threats, the most important being habitat destruction. The chief wintering grounds face the threat of land reclamation, particularly in China—where the booming economy has resulted in many coastal wetlands being converted to industrial sites and fish-farming ponds—and also in South Korea and Japan. Other key sites could soon be lost to industrial developments in China and on the island of Taiwan.

In the south of Taiwan developers want to build a huge industrial project (including a steel-making facility, petrochemical plant, and harbor) next to the spoonbill's main wintering site at the Chiku lagoons. If this goes ahead, it would deal a severe blow to the

The black-faced spoonbill, *in common with all species of spoonbills, has a remarkable bill. It is long and flattened, expanding to a spatula-shaped tip.*

species' chances of survival, since the harbor is likely to encroach onto the lagoons, and pollution from the complex could wipe out the fish stocks that provide the bird's main food resource. Pollution is also a problem for spoonbills wintering in Hong Kong. Other threats faced by the birds are increased levels of disturbance and hunting in China and Vietnam.

Recommendations for saving the species have been drawn up by conservationists. They include a plan to survey coastal wetlands in China for unknown wintering sites. Another suggested measure is to improve the protection of known wintering sites (especially on Taiwan) and the new Chinese breeding sites. Assessing the population is difficult. Although there have been apparent increases, they may be due to increased coverage by birdwatchers or displacement of birds from other already degraded sites.

Squirrel, Eurasian Red

Sciurus vulgaris

Red squirrels are common across Europe, but are rapidly being replaced by American gray squirrels in Britain. Such a fate may also overtake their continental cousins.

Only 100 years ago the red squirrel was common and the only squirrel in Britain and across continental Europe. Now it is extinct in southern England, except on three islands off the coast. It is still found in Scotland and remains widespread in northern England, although its numbers there are declining fast. Apart from these areas, it survives in a few scattered localities in Wales and eastern and central England. In its place has come the American gray squirrel, introduced to Britain between 1876 and 1929. The American gray has proved a highly successful invader, becoming the squirrel commonly seen in most British woodlands, parks, and gardens.

Many people blame the grays for attacking and driving out the native red squirrel or for passing on fatal diseases. In fact, there is no evidence that it is guilty of either of these crimes, although one natural disease that kills red squirrels does not affect grays. The main problem seems to be that while the European red squirrel is satisfactorily adapted to life in coniferous woodlands, it is simply less well equipped than the gray to survive in deciduous forests.

Gray squirrels originated in the hardwood forests of North America and are at home in similar woodland areas of lowland Britain. While the reds can survive in deciduous forests on their own, they are at a disadvantage in such environments when they face competition from the grays. The result is that once the grays spread into an area, the reds disappear within about 15 years. Attempts to reintroduce them back into the areas from which they disappeared have not been successful.

A Question of Adaptation

One major problem is that red squirrels cannot digest acorns properly. Acorns are the main food available in the fall in most lowland forests. Grays thrive on them, and they also compete for hazelnuts, the reds' favorite food in deciduous woodland. Since gray squirrels normally live at double the population densities of reds, they eat at least twice as many nuts, leaving the latter with insufficient food resources. Eurasian red squirrels feed mainly in the treetops, so they cannot afford to store much fat for the winter without running the risk of becoming clumsy

DATA PANEL

Eurasian red squirrel (European red squirrel)

Sciurus vulgaris

Family: Sciuridae

World population: Probably at least 2 million spread over a huge area

Distribution: Europe and Asia, from Britain east to China and northern Japan

Habitat: Forest, especially coniferous forest

Size: Length head/body: 7–10 in (18–24 cm); tail: 5–8 in (14–20 cm). Weight: 9–12 oz (250–350 g)

Form: Bright chestnut red in summer, darker in winter; large bushy tail and (in winter) prominent ear tufts

Diet: Pine seeds, nuts, fruit, and fungi; occasionally insects and birds' eggs

Breeding: Usually 3 (but up to 8) young per litter; 1 or sometimes 2 litters per year after a gestation period of 5–6 weeks. Life span up to 7 years in the wild, but many die young; 10 years in captivity

Related endangered species: Some local populations and subspecies of squirrels and chipmunks in the U.S. are Critically Endangered, Endangered, or Vulnerable, but (as with the Eurasian red squirrel) whole species are not at risk

Status: IUCN LRnt (except in Britain where it is classified as EN); not listed by CITES

See also: Introductions **1:** 54; Rat, Black (see text on moral dilemmas) **8:** 24; Souslik, European **9:** 18

SQUIRREL, EURASIAN RED

The Eurasian red squirrel *spends much of its time foraging in trees; it comes down to the ground occasionally to bury nuts.*

climbers. Grays, on the other hand, forage more on the ground and so can accumulate larger fat reserves because agility in the treetops is less important for them. With less fat to tide them over periods of scarcity, reds have to feed regularly, whatever the weather. Since they do most of their foraging in the trees, they are also limited in the range of food available to them. In contrast, the ground-feeding grays not only have access to a wider selection of forage but can also find enough to meet their needs in a much shorter time, a substantial advantage in spells of bad weather.

Ironically, native red squirrels have simply turned out to be less well adapted to cope with the British weather and living conditions than the invasive grays, and so they have lost out in competition with the newcomers. Sadly, the same story has been repeated in Ireland, where the gray squirrel was first released in 1913; it has now spread through the country, again at the expense of the red.

Still more alarmingly, grays are now spreading across northern Italy. The species was introduced there in 1948 and in 1966, near Turin. If they spread, the grays will threaten red squirrels throughout the rest of Europe. Attempts to curb the threat to Eurasian red squirrels by eliminating the grays have been stopped by animal-rights supporters, who have managed to win legal backing for their efforts to halt the killings.

The situation raises a difficult moral dilemma. If the few hundred introduced gray squirrels have a right to life, should the threatened red squirrel population not benefit from similar protection? And if so, how can their future be assured in the face of a challenge from outside, except by culling the newcomers?

Starling, Bali

Leucopsar rothschildi

The beautiful Bali starling's tiny surviving population is confined to a minute area of a national park. For over 70 years large numbers have been taken from the wild to supply the international cage-bird trade, a threat that could still result in its extinction.

The Bali starling is the only bird species to be found exclusively on the Indonesian island of Bali. It has probably always been restricted to the northwestern third of this small island and was probably already very scarce when first discovered in the early 1900s. The population of the Bali starling has been greatly reduced over the last century by relentless trapping for the worldwide cage-bird trade, and increasing habitat loss has been an important secondary threat. As a result, it is now one of the world's rarest and most threatened birds.

DATA PANEL

Bali starling (Bali myna, Rothschild's myna)

Leucopsar rothschildi

Family: Sturnidae

World population: 12 birds in 1999

Distribution: Endemic to the island of Bali, Indonesia. Confined to Bali Barat National Park, northwestern Bali

Habitat: During the breeding season open shrubland and savanna with many trees, including palms, and adjacent tropical moist deciduous monsoon forest below an altitude of 575 ft (175 m); at other times disperses to the edges of the forest and flooded savanna woodland

Size: Length: 10 in (25 cm). Weight: 3–3.2 oz (85–90 g)

Form: Plump, thrush-sized bird. Whole body has white plumage; bright-blue bare skin around each eye tapers to a point; has a long crest, especially in males, that the bird can erect; tail and wings white with black tips; strong gray or brown bill and pale blue-gray legs

Diet: Caterpillars, termites, ants, and other insects; also seeds and fruit

Breeding: October–November; nests in tree holes, often old woodpecker nesting holes lined by male with dry twigs; female incubates 2–3 pale-blue eggs for 12–14 days; young fledge in about 3 weeks

Related endangered species: Black-winged starling (*Sturnus melanopterus*) EN; white-faced starling (*S. albofrontatus*) VU; Pohnpei mountain starling (*Aplonis pelzelni*) CR; white-eyed starling (*A. brunneicapilla*) EN; helmeted myna (*Basilornis galeatus*) LRnt

Status: IUCN CR; CITES I

In Great Demand

The dazzling white plumage, a contrasting patch of bare, bright-blue skin around the face, and a luxuriant crest ensure that the Bali starling is highly sought after by bird collectors. In 1928, less than 20 years after the species became known in the West, the first Bali starlings were being exported to Europe, and they first bred in captivity three years later. Over succeeding decades the collectors' demands for wild-caught individuals of the beautiful birds grew—despite the fact that they proved easy to breed in captivity.

During the 1960s and 1970s the cage-bird trade in Bali starlings was vigorous, and many hundreds of birds were caught to be exported overseas. The trade in the Bali starling continues today, despite the fact that it was placed on Appendix I of CITES in 1970, has been protected under Indonesian law since 1971, and the species' entire population occurs in a national park where it is the subject of a special conservation program. As numbers have dwindled, owning a Bali starling has become a sign of prestige to some collectors. In the mid-1990s a single bird could fetch $2,000 on the black market.

Today most birds are sold to collectors in Indonesia, where many people keep cage birds. Methods of capture involve smearing sticky "bird lime" on branches to glue unsuspecting birds when they land, using a tethered bird as a decoy, or raiding nests at night. Recently, poachers have equipped themselves with telescopes, walkie-talkies, and fine-mesh mist nets to help entrap the starlings.

See also: Exploitation of Live Animals 1: 49; National Parks 1: 92; Bird of Paradise, Blue 2: 84

Serious Setbacks

Although the primary threat to the Bali starling is from illegal trapping, the dwindling population is placed at further risk by long-term destruction of its habitat. Unlike other restricted-range birds in Java and Bali that are found in rain forest at higher altitudes, the Bali starling prefers drier, more open lowland, deciduous monsoon forest, and densely wooded savanna with an understory of grasses. During the early 20th century such areas were mainly undisturbed, but the spread and growth of settlements have destroyed much of the species' habitat. With fertile volcanic soil Bali and Java support some of the world's most intensive agriculture and about 60 percent of the human population of Indonesia.

Of an original area of 1,370 square miles (3,550 sq. km) of monsoon forest, only an eighth is left. Much has been converted to plantations of kapok and coconut trees and for settlements. Even in the Bali Barat reserve—to which the birds have been confined since the early 1980s—about a third of the 38 square miles (100 sq. km) of suitable habitat has been converted into plantations and settlements. Other threats to the park include tourism.

Alarming Decline

The Bali starling largely disappeared from the southern part of its range during the 1960s and from the northeastern part in the 1970s. Until 1974 the lack of research into the bird life of Indonesia meant that no one knew how many Bali starlings remained. The first census produced an estimate of 100 birds before the breeding season. Through the late 1970s and early 1980s counts suggested there were about 200 birds, but by 1989 there were just 28—largely as a result of poaching. The alarming decline continued until 1990, when the estimate was of just 15 wild birds. By contrast, about 1,000 exist in captivity worldwide.

A conservation program was launched in 1983 involving the Indonesian government, BirdLife International (a global partnership of conservation organizations), the American Zoo and Aquarium Association, and the Jersey Wildlife Preservation Trust. It helped strengthen protection of the birds in Bali Barat National Park and achieved major advances in techniques for releasing captive-bred birds. However, it has not removed the threat of extinction because of mismanagement associated with both the park and the conservation program. The few wild birds left may face additional threats, including native predators, disease, competition with other birds, and the effects of climate change in long periods of drought.

The Bali starling *is still being poached for the cage-bird trade, despite protective legislation.*

Stilt, Black

Himantopus novaezelandiae

With a population of below 50 individuals, the distinctive black stilt of New Zealand is one of the rarest of all the world's waders. This is despite 20 years of effort by conservationists to make good its losses to habitat destruction, introduced predators, and interbreeding with other species.

The black stilt is the only globally threatened member of its family, the stilts and avocets. Until the late 19th century it was a common and widespread breeder in New Zealand. By the turn of the century the black stilt nested only on South Island. Within another 30 years nests could be found only on inland riverbeds and associated wetlands in the lowland parts of southern Canterbury and central Otago regions and the Mackenzie Basin.

By 1940 the total population was down to an estimated 500 to 1,000 individuals. The real crash, however, began in the early 1950s, when numbers plummeted; just 50 to 100 birds were left by 1960, all of them breeding in the Mackenzie Basin. Today black stilts nest only along rivers in the upper Waitaki Valley. Of the total population only 18 are breeding adults.

After breeding most of the birds move short distances to ponds or lakes before wintering on nearby river deltas around large lakes, although a few migrate to the northern harbors of North Island.

Introduced Predators

The major cause of the black stilt's decline has been the introduction by human settlers of nonnative predators. In a land with no natural mammalian predators the stilts had evolved no antipredator behavior, and proved easy targets for invading cats, ferrets, weasels, stoats, brown rats, and hedgehogs. Mammals such as rabbits provided a new food source for native bird predators, notably Australasian harriers and kelp gulls, increasing their numbers and so putting extra pressure on the stilts.

In addition to their fearlessness of predators

DATA PANEL

Black stilt

Himantopus novaezelandiae

Family: Recurvirostridae

World population: 40 birds in 1999

Distribution: New Zealand; entire population now breeds only in upper Waitaki Valley, South Island, although small numbers migrate to winter on North Island

Habitat: Breeds on the banks of intertwining rivers and side streams; also occurs in swamps and other wetlands

Size: Length: 14.5–15.8 in (37–40 cm). Weight: about 7.8 oz (220 g)

Form: Elegant wader with long, thin, black bill and long, pinkish-red legs; plumage entirely black with greenish gloss to back and wings; female has shorter legs on average; nonbreeding adults may show grayish or whitish forehead and chin; juveniles have white head, neck, and breast, becoming progressively darker

Diet: Chiefly small aquatic invertebrates; also small fish

Breeding: September–January, usually solitary; both sexes build a nest near water; nest is a shallow scrape that is often well lined with vegetation; usually 4 greenish eggs with dark-brown or blackish blotches and streaks are laid; incubation by both sexes for 3–4 weeks; fledging period 4–8 weeks

Related endangered species: No other species in the stilt and avocet family

Status: IUCN CR; not listed by CITES

See also: Speciation 1: 26; Drainage and Irrigation 1: 40; Introductions 1: 54; Sandpiper, Spoon-Billed 8: 54

the stilts have other traits that make them vulnerable: They nest as solitary pairs on banks that are accessible to predators, and the young remain flightless for a long period—up to eight weeks.

Habitat Loss and Hybridization

Another factor affecting the stilt is habitat destruction and alteration. Many of New Zealand's swamps and other wetlands have been drained over the past few hundred years. The process continues today in the birds' last refuge in the MacKenzie Basin. Another threat comes from hydroelectric power projects, which have also dramatically modified the habitat. Reduced flows in rivers have allowed predators to reach nesting islands more easily, while floods destroy nests. Habitat changes have also affected the stilts' feeding areas. The result is that the stilts have been forced to abandon sites by water for drier areas where they are more likely to suffer plundering by predators.

Also, introduced plants, such as lupins and willows, have quickly spread along rivers, replacing native vegetation and making the habitat unsuitable for the stilts.

As the numbers of black stilts declined, their populations became fragmented. The birds became so widely separated from one another that there were often too few of them on a particular stretch of river for all the adults to find mates. At the same time, the other stilt species in New Zealand, the pied stilts, were becoming more abundant. Because the geographical separation of the two species was fairly recent, black stilts had not evolved sufficiently different courtship rituals to prevent interbreeding, which reduced the species numbers further. There is also a skewed sex ratio, with about three times as many males as females, because the males breed with the pied stilts or hybrids.

Reversing the Decline

Conservationists have tried to reduce predation by trapping predators around the nests or fencing off nest sites. Captive breeding, which began in 1979, also plays an important role in the species' survival, and targets include increasing the number of captive birds still further to help boost the wild population. Other aims are to establish a self-sustaining population on a suitable predator-free island and to raise public awareness about the bird.

The black stilt's long legs enable it to wade into relatively deep water to feed. It uses its long, needlelike bill to snap up mayflies, caddisflies, stoneflies and their larvae, other invertebrates, and even small fish.

Stork, Greater Adjutant

Leptoptilos dubius

The greater adjutant stork population suffered a huge decline during the first half of the 20th century. An increase in the level of human interference is likely to result in even greater losses.

One of the world's largest flying birds, the greater adjutant stork has a common name that refers to its habit of striding up and down with a measured military gait, like an adjutant (army officer who acts as an administrative assistant).

The greater adjutant stork was, until the 1940s, common and widespread in northern India and continental Southeast Asia: Large numbers could be seen in many places, even rooftops in Calcutta, India's largest city. The bird served a valuable function as a scavenger of animal carcasses and other edible human garbage and was a common sight on the outskirts of urban areas, especially at garbage dumps and abattoirs. However, it has suffered such a catastrophic decline in numbers and range that it is now classified as Endangered.

In flight the greater adjutant is graceful, soaring effortlessly on its great broad wings. On the ground, however, it is a rather ungainly bird, with its disproportionately huge bill, a bare-skinned face and neck, and a pendulous gular (throat) pouch. It spends much time squatting on its tarsi (the lower parts of each leg) with its long neck hunched into its shoulders and its bill wide open.

The massive conical bill, like a meat-cleaver, is not effective at tearing into or dismembering animal carcasses—an important part of the greater adjutant's diet—but is well suited to snatching morsels of meat or even bone from a carcass: The bird usually waits until vultures have opened up the carcass with their hooked bills; one bird was seen to swallow two buffalo vertebrae in about five minutes!

An odd habit of the greater adjutant, shared with other storks, is that of coping with high temperatures by defecating onto its legs to lose heat by evaporation. Along with the marabou of Africa, it is the only stork to have inflatable air sacs: There are

DATA PANEL

Greater adjutant stork

Leptoptilos dubius

Family: Ciconiidae

World population: 700–800 birds

Distribution: Breeds in Assam (northeastern India) and at Tonle Sap Lake, Cambodia; wandering individuals recorded from Bangladesh, Nepal, Thailand, and Vietnam

Habitat: In Assam on outskirts of urban areas; breeds at marshes, lakes, and other wetlands; spends rest of year at garbage dumps, abattoirs, and burial grounds. In Cambodia breeds in freshwater flooded forest; disperses to seasonally flooded forest, wet grassland, mangroves, and intertidal flats

Size: Length: about 5 ft (1.5 m); wingspan: 8.5–9.5 ft (2.6–2.9 m)

Form: Huge bird with blackish, gray, and off-white plumage; naked skin on head and neck; naked skin pouch from throat; ruff of white feathers at base of neck; wedge-shaped, dirty-yellow or pale-gray bill; legs pale grayish brown. Juveniles have narrower bills, more down on head and neck, and all-dark wings

Diet: Mainly carrion, garbage, and fish; also frogs, reptiles, large insects and crustaceans, and injured birds such as ducks

Breeding: Usually October or December to January; builds a huge nest of sticks 40–75 ft (12–23 m) up in large tree; once nested on cliffs. Female lays 2–4 (usually 3) white eggs. Sexes share nest-building, incubation, and feeding of young

Related endangered species: Lesser adjutant stork (*Leptoptilos javanicus*) VU; milky stork (*Mycteria cinerea*) VU; painted stork (*M. leucocephala*) LRnt; Storm's stork (*Ciconia stormi*) EN; oriental stork (*C. boyciana*) EN; black-necked stork (*Ephippiorhynchus asiaticus*) LRnt

Status: IUCN EN; not listed by CITES

See also: Habitat Loss 1: 38; Education 1: 94; Bittern, Eurasian 2: 90; Flamingo, Andean 4: 80; Spoonbill, Black-Faced 9: 26

two of them, one on the upper back and a prominent one hanging from the throat. Once thought to act as a support for the huge bill, they are now known to be used as cooling devices and in breeding displays, when they change—along with the other areas of bare skin—from a dull yellowish to a bright-reddish color.

A Variety of Threats and Solutions

The greater adjutant stork suffered huge declines during the first half of the 20th century and continues to disappear at an alarming rate. Today it breeds only in Assam, northeastern India (its remaining stronghold, with at least 600 birds), and at Tonle Sap Lake in Cambodia (with at least 150 birds). There are now only a few small sites and scattered pairs of birds.

The declines are the result of increasing human activity. A major threat is direct persecution, especially at the birds' nest sites. Another is habitat destruction, in particular the deforestation of lowlands and loss of nesting trees. The demand for timber for house building or fuel, together with the constant noise and odor from the colonies, has sometimes caused local people to cut down traditional sites. Drainage and pollution of wetlands, along with the intensive exploitation of fish and other food sources, are also damaging. Also, with fewer open garbage dumps in India it is now harder for the storks to obtain carcasses and discarded food.

The species' future depends on detailed studies of its requirements, protection of its nesting and feeding sites, and the control of pesticide use on wetlands where the birds feed. Since 1991 conservation-awareness programs have been ongoing in Assam and, with other species, in Laos and Cambodia too. In 1997 about 80 percent of waterbird egg and chick collection, including that of the storks, was stopped in Prek Toal, Cambodia.

The greater adjutant stork.
The bare skin of the head and neck that makes the bird seem repulsive to most humans is simply an adaptation to avoid becoming soiled as the bird plunges headfirst into a bloody carcass. It is often flecked with dried blood.

Sturgeon, Common

Acipenser sturio

It is difficult to imagine that some European rivers can hide giant fish measuring up to 20 feet (6 m) long that are capable of producing many millions of eggs in a single spawning. Such a fish is the common sturgeon. In spite of its prolific breeding habits, the species is at risk.

The common sturgeon usually grows to a length of 3.3 to 6.6 feet (1 to 2 m), but can be longer. At least one report indicates that the species can attain a length of 20 feet (6 m) and a weight of about 1,300 pounds (600 kg). Despite this report, probably the largest specimen actually on record was 11.3 feet (3.4 m) long and 705 pounds (320 kg). The female has the potential to deliver close to 2.5 million eggs in a single spawning episode.

As with some 40 or so other sturgeon species, the common sturgeon is under severe threat. It was once found in large numbers along the coast of Europe, from the North Sea to the Mediterranean and Black Seas. Today it is scarce throughout its range.

Sturgeons are famous primarily for their eggs, known universally as caviar. However, many species have also been fished for their flesh. All species are long-lived, with ages beyond 50 years being common.

Double Life

The common sturgeon is anadromous, which means that it spends its life at sea but migrates into freshwater habitats during the spawning season. One notable exception to the rule is the common sturgeon population that lives in Lake Ladoga in Russia. Another is the sterlet, which lives permanently in fresh water.

Spawning migrations upriver occur in early or mid-spring, with actual breeding taking place during early summer. Spawning is usually in pools that are several feet deep and have a flow of water. Alternatively, it may occur along river banks covered by spring floods. The eggs—up to 2.5 million for a largish female—are scattered over a gravelly bottom and abandoned.

By now the condition of the adults has deteriorated, since they do not feed during their migrations: Many, in fact, will not make it back to sea to resume feeding. In better days such losses would not have been a problem, owing to the large number of adults in the population, not to mention the high numbers of offspring. Today every adult that dies adds to the scarcity of the species as it struggles to survive in the modern world.

DATA PANEL

Common sturgeon (Baltic sturgeon)

Acipenser sturio

Family: Acipenseridae

World population: Unknown, but close to extinction in parts of its range

Distribution: Atlantic Ocean from Norway south to North Africa and into the western Mediterranean; Baltic, and Black Seas

Habitat: Relatively shallow, mainly coastal seas, usually over sandy or muddy bottoms; some specimens move to deeper waters

Size: Length: on average 3.3–6.6 ft (1–2 m). Weight: a 10-ft (3-m) specimen may weigh about 440 lb (200 kg)

Form: Elongated body with distinct snout and characteristic caudal (tail) fin in which upper lobe is larger than lower one. Five rows of large, stout scales down body. Underslung mouth has distinctive barbels (whiskers)

Diet: Adults feed on bottom-dwelling marine invertebrates, but will also take small fish; juveniles feed mostly on bottom-dwelling freshwater invertebrates

Breeding: Migrates up to 620 miles (1,000 km) upriver in early to mid-spring; spawning occurs over gravel or pebbles, usually in flowing water pools. Each female is usually accompanied by more than 1 male. Hatching takes about 7 days, and juveniles may stay in their river of birth for up to 4 years

Related endangered species: Over 40 populations of the 25 species are under varying degrees of threat, including the ship sturgeon (*Acipenser nudiventris*) CR

Status: IUCN CR; CITES I

See also: Pollution 1: 50; Captive Breeding 1: 87; Paddlefish 7: 46; Salmon, Danube 8: 52

Young common sturgeon stay fairly close to the spawning grounds at first, but gradually move downriver as they grow. Some reports suggest that by the fall of the same year they move out to sea; others state that this may be delayed for one to four years. Whatever the case, males mature at between seven and nine years (some estimates indicate later maturation between nine and 13 years), while females may take eight to 14 years (some estimate it to be between 11 and 18 years) to mature and return to their waters of birth to breed for the first time.

Overfishing and Habitat Destruction

Overfishing is usually cited as the main reason for the sharp decline in numbers. Undoubtedly, fishing has had a severe effect on natural populations, not just of the common sturgeon, but of many of its relatives. Some of the eastern populations and species in particular are still the focus of illegal trade in caviar. In some cases arguments have been put forward to ban fishing altogether. However, others argue that to do so would drive the market underground and into the hands of organized illegal groups, thus probably accentuating rather than solving the problem.

The common sturgeon's best hope for the future appears to lie in coordinated captive-breeding programs to rear stocks for commercial exploitation of the roe (caviar). Such farms are likely to produce more fish than may eventually be needed for harvesting purposes, thus acting as a potential source of fish for restocking former habitats. A beneficial spinoff from such programs is that they also reduce pressure on existing wild stocks.

However successful such breeding projects may be, the survival of the species in the wild needs to be urgently addressed. One problem is the pollution of watercourses. While it presents a daunting challenge, there are other potentially more difficult pressures facing the common sturgeon, including the building of dams, water channeling, and allied habitat-altering developments that plague the waterways.

The common sturgeon has a number of distinctive features, including an elongated snout and barbels (whiskers) below its underslung mouth.

Sucker, Razorback

Xyrauchen texanus

In 1949 a single fisherman caught nearly 7,000 pounds (3,200 kg) of razorback suckers in Saguaro Lake. By 1966 the same lake yielded no razorbacks. Such a dramatic decline has been mirrored elsewhere in the species' range, and the fish is considered to be in danger of extinction.

The razorback sucker is one of the largest suckers found in the United States: Mature specimens can grow to lengths of over 24 inches (60 cm). As a result of its size and abundance, it formed one of the most important components of the Mojave Indians' diet until the early years of the 20th century. It was even used as a fertilizer.

Fast-Water Adaptations

The razorback sucker is a most unusual-looking fish. As its common name suggests, the area behind the head forms a pronounced keel (ridgelike part) or razor. Muscles attached to bones that form the skeleton of the keel are thought to allow the fish to maintain its position in fast-flowing, turbulent waters. The flattened, sloping head, which tends to keep the razorback's body close to the bottom in such environments, is also a fast-water adaptation.

Nowadays, while the species still inhabits some flowing waters, it is often found in pools or stretches of water that are free of main-channel currents. It is therefore possible that the keel and head adaptations evolved at a time when the Colorado River flowed much faster than it does today.

The razorback sucker is a long-lived species, often living for 40 years or more. Some individuals are nearer 50 when they die. Growth during the fish's life span is variable, with rates being influenced by environmental conditions. In the Middle Green River, for instance, young razorbacks grow to about 4 inches (10 cm) in their first year, while in the Lower Colorado River basin growth is almost four times as rapid.

A Variety of Threats

Among the most serious threats to the continued survival of the razorback sucker are at least three nonnative fish species that have been introduced at different points in the razorback's range. Of particular note are two larger, predatory species introduced to cater to the needs of sport anglers. Both the large-mouth bass and the channel catfish soon began to have a damaging effect on the resident razorback suckers,

DATA PANEL

Razorback sucker

Xyrauchen texanus

Family: Catostomidae

World population: Lake Mojave population estimated at 20,000 (1993). Green River population estimated at fewer than 500 (1993)

Distribution: Lower Colorado River basin: Lakes Mojave, Mead, and Havasu. Upper Colorado basin: Green River; small numbers known in Lower Green River and Upper Colorado River in Grand Valley, as well as in San Juan and Colorado sections of Lake Powell

Habitat: Warm, flowing waters; deep pools and eddies away from main channels; juveniles tend to inhabit slow-flowing backwaters

Size: Length: 24 in (60 cm); mature specimens can grow to about 39 in (100 cm). Weight: up to 10 lb (4.5 kg)

Form: Pronounced keel starts behind head and extends to front edge of dorsal (back) fin. Head flattish; mouth underslung. Body dark brownish black above, fading through lighter colors to white or yellow below; throat yellow

Diet: Algae, zooplankton, detritus, and aquatic invertebrates

Breeding: In Lake Mojave: November–May (after upriver migration). Mid-April–mid-May in Middle Green River, where water is cooler. Spawns near shore over pebbles or gravel. Mature at 4–7 years

Related endangered species: Harelip sucker *(Moxostoma lacerum)* EX

Status: IUCN EN; not listed by CITES

to the extent that large populations in lakes and reservoirs were totally wiped out. In a less spectacular, but equally effective manner, introduced baitfish species such as the red shiner had a profound effect on razorbacks by preying on their fry (young).

One of several naturally occurring threats was detected as long ago as the 19th century, but is still regarded as a significant factor in the species' decline. It comes from a nonpredatory, closely related species: the flannelmouth sucker with whom the razorback freely mates. Hybridization is so frequent in parts of the razorback sucker's range that affected populations may become extinct.

Habitat alteration is another factor in the razorback sucker's decline. Dams and the reservoirs they create form major barriers to spawning migrations. They also remove the tributaries that have traditionally aided the fish's upriver migrations.

Other water-management projects have altered environmental conditions in such a way that they have eliminated seasonal variations in water temperature and flow, and replaced them with more constant, but colder temperatures and more even water flow throughout the year. Such conditions appear to tip the reproductive balance against the razorback and in favor of some of its competitors.

To a lesser extent pollutants—some of which are believed to impair the reproductive viability of the species—have been detected in the water and in the tissues of some razorback suckers tested for toxicity.

Recovery Measures

Although the decline in razorback sucker numbers had been known about for some time, it was not until the 1980s that official moves were made to protect the species. Indeed, some activities previously carried out on razorback rivers—such as poisoning a section of the Green River to create better conditions for trout—were directly harmful to the species.

During the 1980s about 15 million razorbacks were released into former habitats in Arizona in an attempt to help wild populations recover. Yet despite such efforts, populations failed to reestablish themselves, largely because of introduced species that preyed on the razorbacks.

In 1988 a program aimed at protecting not just the razorback but other threatened native species was implemented for the Upper Colorado River. The 15-year project includes restoring watercourse flows, habitat development and management, restocking, control of nonnative "sport" species, and a long-term monitoring and research program.

The razorback sucker *can be recognized by the pronounced keel or projection behind its head. It is thought that the keel and flattened head help the fish swim in fast-flowing, turbulent waters.*

Sunfish, Spring Pygmy

Elassoma alabamae

True to its name, the spring pygmy sunfish is tiny. It lives among dense vegetation and is often hard to find. Yet it has received an enormous amount of interest over the years, mainly because for about three decades it was believed to be extinct.

Although pygmy sunfish have been known and studied for well over 100 years, their relationship with their presumed close cousins, the much larger sunfish (family Centrarchidae), has been the focus of considerable controversy. The closeness of their kinship—and whether it is close enough for them to be regarded as members of the same family—has been hotly disputed ever since the first species, the banded pygmy sunfish, was described by scientists in 1877.

Currently, size and skeletal differences between the two groups are generally accepted as being marked enough for the pygmies to have their own family, the Elassomatidae, consisting of just six species.

However, new evidence now seems to indicate that the relationship between the pygmy sunfish and the other sunfish may not be close at all; they could even be more closely related to sticklebacks and swamp eels instead. It appears, therefore, that new controversies lie ahead.

Limited Distribution

In 1937 a scientific collection at Cave Spring in Lauderdale County, Alabama, revealed the presence of spring pygmy sunfish for the first time. At the time the spring was the only known location for the as yet undescribed species, which was referred to as "*Elassoma* species." It was later given the name *Elassoma alabamae*. Four years later a collection was made at a second location, Pryor Spring in Limestone County, Alabama.

In the years that followed the fish was, to all intents and purposes, lost—apparently forever—and it was presumed to be extinct. It was not until 1973 that the species was rediscovered (albeit as a single specimen) in Moss Spring, a tributary of the larger

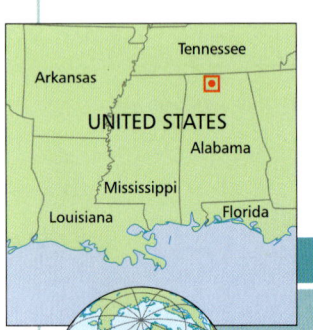

DATA PANEL

Spring pygmy sunfish

Elassoma alabamae

Family: Elassomatidae

World population: Numbers unknown, but abundant in the very few and restricted localities where it is known to exist

Distribution: Pryor Spring and several other springs and small waterways in Beaverdam Creek, Limestone County, Alabama

Habitat: Densely vegetated clear spring waters

Size: Length: 1.2 in (3 cm)

Form: Male dark brown or blue/black, with 6–8 vertical golden bars on body; female is less colorful. Mature male has a transparent small "window" on posterior section of the dorsal (back) and anal (belly) fins

Diet: Small aquatic invertebrates

Breeding: Territories established by males, whose colors intensify, and attract females.

Intricate courtship display is followed by the spawners aligning themselves side-by-side among fine-leaved vegetation. Eggs are released and fertilized. Most stick to vegetation where they are guarded by the male until they hatch some days later

Related endangered species: Carolina pygmy sunfish (*Elassoma boehlkei*) LRnt; blue-barred pygmy sunfish (*E. okatie*) VU

Status: Not listed by IUCN; not listed by CITES

See also: Drainage and Irrigation **1**: 40; Reintroduction **1**: 92; Caracolera, Mojarra **3**: 26; Darter, Watercress **4**: 4

Beaverdam Creek in another part of Limestone County. Since then, other locations in the region have yielded further stocks of the spring pygmy sunfish. Despite the newer finds, however, the geographical range of the species remains restricted.

Multiple Threats

The population of spring pygmy sunfish at Cave Spring was discovered during a survey that was carried out by the Tennessee Valley Authority in advance of the construction of a large reservoir, Pickwick Lake. As the lake began to fill up, Cave Spring was gradually flooded, thus wiping out the species from this habitat.

The one other remaining known locality, Pryor Spring, suffered a different, though similarly terminal, fate. An exotic plant species known as Parrot's Feather swamped both the spring and its outflow, leading to widespread flooding of neighboring forests.

Physical removal of the weed proved ineffective. It was followed by chemical treatment, which had more lasting effects, but did not save the spring pygmy sunfish from its last (presumed) refuge in Pryor Spring. Habitat alteration (channeling of the spring), along with pollution as a result of waste dumping, also contributed to the species' disappearance from the area, where it has not been seen since 1941.

All that remained were the more recently discovered populations in Moss Spring and other small springs and tributaries, as well as those in man-made ditches, such as Lowe's Ditch in the Beaverdam Creek system. Even some of these habitats have experienced severe threats, however. In 1976, for example, dredging to create waterholes for cattle led to the destruction of some of the few remaining habitats.

Rescue Plans

As the situation became ever more critical, measures were set in motion to save the species from further decline and possible extinction. In 1984 landowners,

The spring pygmy sunfish has been variously threatened by the construction of a reservoir, the use of chemicals to remove weeds, and dredging to create waterholes for cattle. Its survival has been helped by a successful captive-breeding program.

researchers, and both state and federal scientists were involved in a project that has resulted in the successful reintroduction of the species into one of its former habitats, Pryor Spring. In addition, at least one captive-bred population of the species is being maintained at Conservation Fisheries, Inc., as a backup measure and in an attempt to learn more about the biology of the minuscule egg-layer, which is notoriously difficult to observe in the wild.

The problems in carrying out field observations do not, however, mean that the species is rare in the localities where it exists. Indeed, it is very abundant at these sites; the difficulty arises from both the small size of the fish and the thick aquatic vegetation that obstructs direct studies, as scientists from the Fisheries Section of the Division of Wildlife and Freshwater Fisheries have discovered.

The future for the spring pygmy sunfish looks more hopeful than it did some years ago. Nevertheless, its very restricted distribution in an area that can be dramatically upset by runoff from crop-spraying, fertilizers, siltation, and other habitat-deteriorating factors means that a careful watch must be kept on the remaining wild populations.

Swallow, Blue

Hirundo atrocaerulea

Perhaps the most beautiful of all the world's swallows and martins, the blue swallow is also one of the rarest. It is threatened by the human impact on its dwindling breeding habitat.

The blue swallow spends much of its life in the air, twisting and turning over the ground in pursuit of flies with the help of its long, wirelike tail streamers; those of the male are the longest of any swallow. It drinks and bathes on the wing, dipping its bill or body skillfully into the water and flying up again with scarcely a pause.

During courtship a male will chase a female in flight, fluttering his wings or holding them up in a "V" and fanning his tail to show off his splendid streamers. He then reaches downward with his head toward hers so that the pair almost touch bills, while singing a brief, monotonous song consisting of several plaintive high-pitched notes.

Uncommon

Although it is unlikely that it was ever a common bird, the blue swallow seems to have declined greatly in many parts of its fragmented range, particularly in South Africa and Swaziland, where it is close to extinction, and in Zimbabwe and Zambia, where it is rare. It is reported as uncommon in Kenya and Uganda and is reasonably common only in Malawi (which has the largest population) and Tanzania.

Where its specialized nesting and feeding requirements still exist, the blue swallow can survive in good numbers; but in many areas it faces dramatic changes in the landscape. In many parts of its range suitable grassland in mountainous regions is disappearing with the spread of commercial forestry and intensive agriculture. Land is used for livestock rearing and grazing, planting of sugarcane, and grass-burning. Another threat is the invasion of the upland grasslands with nonnative trees and bracken. A potential problem is presented by small-scale mining operations near nest sites.

Although some areas are likely to stay safe from development because of their poor soils and cold climate, and despite some birds receiving protection

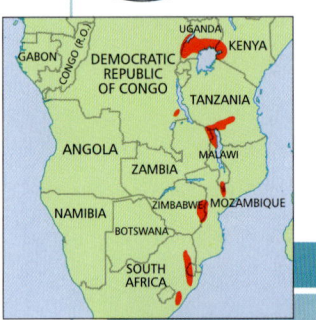

DATA PANEL

Blue swallow

Hirundo atrocaerulea

Family: Hirundinidae

World population: About 3,000 birds

Distribution: Breeds in relatively few scattered upland areas of southern Africa, in the Democratic Republic of Congo (DRC), Zambia, Tanzania, Mozambique, Malawi, Zimbabwe, Swaziland, and eastern South Africa. Migrates within Africa, visiting northeastern DRC, southern Uganda, and western Kenya

Habitat: Breeds in montane grassland, migrating to open grassland and savanna

Size: Length head/body: 7–10 in (18–25 cm); tail streamers of male: 4.8–5.5 in (12–14 cm), of female: 2.3–3 in (6–8 cm)

Form: Slim swallow with long outer tail feathers (streamers) in male; shorter in female and short in juveniles. Adult plumage often looks all black, but in sunlight appears deep, glossy blue; flight feathers are brownish black with a greenish-blue tinge

Diet: Aerial insects; mainly small flies

Breeding: Usually November–January; builds open-cup nest of mud and grass. Female usually lays 2–3 brown and purplish spotted white eggs, incubating them alone for 15–16 days; young fledge at 20–26 days; usually second brood reared later in breeding season

Related endangered species: Another 4 species in the swallow and martin family are threatened, the most closely related being the white-tailed swallow *(Hirundo megaensis)* VU

Status: IUCN VU; not listed by CITES

SWALLOW, BLUE

The blue swallow *chases flies and other small aerial insects at high speed with the help of its long, wirelike tail streamers.*

within national parks or nature reserves, there is an urgent need to locate the swallows' key wintering sites and preserve them. The spread of nonnative plants, such as wattle and pine, also needs investigation, and efforts must be made to control them. Already a project is underway in Zimbabwe with the aim of surveying suitable habitat, assessing the swallows' distribution and numbers, and addressing the problem of invasive plants.

Nesting Instinct

Many members of the swallow and martin family nest in holes, but they choose sites that are off the ground, in cliffs, earth- or sand banks, or trees. Of the blue swallow's closest relatives—the other species in the genus *Hirundo*—almost all build bowl-shaped nests of mud attached to a cliff, cave roof, tree, or artificial support, such as the eaves of a house roof or the underside of a bridge. The blue swallow, by contrast, usually nests in holes or overhangs below ground, selected if they are not surrounded by vegetation; suitable sites include old burrows of aardvarks or other mammals, potholes, within dongas (steep-sided gullies created by soil erosion), or beneath earth banks. Nests have been found 16 feet (5 m) below ground level.

Sites that are not surrounded by vegetation are relatively restricted. The bird is further limited by its need for open grassland around the nest site, where it can hunt unimpeded. A few pairs have been recorded over the past 30 years using artificial nest sites, including road culverts, mine shafts, and the eaves of houses. However, they face competition with other birds at such sites, and there is unlikely to be suitable habitat nearby where they can feed.

As with other swallows, blue swallows return year after year to the same nest sites, often repairing and reusing the nest. In contrast to other *Hirundo* species, blue swallows mix the mud with the grass as they collect it rather than compacting the mud into pellets first. Some birds have been known to come back to the same nests for up to 30 years. Many eggs or young are destroyed by weather problems such as flooding and heavy rain, leading to erosion and the collapse of the burrows.

Swan, Trumpeter

Cygnus buccinator

The largest of native North American wildfowl and the biggest of the world's seven species of swan, the magnificent trumpeter came close to extinction through hunting.

The trumpeter swan is named after its loud, deep, trumpeting calls. Largely as a result of hunting, it is the rarest of all the world's swans. In the past the trumpeter swan nested from Alaska across much of Canada and into the United States as far east as Indiana and south as Missouri. However, from the European settlement of North America in the 17th century to the early years of the 20th century the trumpeter swan was hunted for its meat, skin, and feathers, and its eggs were taken, too. The meat and eggs were regarded as delicacies, while the tough skins, with their warm, soft, downy feathers, were made into boas, hats, and other articles of dress, and the down into powder puffs.

In the Nick of Time

In 1918, as a result of alarm at the catastrophic decline of various birds, including the trumpeter, hunting was outlawed by the Migratory Bird Treaty Act. The act almost came too late. By 1932 only 69 trumpeter swans were known to exist, all of them in one area, near Yellowstone National Park. In 1935 the federal government designated about 22,000 acres (9,000 ha) of prime trumpeter nesting habitat in southwestern

DATA PANEL

Trumpeter swan

Cygnus buccinator

Family: Anatidae

World population: About 16,000 birds

Distribution: Major breeding areas in Alaska and northwestern Canada; isolated breeding populations elsewhere, including Michigan, Wisconsin, Minnesota, and Oregon. Some populations migrate: main wintering areas are on the coasts of Alaska, British Columbia, and Washington State

Habitat: Breeds by freshwater lakes, ponds, and marshes; winters on shallow lakes and reservoirs, and by streams and rivers; also on estuaries and sheltered coasts; forages in croplands and pastures

Size: Length: 4.9–5.1 ft (1.5–1.8 m); wingspan: 7.3–8.2 ft (2.2–2.5 m). Weight: 16–27.5 lb (7.3–12.5 kg)

Form: Large swan. Adult plumage entirely white, contrasting with black bill, short black legs, and black webbed feet. Heads and necks often stained a rusty color due to immersion in iron-rich waters when feeding. Juveniles have gray-brown plumage and a mainly pinkish bill

Diet: Plant food, especially sago pondweed and duck potato tubers; also stems, young shoots, leaves, seeds, roots, and tubers of other aquatic plants; grasses and grain crops in fields. Young are fed on aquatic invertebrates and fragments of vegetation

Breeding: Establishes mate for life when about 3 years old; breeds the following year. In late March to early May male gathers marsh plants and brings them to female, who builds a huge nest mound on a shore or islet or on a beaver or muskrat lodge. Female lays 3–9 large, white eggs which she incubates for about 5 weeks; her mate stands guard. Downy young (cygnets) grow quickly; by 8–10 weeks they have reached half their adult size and are fully feathered. Young fly at 3–4.5 months; stay with parents for their first winter and then return to the breeding areas

Related endangered species: None

Status: Not listed by IUCN; not listed by CITES

See also: Hunting 1: 42; The Feather Trade 1: 46; Duck, Labrador 4: 42; Nene 7: 10

Montana's Centennial Valley as the Red Rock Lakes National Wildlife Refuge. The Red Rock Lakes population served as a source of breeding stock for reintroductions of the species to parts of its original range, chiefly to wildlife refuges in the Midwest.

Against the Odds

Trumpeter swans are still vulnerable to shooting, even in error: The much smaller tundra or whistling swan, and even the snow goose, can be mistaken for the trumpeter at long range. Trumpeters are also killed by lead poisoning as a result of swallowing lead shot in cartridges and sinkers used by anglers to keep their lines underwater. Lead shot has been banned nationally for wildfowl hunting in the United States since 1991, but trumpeters still succumb, since old pellets can stay in the sediment at the bottom of lakes and wetlands for decades. Other threats to the swans include collision with power lines and wire fences that

The trumpeter swan *has a wingspan of 8 feet (2.4 m) and a long neck, which it holds erect when swimming, not curved, as in the mute swan.*

snake across the land. Pollution and disturbance by boats and even birdwatchers can cause problems. The swans' winter habitat is under threat from pollution. Another problem today is that some of the reintroduced flocks have lost most of their migratory instinct and move only short distances south to become crowded in unsuitable wintering areas where they may suffer freezing and starvation.

Despite such threats, populations of trumpeter swans have increased from about 2,000 birds in the early 1960s to about 16,000 today, with some populations showing ongoing increases. Conservation steps have included reestablishment of swans in breeding haunts and wintering quarters, protection of their habitat, and public education programs.

Tahr, Nilgiri

Hemitragus hylocrius

A close relative of the Himalayan tahr, the fairly large Nilgiri tahr is found only on a very few hilltops of the Western Ghat Mountains in southern India.

The Nilgiri tahr lives high up in the Western Ghat Mountains of southern India, in a landscape of rolling hills and dramatic cliffs. The barely accessible ledges where the tahr spends much of its time have the significant advantage of being relatively safe from predators. Killing by other animals does not seem to have been a major factor in the tahr's decline. There are hardly any tigers or leopards left in its range, and even the adaptable Asian wild dog, the dhole, does not appear to favor tahr as prey.

Apparently, young tahr make very good eating, but the meat of old males is barely edible. If they were not so rare, Nilgiri tahrs could be an important source of meat protein for undernourished local people.

Population Management

Hunting may seem like the last thing such an endangered animal would need, but there is some evidence to suggest that the tahr were better off when their habitat was managed by local hunting associations. In the days of the hunt access was strictly restricted so that numbers of game animals were allowed to build up for the sport of a few privileged members. Later, when the management passed from the hunting clubs to the overstretched government forest department, things deteriorated fast. Even though the tahr was officially protected, access to its habitat was easy and largely unrestricted, so many animals were poached for meat. This sort of unmanaged exploitation caused a rapid population decline, whereas carefully managed harvesting could have maintained secure and healthy populations.

Wild tahr do not like disturbance; and although few people or livestock venture on to the precipitous cliffs where they live, crops such as tea, cardamom, plantain, and wattle are planted right up to the cliff edges, and cattle are grazed on almost every other available patch of land. The

---

DATA PANEL

Nilgiri tahr (Nilgiri ibex)

Hemitragus hylocrius

Family: Bovidae

World population: 1,000–2,000

Distribution: Scattered populations in highlands of southern India

Habitat: Steep, grassy and tree-covered slopes and cliffs at altitudes of 4,000–6,000 ft (1,200–1,600 m)

Size: Length head/body: 36–54 in (90–140 cm); tail: 3.5–4.5 in (9–12 cm); height at shoulder: 24–40 in (60–106 cm). Weight: 110–220 lb (50–100 kg); bucks heavier than does

Form: Brownish goat; males are darker than females and have a pale saddle-patch

Diet: Mostly grasses and leaves

Breeding: One (occasionally 2) kids born at any time of year

Related endangered species: Arabian tahr *(Hemitragus jayakari)* EN; Himalayan tahr *(H. jemlahicus)* VU

Status: IUCN EN; not listed by CITES

comings and goings of plantation workers and livestock disturb the tahr, and restrict their activities to small patches of inaccessible habitat surrounded by areas of farmland.

It became clear that the tahr was in need of help in the mid-1970s, when surveys indicated that the total wild population had dropped to about 1,000 animals. In some areas this represented a 97 percent decline in only 30 years. Conservationists were appalled, and just in time several areas were declared sanctuaries for the tahr. Fortunately, even though tahr populations are still extremely small, they seem to have a good mixture of ages and sexes, and the birth rate is relatively high.

The dramatic scenery in which the Nilgiri tahr lives has always made the area a popular retreat from the hot lowlands, and the growing tourist industry is showing signs of becoming a major positive factor in the tahr's survival. If tourists can be drawn to an area for its scenery and wildlife, the benefits of conserving rare species will begin to outweigh those of farming, or even poaching, and the tahr may stand a good chance of recovery.

Plantations are now managed with the tahr's welfare in mind, and in some places the animals have overcome their fear of people. Semitame herds are becoming an important tourist attraction. With careful management there is no reason why the Nilgiri tahr should not once again roam the hills and cliffs of the Western Ghat range in substantial numbers.

The Nilgiri tahr *is extremely nimble and puts its agility to good use, living on exposed cliff edges and precipices that few other animals can reach.*

Takahe

Porphyrio mantelli

Once believed extinct, the flightless takahe of New Zealand was rediscovered in 1948 in the cold, wet, and remote mountains of Fiordland on South Island. Since then its numbers have fluctuated fairly constantly between 100 and 160, but a recent steady increase offers hope for the future.

Isolated in the South Pacific, between the coral seas of Polynesia and the windswept pack ice of Antarctica, New Zealand has been cut off from the rest of the world for 80 million years. Inaccessible to the mammals that spread over other regions of the world during this time, it became the home of an extraordinary variety of birds adapted for every conceivable lifestyle. Since the birds had no need to escape from enemies such as cats, foxes, or humans, many of them lacked any fear of predators and the power of flight.

One of the most spectacular of these flightless islanders is the takahe, a giant bird that once ranged all over the North and South Islands, originally occurring throughout the islands' forests and grasslands. Its troubles began with the arrival of Polynesian colonists about 1,000 years ago. These colonists—the Maori—found the takahe easy meat and probably wiped out local populations by hunting them. This probably drove the birds into suboptimal grassland habitats, where there was little hunting.

The Maori also brought the first of many mammal invaders: pigs, rats, and dogs. Some 800 years later European settlers arrived and began introducing a whole menagerie of cats, foxes, stoats, possums, rabbits, deer, cattle, and sheep to the islands. While predators such as the stoat attacked the takahe, the grazers destroyed its food supply. By degrees the takahe disappeared, and by the 1930s the species was believed to be extinct.

DATA PANEL

Takahe (notornis)

Porphyrio mantelli

Family: Rallidae

World population: About 150–220 birds

Distribution: Occurs naturally on South Island, New Zealand, but has been introduced to 4 predator-free islands off New Zealand

Habitat: Mountain tussock grassland in summer; beech forest and scrub in winter

Size: Length: 25 in (63 cm). Weight: male 4.8–8.8 lb (2.2–4 kg); female 4–7.7 lb (1.8–3.5 kg)

Form: A bulky, flightless bird with a large red bill and frontal shield, reduced wings, and a short tail. Head and neck iridescent blue; peacock-blue shoulders; green and blue back and wings; red legs. Juveniles duller

Diet: Mainly juices from the tender bases of snow tussock grasses; grass seeds and fern rhizomes in winter; also some insects and small lizards

Breeding: Pairs mate for life and usually breed October–December. A nest is built on the ground; 2 brown-blotched, pale-buff eggs are incubated for 4–4.5 weeks by both parents. Chicks depend on parents for 4 months

Related endangered species: One of 33 threatened species in the family Rallidae, including Invisible rail *(Habroptila wallacii)* VU; Guam rail *(Gallirallus owstoni)** EW; Makira moorhen *(Gallinula sylvestris)* CR; Samoan moorhen *(G. pacifica)* CR; and horned coot *(Fulica cornuta)** LRnt

Status: IUCN EN; not listed by CITES

See also: Introductions 1: 54; Reintroduction 1: 92; Coot, Horned 3: 62; Rail, Guam 8: 18

Rediscovery

In fact, the takahe had retreated to the remote Murchison Mountains in the Fiordland of South Island. When it was rediscovered in 1948, there were between 250 and 300 birds left, surviving in a region of heavy snows and high rainfall. It is a hard life, and it has been made harder by introduced red deer that overgraze and eliminate the most nutritious grasses, leaving little for the takahe to eat. The takahe also suffers predation by stoats, and as a result it has a low breeding success rate. Since 1980 the wild population has fluctuated at levels of 100 to 160 birds, and without intensive conservation actions its chances of survival would have been slim.

Conservation

Red deer have been controlled in the Murchison Mountains since the 1960s, but despite this the takahe population failed to recover. In an effort to boost its numbers, a captive-breeding unit was established in the 1980s and captive-bred birds were released into the wild. From 1984 to 1991 small populations were also established on four predator-free islands and intensively managed to maximize their breeding success. Even so, these islands' populations have reached a total of only about 60 adults.

There is a plan to establish a second mainland population. The ultimate goal is to reach a total, self-sustaining population of over 500 birds; if the recovery program achieves this, the takahe will be off the Endangered list, but will be classified as Vulnerable.

The takahe *is the largest and one of the most colorful members of the rail family.*

Takin

Budorcas taxicolor

The takin is struggling to survive in the wild areas around the foothills of the Himalayas. It is preyed on not only by wolves and bears, but by humans for its meat. The combined pressures of predation and habitat destruction have taken a severe toll on numbers.

The takin is also known as the golden-fleeced cow, the gnu-goat, and the chamois cattle, an indication that it is a difficult animal to classify. It shares many characteristics of other members of the Bovidae family, which include sheep, goats, cattle, and antelopes.

The takin's shaggy coat and short, powerful legs are adaptations to the harsh mountainous landscapes of southwestern China, Tibet, Myanmar (Burma), and northern India where it is still found. There are four subspecies of takin found in different parts of the range, but all are under pressure from the loss of habitat and from competition for food with domestic livestock that eat huge amounts of vegetation.

Hunting for meat is still a major threat to the takin. The animal has a stocky body, which makes it attractive quarry for any hunter. It has been hunted for centuries by humans; the animals are caught in snares and pitfall traps or are killed with spears and guns. The takin's natural predators are wolves and bears.

Balancing Act

The takin has remarkable feet, similar to those of a yak, with broad cloven hooves that splay to give grip on rocky ground. In addition, there is a kind of spur, or highly developed dewclaw. The dewclaw in most bovids is small and insignificant, having been reduced from the ancestral thumb. In the takin, however, this otherwise redundant digit has been reinstated and now serves as a useful third toe, helping the animal maintain its balance in the rocky landscapes.

DATA PANEL

Takin (golden-fleeced cow, gnu-goat, chamois cattle)

Budorcas taxicolor

Family: Bovidae

World population: Unknown, perhaps several thousand

Distribution: Tibet, Myanmar (Burma), parts of central and southern China, Bhutan, and the Assam and Sikkim regions of India

Habitat: Mountain slopes between 3,300 and 15,000 ft (1,000–4,500 m) at upper limit of trees

Size: Length: 5.5–7.2 ft (1.7–2.3 m); height at shoulder: up to 3.3–4.3 ft (1–1.3 m); females about 20% smaller than males. Weight: up to 790 lb (350 kg)

Form: A dumpy, cowlike animal with a dense shaggy coat, stumpy legs, and broad feet. Both sexes bear sturdy, backward-pointing horns

Diet: Browses leaves from deciduous trees and shrubs; also grazes grasses and herbs

Breeding: Calves born singly (twins rare) in March after gestation of 7–8 months. Life span up to 15 years

Related endangered species: Mountain anoa (*Bubalus quarlesi*)* EN; wild yak (*Bos grunniens*)* VU; kouprey (*B. sauveli*) CR; gaur (*B. frontalis*)* VU; other wild cattle

Status: IUCN VU; CITES II

See also: Pasture 1: 38; Gaur 5: 18; Yak, Wild 10: 90

The takin *is found around the tree line in the Himalayan foothills. It lives in small herds of between 10 and 15 animals.*

Takin live in small herds and appear to be wilier than many of their close relatives; they are certainly more cunning than their domestic equivalents. At the first sign of danger takin raise the alarm with a loud, coughing snort, at which the entire herd will head for cover. They cannot run fast, but their yellowish-brown coat offers effective camouflage, especially when the animals lie down among dense bamboo.

Scent and Taste

Takin do not have specialized scent glands, yet scent is an important part of their lives, a trait that makes them more similar to goats than to other wild cattle. The animals secrete a smelly, oily substance from their skin and spray urine all over the underside of their body, which enhances their personal scent for others to interpret. Hormones in the urine may help advertise the breeding condition of an individual.

Another goatlike characteristic of the takin is its very broad diet. The animals will eat just about any plant material, favoring leaves and tender shoots, but they will also eat tough and even woody material if no alternative is available. If food is above head height, takin rear on their hind legs to reach it, something cattle do not do. Salt is also very important in the takin's diet, and the animals will travel long distances to find places where they can lick naturally occurring salt deposits.

Tamarin, Golden Lion

Leontopithecus rosalia

Most of the coastal forests in which the golden lion tamarin lives have been felled. Reintroductions of captive-bred animals have focused attention on the need to conserve the remaining habitat.

The tropical forests of Brazil's Atlantic coast used to be rich in wildlife, but since the early 19th century over 90 percent of the forest has been felled for timber and for fuel or to create space for people and agriculture. The forests have always been the only home of the golden lion tamarin, whose habitat was eventually reduced to barely 350 square miles (900 sq. km) and divided into more than a dozen separate patches. To make matters worse, many of these attractive creatures were captured for zoos or for sale as pets.

Golden lion tamarins are social animals that breed in small groups of about five individuals. All members of a group help care for the few young that are produced by the breeding females. If the group is disturbed or reduced to only two or three animals, the survivors will inevitably be less successful in raising young. Any reduction in numbers therefore leads to a downward spiral of ever fewer animals with even lower breeding success.

Numbers of the species as a whole fell to a critically low level in the 1970s, when the golden lion tamarin became one of the world's rarest mammals. A captive-breeding program involving zoos in several countries was begun in 1973. Within 10 years the number of animals involved had risen from about 70 to nearly 600, enabling some to be taken back to Brazil for reintroduction into the wild. The release project began in 1984, when 15 animals were set free in the coastal forest. Several soon died from disease, snakebite, or dog attack, but the first baby was born within a few weeks.

Back to the Wild

Initially the released tamarins found it difficult to cope with the challenges of survival in the wild. Used to being cared for by humans, they had lost crucial food-gathering skills. In recognition of the problems they faced, scientists took care to give subsequent animals some experience of conditions in the wild before releasing them. A period of adjustment helped improve the reintroduction program's success rate. By the early 1990s golden lion tamarins that had been released into the wild were breeding more successfully than their cousins in captivity. It was anticipated that in time the wild population could

DATA PANEL

Golden lion tamarin

Leontopithecus rosalia

Family: Callitrichidae

World population: About 800–900

Distribution: Coastal forest of Brazil

Habitat: Lowland tropical forest from sea level to about 3,000 ft (1,000 m)

Size: Length head/body: 8–13.5 in (20–34 cm); tail: 12.5–15.8 in (32–40 cm). Weight: 21–28 oz (600–800 g)

Form: Tiny monkey with long, silky golden hair and a long tail

Diet: Mostly fruit and insects; also small animals; occasionally birds' eggs

Breeding: Average of 2 young born September–March each year after 4-month gestation; mature at 2–3 years. Life span up to 15 years in captivity, less in the wild

Related endangered species: Black-faced lion tamarin (*Leontopithecus caissara*) CR; golden-headed lion tamarin (*L. chrysomelas*) EN; golden-rumped lion tamarin (*L. chrysopygus*) CR

Status: IUCN CR; CITES I

See also: Life Strategies 1: 24; Reintroduction 1: 92; Monkey, Goeldi's 6: 88

stop being dependent on humans to provide extra food and protection.

At present the population is still centered on the Poco das Antas Reserve in Rio de Janeiro Province, although as numbers have built up, and more animals have become available from zoos, additional populations have also been established in other parts of the coastal forest. Spreading the population reduces the risk of disease or fire wiping out the whole species at once.

Tamarin social groups are territorial, each needing an exclusive range of about 100 acres (40 ha). Tiny remnant patches of forest are consequently of little use to the animals and do not allow the population to expand. It therefore becomes vital to link up habitat patches by planting more trees. Thanks to conservation efforts since the project began, there has in fact been a 38 percent increase in forest cover in the areas where the tamarins live. Replanting is also bringing benefits to many other species.

Fortunately, local people—including major ranch owners in the region—have adopted the cause of the golden lion tamarin and are proud of the part they have played in helping conserve the species. An educational program has involved schoolchildren in the campaign to protect the animal's future.

The success of the conservation project has had the added benefit of focusing attention on the plight of other tamarin species. In 1998 Brazil's Superagui National Park was extended by more than 50 percent to accommodate the endangered black-faced lion tamarin. Several zoos are now breeding tamarin species that may one day be released to supplement wild populations elsewhere in South America.

Golden lion tamarins *are so called on account of their long mane of hair. All four species have a golden coloration, but only the golden lion tamarin is golden from head to toe.*

Tanager, Seven-Colored

Tangara fastuosa

Found only in the dwindling Atlantic forests of Brazil's northeastern states, the seven-colored tanager could disappear for good unless trapping and the destruction of its habitat are stopped.

One of the charms of the tropical evergreen forest in eastern Brazil is the sight of fruiting shrubs being raided by multicolored flocks of feeding tanagers, glowing among the foliage like feathered jewels. There are over 250 species of these colorful, finchlike birds, found only in the Americas and mostly in the tropics. Many have limited geographic ranges with little overlap and live in the high forest canopy, descending to the bushes to feed.

Of these birds the most dazzling is arguably the seven-colored tanager. It lives in the Atlantic forests of northeastern Brazil, nesting mainly in bromeliads and other epiphytic plants (those that grow on others) high up in mature forest trees, in much the same way that mistletoe does. The bird has probably always had a restricted range, being replaced by other tanagers to the north, west, and south; but in the past the richness of its habitat enabled a dense population to live within a relatively small area. Today that natural wealth is disappearing, and the bird is in serious danger of becoming extinct.

Dwindling Habitats

Brazil's Atlantic forests are enormously rich in plant and animal diversity, and provide a home for many endemic species. Now, however, they are widely regarded as one of the most threatened ecosystems in the world. They were among the first parts of Brazil to be settled by Europeans, and woodlands were the first to be exploited on an industrial scale. The Portuguese were shipping thousands of hardwood trees back to Europe each year as long ago as 1519; and once the trees were felled, the land was cleared for agriculture. The soil beneath the coastal lowland forests proved particularly fertile, with the result that over the centuries nearly all the lowland tree cover has been swept away. In the states of Pernambuco and Alagoas, where the seven-colored tanager lives, all but 2 percent of the original forest has now been felled. The lowlands are now a sea of sugarcane, while logging and smaller-scale farming of coffee, banana, and rubber are steadily eroding the wooded areas that remain on the steeper mountain slopes.

As a result, the once-continuous forest has become fragmented into

---

DATA PANEL

Seven-colored tanager

Tangara fastuosa

Family: Emberizidae

World population: 2,500–10,000 birds

Distribution: Restricted to the states of Pernambuco and Alagoas in extreme northeastern Brazil; also (at least formerly) Paraíba

Habitat: Breeds in primary Atlantic forest; forages in forest and adjacent scrub

Size: Length: 5 in (13 cm). Weight: about 0.3 oz (8 g)

Form: A small perching bird with a stout, seed-cracking bill and striking plumage. Turquoise-blue head, neck, and wing coverts; bright-blue breast; ultramarine belly; black back; blue-black tail; orange rump, lower back, and edges to tertial wing feathers

Diet: Mainly seeds and berries

Breeding: Nests October–March in tall, mature forest trees, often in epiphytic bromeliads. Breeding details little known, but *Tangara* species typically lay 2 eggs that hatch after 13–14 days, with a nestling period of 15–16 days

Related endangered species: Many species in the tanager subfamily Thraupinae, including the azure-rumped tanager (*Tangara cabanisi*) EN; green-capped tanager (*T. meyerdeschauenseei*) VU; black-backed tanager (*T. peruviana*) VU; Sira tanager (*T. phillipsi*) LRnt

Status: IUCN EN; CITES II

See also: Communities and Ecosystems **1:** 22; Saving the Habitats **1:** 88; Finch, Mangrove **4:** 76; Manakin, Black-Capped **6:** 66

small islands surrounded by plantations and the degraded secondary forest that grows on cleared land. The shrubs growing in the degraded areas do at least offer the tanagers food, even if not in such variety as the virgin forest they have replaced; but the birds still rely on the primary forest canopy for nesting sites. The surviving population of seven-colored tanagers is consequently being fragmented.

Habitat fragmentation greatly increases the species' vulnerability because each pocket of forest is itself dwindling. In one of the bird's few remaining strongholds, at Murici, primary forest that extended over 27 square miles (70 sq. km) in the 1970s had been reduced to a discontinuous 12 square miles (30 sq. km) by 1999. This perilously small area could easily disappear altogether, along with the tanagers that live in it, either as a result of accidental fires spreading from nearby plantations or because of logging or agricultural conversion.

Brazil also has a strong cage-bird tradition, and almost every household keeps a songbird. The custom supports a lucrative trade in wild-caught birds, and the seven-colored tanager's glorious plumage makes it one of the most valuable catches. Many are trapped illegally, further reducing the species' chances of long-term survival. Captive birds have been confiscated and returned to reserves, but until such areas receive effective protection, they will not be out of danger.

The seven-colored tanager *is one of many tanager species that are currently at risk. A few thousand individuals survive in pockets of residual forest in northeastern Brazil.*

In recent decades the rate of habitat destruction has accelerated. Much of the remaining virgin forest is privately owned; and although many areas are legally protected, the value of the timber far outstrips the fines levied for felling it. Illegal logging has, until recently at least, been occurring even at Murici.

There is now a move to make Murici a fully protected reserve. In March 2000 BirdLife Brazil began a site conservation project there, partly funded by money raised at the 1999 British Birdwatching Fair, where the seven-colored tanager was the flagship species for conservation in northeastern Brazil. Such initiatives may yet preserve the remaining forest that supports tanager populations, but this is only the beginning in the bid to conserve this lovely bird.

Tapir, Central American

Tapirus bairdii

With conservation laws rarely enforced and a high price on its hide, the Central American tapir is illegally hunted over much of its range. The animal's habitat is shrinking fast as farmers and engineers seek to adapt the land to their own uses.

Although they look something like a cross between a pig and an elephant, tapirs are in fact more closely related to horses and rhinoceroses, and are far more nimble and adaptable than their appearance would suggest. In fact, the trails they blaze across difficult terrain often provide the only passageways for other animals and for humans. There are two species of American tapir, and both face similar problems. The mountain tapir is highly endangered; there are possibly fewer than 2,000 left. The Central American tapir is probably more numerous, but it is still threatened.

American tapirs have been hunted for sport and also for their meat, which is considered a delicacy. They are particularly sought after for their hides, which can be tanned to make fine leather. Unfortunately for the tapirs, the trails they create make them relatively easy to track down. Although they are wary animals, with good hearing and a superb sense of smell, they give themselves away only too easily by responding to imitations of their distinctive, whistling call, or else by crashing through the undergrowth.

The tapir's best defense against predators is to take to the water. They are excellent swimmers and can remain submerged for several minutes at a time. In fact, water plays a vital role in the tapir's ecology. The areas where they live are crisscrossed with rivers and streams, and most of their food comes from the river or the dense vegetation that grows at the water's edge. The Central American tapir's dependence on this "riparian" waterside habitat is one reason why the species is becoming rare. Logging and land clearance not only destroy swathes of forest, but also

DATA PANEL

Central American tapir (Baird's tapir)

Tapirus bairdii

Family: Tapiridae

World population: Unknown and almost impossible to estimate, but probably in the low thousands

Distribution: Southern Mexico south to Ecuador and Colombia

Habitat: Riverine forest and grassland

Size: Length: 6–8 ft (1.8–2.5 m); height at shoulder: 29–47 in (74–120 cm). Weight: 330–660 lb (150–300 kg)

Form: Long-nosed, piglike animal, with short, coarse, brown hair and sparse mane on back of neck and shoulders. Short legs, with 4 toes on front, 3 on hind feet

Diet: Leaves, buds, shoots, and fruits of terrestrial shrubs and aquatic vegetation

Breeding: Single offspring born after gestation of 13–14 months; weaned at 6–8 months; mature at 1.5–2 years. May live for up to 30 years

Related endangered species: Mountain tapir *(Tapirus pinchaque)* EN; Malayan tapir *(T. indicus)** VU

Status: IUCN VU; CITES I

See also: Drainage and Irrigation 1: 40; Ecotourism 1: 90; Tapir, Malayan 9: 58

have a carry-over effect farther inland as drainage patterns and nutrient levels change. Many waterside habitats are severely affected by these developments, which have a serious impact on tapir numbers.

The Dangers of Encroachment

As people encroach further into the tapir's habitat, encounters between tapirs and domestic stock will undoubtedly increase. While there is little evidence that contact between the animals could harm the livestock, it seems that tapirs are vulnerable to some diseases carried by horses. Having had no chance to build up an immunity to such infections, and without the veterinary help available to their domestic relatives, tapir populations risk being seriously affected by relatively minor ailments.

Young tapirs *like this one spend 13 to 14 months developing inside the mother and are born singly. It is a further 10 months before they can fend for themselves. This slow reproductive rate is a factor in the species' decline.*

Large areas of prime tapir habitat are also under threat from plans to create huge reservoirs in the forest. One such project in Belize will flood 90 percent of one of the tapir's few remaining strongholds.

On a more hopeful note, ecotourism is becoming big business in parts of Central America, and tourists want to see large mammals such as tapirs. This could be a positive step as long as the needs of the environment are respected. If the tapir's habitat continues to be destroyed, however, there will be little wildlife left to see.

Tapir, Malayan

Tapirus indicus

The black-and-white tapirs of Southeast Asia are still widespread. However, because they are thinly distributed among small islands of habitat, they are highly vulnerable to hunting and to the danger of further habitat loss.

Fossils and other remains suggest that Malayan tapirs were once widespread throughout Southeast Asia. Ten thousand years ago their range probably extended from northern India across southeastern China to Laos and Vietnam, and through Thailand, Myanmar (Burma), and Malaysia to Indonesia. There was even a report in 1929 of tapirs living on Borneo, but their presence there was never confirmed; if the sighting was indeed of a Malayan tapir, it must have been one of the last on the island. For the most part, tapirs have been eliminated from all of the edge of their former range, leaving them only in its center in Myanmar, Thailand, Malaysia, and Sumatra. The decline took place over many hundreds of years, and scientists generally agree that the animals' range had already shrunk considerably before humans began to interfere with the environment.

If we were to consider range alone as a measure of the tapir's status, we might draw the conclusion that little has changed in recent times, so there is little cause for concern. However, this is far from the case. What was once a vast tract of forest habitat, broken only by mountains and floodplains, is now a mixture of agricultural land, grazing pasture, and human settlement, interspersed with scattered patches of degraded or regenerating forest. None of the land is good tapir country. Islands of pristine jungle suitable for tapirs are shrinking, and the resident animals form small clusters, isolated from populations elsewhere.

Malayan tapirs are preyed on by tigers and leopards, a fact that poses something of a conservation puzzle: what to do when one endangered species threatens another. However, native predators cannot be held responsible for the overall decline of the tapir, especially since they themselves are now so rare.

DATA PANEL

Malayan tapir (Asian tapir)

Tapirus indicus

Family: Tapiridae

World population: Unknown, perhaps up to 5,000

Distribution: Myanmar (Burma), Thailand, mainland Malaysia, Indonesia (Sumatra only)

Habitat: Dense tropical rain forest; grasslands close to water

Size: Length 6–9 ft (1.8–2.7 m); height at shoulder: 29–47 in (73–120 cm). Weight: 330–700 lb (150–320 kg)

Form: Robust, piglike animal with long, fleshy snout and short, sturdy legs. Striking markings: white body, with black head and legs

Diet: Grass, leaves of shrubs and aquatic plants, twigs; also seeks out salt licks

Breeding: Single young born every other year in May–June after 13–14 month gestation; mature at 3 years. May live as long as 30 years

Related endangered species: Central American tapir *(Tapirus bairdii)** VU; mountain tapir *(T. pinchaque)* EN

Status: IUCN VU; CITES I

See also: Communities and Ecosystems 1: 22; Natural Extinction 1: 34; Money Problems 1: 88; Tapir, Central American 9: 56

Tapirs are prized for their flesh by humans too, although in some parts of their range they are spared the additional pressure of hunting for meat because Muslims do not eat them. Elsewhere tapir meat is highly valued, despite the fact that selling it without a license is illegal. There is also a continuing trade in live animals. Malayan tapirs are both striking in appearance and very docile. They seem to take to captivity well, making them popular with private collectors. Their adaptability is a mixed blessing; since they can be bred in captivity, they are unlikely to become extinct. At the same time, the continued illegal trade threatens the vulnerable wild population.

Keeping Track of Tapirs

The Malayan tapir has been far less researched than the New World species of Central and South America. Expeditions to study the animals are expensive and sometimes dangerous. In recent years, however, technology has provided a solution in the form of camera-trapping. Automatic cameras set up along well-used animal trails are triggered when a beam of infrared light is broken by a passing animal. The photographs have provided useful information about many species, including tapirs.

The tapir shares parts of its range with several other high-profile endangered animals, and it could be that efforts to save such "flagship" species will prove the tapir's best hope for preservation. Meanwhile, their decline in Asia as in America removes one of the key species involved in dispersing the seeds of large trees. Their loss thus interferes with the natural processes of forest regeneration, with potentially disastrous long-term consequences.

The Malayan tapir's *striking markings are conspicuous in daylight, but come into their own after dark. By night the animal blends in well with the bright pools of light and deep shadows created by the moon.*

Tarantula, Red-Kneed

Euathlus smithi

Although there are many species of tarantula, the different forms generally share similar characteristics. Their large, hairy bodies are often strikingly marked, and some species have become popular as pets. Collection of the red-kneed tarantula has put the wild population at risk.

The red-kneed tarantula is arguably the most popular of all pet tarantulas, and people have been collecting specimens since the 1970s. First discovered in 1888, the spider was soon recognized as having potential as a pet. It was also used to heighten tension in films such as *Raiders of the Lost Ark*. Such publicity encouraged collection, and tarantulas were sold in pet stores for many years.

The red-kneed tarantula is found mainly in Mexico and Central America. Its natural habitat is scrubland and desert that provide temperatures of 70–90°F (20–30°C) and humidity of about 60 percent. The spider is found near cacti and bushes, and among logs, rocks, and other debris. It digs burrows in the ground that it lines with spider silk.

For most of the time the spider is relatively docile. However, a threatened red-kneed tarantula will rear up and display the red bristles on its body. As a defensive measure it will flick off urticating (irritant) hairs in the direction of its predator. The hairs are microscopically barbed (having tiny hooks) and can be irritating to the skin and lungs, causing a form of urticaria (an allergic disorder). Serious damage can occur if any hairs become embedded in the eye. Although most people are not seriously affected by the spider's venom, some are allergic to it and can have a strong adverse reaction.

Intriguing Habits

The red-kneed tarantula has a typical spider form, including a pair of fangs (chelicerae) that it uses to stab prey and inject venom. Pedipalps—small appendages near the mouth—have a number of functions, including handling prey. The spiders have poor vision, but sensory structures on the end of the legs allow them to smell, taste, and feel.

The tarantula does not spin a web to catch its food; insects, small amphibians, and sometimes mice are actively hunted at night. The prey is subdued with venom and then flooded with digestive juices. Tarantulas are unable to digest food internally, so the digested "soup" of nutritionally valuable parts of the prey are sucked back by the spider.

Males are often eaten by their mates after mating. When mature, a male spider spins a tubular web in which he deposits sperm. He then draws the sperm up into a special receptacle in his pedipalps. When mating is about to start, the male makes courtship signals, which help ensure that the female does not mistake him for prey. He uses tibial spurs (sharp projections) to grip the female's fangs while placing sperm in the female's reproductive tract.

Black Market

Although red-kneed tarantulas are relatively easy to keep, they are not easy to breed in captivity. The females live for a long time, often up to 20 years in captivity, but their reproductive rate tends to be slow. As a result of their popularity with collectors and the tarantula's vulnerability to habitat change, the species has become seriously threatened. Populations could not sustain the demands of the pet trade, and the wild spiders are now difficult to find. Mexico has prohibited their capture and export, but a black market still exists: Smugglers have been caught trying to take them out of their native countries.

See also: Biomes **1:** 18; Exploitation of Live Animals **1:** 49; Spider, Great Raft **9:** 22; Spider, Kauai Cave Wolf **9:** 24

TARANTULA, RED-KNEED

DATA PANEL

Red-kneed tarantula

Euathlus smithi

Family: Theraphosidae

World population: Unknown

Distribution: Central America and Mexico

Habitat: Scrubland and desert

Size: Length: up to 2.5 in (6.4 cm); leg span: up to 5 in (12.7 cm)

Form: Cephalothorax (arachnid with joined head and thorax); opisthosoma (abdomen) with 4 pairs of strikingly patterned legs; claws for gripping. Eight eyes on head allow all-round (but poor) vision. Males have thin body and long legs; mature males have tibial spurs (sharp projections) on pedipalps (appendages on cephalothorax) to grip female's fangs during mating

Diet: Insects; also small animals such as lizards and mice

Breeding: Female produces up to 700 young a year (often fewer). Eggs wrapped in silk and carried by mother. Spiderlings guarded for several weeks after hatching. Life span of males 7–8 years; females 20–25 years in captivity

Related endangered species: None

Status: IUCN LRnt; not listed by CITES

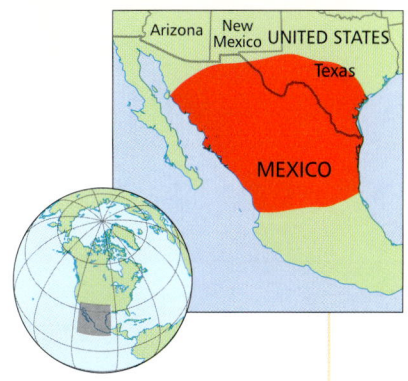

The red-kneed tarantula *is strikingly patterned and has been a favorite with collectors.*

Teal, Baikal

Anas formosa

The world population of this beautiful duck is in rapid retreat—a decline caused chiefly by hunting and the destruction of major wetland sites in its wintering range.

The exquisite-looking Baikal teal has a very apt specific scientific name: *formosa* means "beautiful." The males are particularly handsome in their breeding plumage, while the females have a more sober charm (as with other ducks, their more muted colors provide camouflage and protection from predators while sitting on the nest). The teal's common name refers to Lake Baikal, the largest freshwater lake in the world. On the western fringes of the species' breeding range, the lake was where the first individuals were found by explorers in 1775.

Until the early 1900s it was one of the most numerous ducks in eastern Asia, common across much of the tundra and the boggy taiga regions of Russia. Flocks thousands strong were regularly seen when the birds migrated to their winter quarters farther south, with particularly impressive concentrations being reported from Japan, a major wintering site for the species. In the 1960s one flock of 100,000 birds was reported there; another was estimated to be about 2 miles (3 km) long.

Recent Decline

Since the 1970s, however, ornithologists have detected a major decline in numbers among Baikal teal. Shooting and trapping were probably the main factors that brought about this sorry situation. Early in the winter of 1947, for example, just three hunters in southwestern Japan took a reported 50,000 Baikal teal, including some 10,000 birds in a single day.

Hunting still poses a serious threat. As well as being shot, the ducks are killed in China and South Korea using poisoned grain. Mortality can be high, since the species gathers in large flocks on arable land where huge numbers can be killed at a time.

Such direct persecution is not the whole story, however. Habitat loss is also a threat. At China's largest freshwater lake, Poyang Hu, and on the adjacent Sanjiang plain major declines have occurred

DATA PANEL

Baikal teal

Anas formosa

Family: Anatidae

World population: At least 250,000 birds

Distribution: Breeds in eastern Siberia; migrates through Mongolia and North Korea; winters mainly in Japan, South Korea, and China

Habitat: Breeds in open meadows with grass tussocks near water and in bogs with mosses and clumps of willow and larch; winters on lakes and reservoirs and on farmland

Size: Length: 15–17 in (39–43 cm). Weight: 13–18 oz (360–520 g)

Form: Small, compact dabbling duck; male in breeding plumage (most of year) has striking head pattern. Female resembles females of other dabbling ducks, but more strongly spotted, especially on flanks

Diet: Grasses, sedges, water plants, algae, and crops, including grain and acorns; also snails, insects, and other aquatic invertebrates

Breeding: Begins in May; nests in single pairs or loose groups; female makes hollow concealed in vegetation; lays 6–9 pale-green eggs, which she incubates on her own for 3–3.5 weeks; ducklings fledge in 3.5–4 weeks

Related endangered species: Twenty-two species of duck are threatened, including marbled teal (*Marmaronetta angustirostris*) VU; Eaton's pintail (*Anas eatoni*) VU; Campbell Island teal (*A. nesiotis*) CR; brown teal (*A. chlorotis*) EN; and Madagascar teal (*A. bernieri*) EN. A further 5 have become extinct in historical times

Status: IUCN VU; CITES II

See also: Drainage and Irrigation **1:** 40; Hunting **1:** 42; Duck, Labrador **4:** 42; Duck, White-Headed **4:** 44

not just because of hunting but also as a result of drainage and alteration of habitat for agriculture. Wintering sites in South Korea, too, are threatened by the drainage and development of wetlands.

Saving the Species

Although the Baikal teal is legally protected in Hong Kong, Japan, Mongolia, Russia, South Korea, and some provinces of China, it is still sometimes hunted in its wintering areas. Although some major sites—such as Lakes Bolob and Khanka in Siberia and Katano in Japan—lie within protected areas, others continue to be threatened by habitat alteration or degradation.

To ensure the teal's future, conservationists need to learn more about its decline and the threats it faces. Other targets are to put in place a management plan for the largest wintering population, in South Korea; to research the bird's status as a winter visitor in China; to control hunting of all ducks in China (even where birds are protected, they can be shot in

The Baikal teal's *beautiful plumage has not saved it from hunters, who at one stage threatened its survival, though numbers have recovered in recent years.*

error for commoner species); and to ensure the teal is legally protected by all nations within its large range.

Encouragingly, reports of huge concentrations of Baikal teals have recently come from birders in South Korea via the Korean Wetlands Alliance, a South Korean organization devoted to conserving wetlands. A count in January 1999 at Haenam tidal flats in southwestern Korea recorded a single flock of at least 168,000 Baikal teal, although the most recent total world population estimate at the time, made in 1997, was only 105,000. Then in November 1999 a same-day count at two sites, Haenam and Cheonsu Bay, suggested that the wintering population of the species in Korea alone might amount to more than 250,000 birds, again suggesting that the species' status may be on the mend.

Tenrec, Aquatic

Limnogale mergulus

The aquatic tenrec has evolved specialized characteristics to cope with its environment, but even minor changes to its habitat bring major problems; it is now the rarest of the tenrec family.

The mammals belonging to the order Insectivora are a diverse bunch, including families as different as shrews, hedgehogs, and moles. But there is one family of insectivores—the tenrecs—that appears to reflect this diversity within a single family. There is no typical tenrec; they come in all shapes and sizes from shrewlike long-tailed tenrecs through animals that look just like European hedgehogs to the mink-sized giant otter shrew.

The secret of the tenrecs' diversity lies in the fact that most of them live on the large island of Madagascar (off the east coast of Africa in the Indian Ocean). Here, in the absence of competition from true shrews, desmans, and hedgehogs, the tenrecs have diversified to take over their roles and follow a broad range of insectivore lifestyles.

The aquatic tenrec is the Madagascan equivalent of the semiaquatic desmans of southern Europe and Russia. It is roughly the size of a rat; adults can grow to over 1 foot (30 cm), with a tail of about half the total length. Their webbed feet and flattened tail help make them excellent swimmers. Largely nocturnal animals, their eyesight is generally poor, but they use their whiskers and keen senses of hearing and smell to locate prey.

The aquatic tenrec is extremely rare and apparently restricted to a few scattered sites in and around the Ranomafana National Park in eastern Madagascar. Few live specimens have been recorded, but now concerted efforts are being made to find out more about these threatened animals.

Financial resources for such research are difficult to find, not least because Madagascar itself is a poor country. The aquatic tenrec is of no great importance commercially. It does not cause a nuisance to people; and while its fur is fine and dense—like that of an otter—the animal is too

DATA PANEL

Aquatic tenrec (web-footed tenrec)

Limnogale mergulus

Family: Tenrecidae

World population: Unknown

Distribution: Scattered sites on eastern Madagascar

Habitat: Clean, fast-flowing rivers and streams at 2,000–4,000 ft (600–1,200 m)

Size: Length head/body: 4.5–6.5 in (12–17 cm); tail: 4.5–6 in (12–16 cm). Weight: 2–3 oz (60–90 g)

Form: Large ratlike animal with soft, dense, brown fur and gray belly; eyes and ears small and inconspicuous; feet webbed; tail slightly flattened and with fringe of stiff hairs

Diet: Frogs, fish, aquatic crustaceans, and insect larvae

Breeding: Little known; litters of 1–6 young born December–January

Related endangered species: Giant otter shrew *(Potamogale velox)** EN; Ruwenzori otter shrew *(Micropotamogale ruwenzorii)* EN; Mount Nimba otter shrew *(M. lamottei)* EN; 6 species of long-tailed tenrec *(Microgale* spp.) are Critically Endangered, Endangered, or Vulnerable

Status: IUCN EN; not listed by CITES

See also: Island Biogeography **1:** 30; Desman, Russian **4:** 14; Shrew, Giant Otter **8:** 90

TENREC, AQUATIC

The aquatic tenrec is rarely seen because when not hiding in its burrow, it spends most of its time in or under the water. Its webbed feet provide propulsion, and its long, flattened tail acts as a rudder; these adaptations make it an excellent swimmer.

small and rare to make hunting for its skin a worthwhile undertaking. Consequently, little is known about the tenrec's lifestyle and numbers.

Specific Needs

Captive breeding is not a realistic option for the species. Exporting the tenrecs from Madagascar to zoos elsewhere in the world would be problematic, since every tenrec that died or failed to breed would simply add to the crisis facing the species as a whole.

There is an increasing market in live specimens of other species of tenrec that are kept as pets or in zoos, but as yet there have been no successful attempts to keep aquatic tenrecs in captivity.

Apart from the fact that specimens are hard to come by, it would be difficult to re-create the animal's habitat requirements under artificial conditions. In the wild aquatic tenrecs live in burrows on the banks of fast-flowing rivers and streams from which they emerge to hunt at night. All or most of their prey is caught in the water, and beds of the waterweed *Aponogeton* provide the best hunting grounds. Among the roots and stems of the plants live a variety of small fish, frogs, crustaceans, and insect larvae, all of which make good eating for tenrecs. The fast-flowing water is an important element in the tenrec's natural habitat, since it continually rinses and conditions the animal's fur. Slow-moving or stagnant water would allow the fur to become fouled with algae and other debris, after which it would quickly lose its waterproofing and insulating properties.

Minor Change, Major Impact

The aquatic tenrec's specific habitat requirements are probably the main underlying reason for its decline. The species' specialized lifestyle can become impossible as a result of even fairly minor changes in the local environment. For example, increased mud in the water as a result of deforestation upstream affects the abundance of aquatic prey and also clogs the tenrec's fur. Changes in water flow may also affect the availability of prey.

The wholesale removal of *Aponogeton* beds is probably disastrous to tenrecs. Chemicals such as fertilizers that seep into the water from surrounding farmland may also have a range of consequences, from poisoning of prey to causing the failure of the tenrec's immune and reproductive systems.

Thylacine

Thylacinus cynocephalus

The thylacine—a marsupial—was once prevalent across Australia and Tasmania. Today it seems that domestic dogs and other introduced animals have outcompeted the species. It was also persecuted by farmers and is now probably extinct, although there are continued reports of sightings.

The thylacine appears to have been an unsuccessful evolutionary experiment. The largest marsupial carnivore of recent times, it was a surprisingly clumsy and rather slow-moving creature, ill equipped to be a predator. It is said to have stalked its prey at night or run after wallabies until they got tired and could be killed. Its jaws were longer than a dog's, and it had more teeth, but they were probably unable to deliver a strong bite.

The thylacine has no close relatives. Once placental mammals such as dingoes and, later, foxes and domestic dogs and cats reached Australia, the thylacine was forced to compete with these more efficient hunters and killers. It swiftly disappeared from its former wide range, although there were many reports of sightings on the mainland of Australia, even into the early 20th century.

Forced into Island Isolation

By about 1910 all remaining thylacines were confined to Tasmania, an island that initially lacked competing carnivores. The arrival of Europeans brought about a period of large-scale change to the habitat and to the species profile of the island. Once sheep farming began there, the thylacine was considered to be a serious pest, having a reputation as a livestock killer, particularly of sheep and hens. From about 1840 farmers killed them in large numbers; by about 1860 they had disappeared from the lowlands, surviving only in the more inaccessible mountain forests.

Government-Sponsored Extinction

From 1888 the killing was further encouraged by the Australian government, which offered payments for dead thylacines. Records show that rewards were paid for over 2,000 thylacines during a 20-year period, and many more must have died unrecorded. Most were shot or snared, but many were also poisoned. The species rapidly vanished from Tasmania, perhaps hastened into extinction by a disease that swept through other species of carnivorous marsupials, sharply reducing their numbers. The thylacine was given legal protection in 1936, but by then was probably already extinct in the wild.

DATA PANEL

Thylacine (Tasmanian wolf, Tasmanian tiger, marsupial wolf)

Thylacinus cynocephalus

Family: Thylacinidae (but often considered a member of the Dasyuridae)

World population: 0 (Extinct)

Distribution: Formerly mainland Australia and Tasmania

Habitat: Open woodland

Size: Length head/body: 35–50 in (90–130 cm); tail: 20–25 in (50–65 cm); height to shoulder: 14–24 in (35–60 cm); males larger than females. Weight: up to about 40 lb (18 kg)

Form: Resembles a heavy, sandy-colored dog, with bold black stripes across its haunches. Long, stiff tail

Diet: Small wallabies and kangaroos; probably also smaller mammals, birds, and reptiles

Breeding: Two to 3 young born mainly December–March. Rear-facing pouch housing 4 nipples. Life span in wild unknown; 13 years in captivity

Related endangered species: No close relatives

Status: IUCN EX; CITES 1

See also: Introductions 1: 54; Special Techniques 1: 88; Wombat, Northern Hairy-Nosed 10: 76

The last wild thylacine was captured in 1933 and lived alone in Hobart Zoo, Tasmania, where it died in 1936. There have been many reports of sightings since then, even on the Australian mainland. However, many searches—including a major venture in 1980—have failed to produce any concrete evidence that the thylacine is still alive. Photographs (that may be of another species, or even complete fakes) appear in newspapers from time to time.

A mummified thylacine body was found in a cave in 1949, but there is still disagreement over whether it had died recently or many centuries previously. In 1985 some color photographs and casts of footprints were obtained in Western Australia, but their authenticity has been questioned. Nevertheless, such reports offer the tantalizing possibility that one day a living thylacine might materialize.

In Tasmania a large area of the animal's former habitat has been set aside as a protected reserve just in case any have survived.

It has also been suggested that it might be possible to recreate a thylacine by cloning genetic material (DNA) obtained from a museum specimen. The idea is often proposed for various types of extinct animals, including dinosaurs. However, much depends on how well preserved the DNA is, and whether it is still intact. If more than a few years old, DNA is unlikely to be suitable. The chances of success are greater if it has been preserved by refrigeration or in an appropriate chemical.

The thylacine *was a large animal with bold stripes. The photograph (top) shows the last thylacine in captivity, which died in 1936. No specimens, alive or freshly dead, have been obtained since then, but reported sightings are investigated seriously.*

Tiger

Panthera tigris

Tigers used to occur across Asia as far west as Turkey, and isolated populations developed into eight different subspecies.

Within their huge range tigers have adapted to conditions ranging from bleak mountain forests to mangrove swamps and jungle. Since the beginning of the 20th century numbers have sharply declined, usually through conflict with humans. Tigers are large and fierce animals. They need to kill to eat and will often kill domestic animals and even people. Their own habitat has been reduced by farming and logging to the point where natural prey is difficult to obtain in sufficient quantity. Humans hunt the same prey, leaving few animals for the tigers.

By the 1950s three of the tiger subspecies (Bali, Caspian, and Javan) had become extinct. The remaining populations occur in widely separate places: India, Vietnam, Sumatra, China, and Siberia. The largest subspecies, the Amur (or Siberian) tiger, once ranged throughout the forested areas of China and Korea, north to the forested edges of Siberia. However, in the late 19th century tigers were a major threat to railway construction and increased settlement, so they were persecuted. By the 1940s tigers survived only in about five separated areas. Since then they have benefited from protection, and they have now increased in numbers and distribution again. There were about 450 Amur tigers in 1996. However, climate change now poses new threats.

On Bali and Java the extinction of the tiger was a result of habitat fragmentation, loss of natural prey, and finally, in the 1960s, conflict with groups of heavily armed men hiding in the jungle as a result of civil war. In India tigers used to be a favorite target for big-game hunters, and many thousands were shot.

The tiger *is the largest member of the cat family. There are thought to be about 4,500 in India, the species' main stronghold.*

Throughout Asia the tiger is believed to have magical powers, and many of its body parts are highly prized in traditional Oriental medicine. Killing a single tiger, therefore, can bring huge rewards to a poacher willing to risk the penalties for breaking the law.

Captive Breeding

Tigers breed well in captivity, so they are unlikely to become extinct. However, the captive population has become seriously inbred in the past, and there has been genetic mixing between the different subspecies. In addition, tigers cost a lot to feed, so most zoos give the animals contraceptives as a way of controlling the numbers of young born. It would be relatively easy to breed captive tigers for reintroduction to the wild, but there is not enough suitable habitat left for release of captive-bred stock.

The future lies in careful management of the remaining tiger habitats and reserves. Conservation measures will include linking small, isolated groups of animals and preventing poaching and further habitat loss. It is also vital to have plenty of prey animals; huge areas of land need to be set aside to maintain the prey populations required to support just a few tigers. The dangers of inbreeding may be reduced by using captive-bred animals as a fresh gene source.

See also: What Is an Endangered Species? **1:** 8; Cultural Differences **1:** 94; Leopard **6:** 28; Lion, Asiatic **6:** 34

TIGER

DATA PANEL

Tiger
Panthera tigris

Family: Felidae

World population: 5,000–7,500 (1998 estimate)

Distribution: From India east to China and Vietnam and south to Indonesia (Sumatra)

Habitat: Dense cover: forests, scrub, and tall grass thickets; also mangroves

Size: Length head/body: 4.5–9 ft (1.4–2.7 m); tail: 24–43 in (60–110 cm); height at shoulder: 31–43 in (80–110 cm). Weight: up to 790 lb (360 kg) in the largest Siberian tigers

Form: Unmistakable, large orange cat with black stripes and long tail

Diet: Mostly deer and wild pigs weighing 110–440 lb (50–200 kg). Occasionally smaller animals such as monkeys, fish, and even birds. Needs about 33–40 lb (15–18 kg) per day

Breeding: Two or 3 cubs per litter, born after 14-week gestation; about 2 years between litters. Life span 15 years in wild, at least 26 in captivity

Related endangered species: Snow leopard *(Uncia uncia)** EN; lion *(Panthera leo)* VU; clouded leopard *(Neofelis nebulosa)** VU; also several smaller species of cat, including Iberian lynx *(Lynx pardinus)** EN

Status: IUCN EN; CITES I

Toad, Golden

Bufo periglenes

The golden toad has become a symbol of declining amphibian populations. Although living in a protected habitat, the species disappeared along with several other frog and toad species, and is now probably extinct. The cause of this dramatic decline is unknown.

Most toads belonging to the genus *Bufo* are dull in color. Males and females are generally similar in appearance, with the females slightly larger than the males. The golden toad is highly unusual in that the coloration of the male is strikingly different from that of the female. While the female is greenish-yellow and black, decorated with yellow-edged red spots, the male is bright orange or red. The biological significance of the color difference is unknown.

Golden toads live in "elfin" cloud forest, so called because the trees' growth is stunted by powerful winds. When the forest is shrouded in dense cloud, it creates a damp climate that favors the growth of epiphytic plants and creepers (plants that grow on other plants, but are not parasitic). The toads have been seen only in the breeding season from March to June following the rain and lasting only a few days or weeks. The rain fills small pools—many form around the roots of trees—that are essential for the breeding biology of the species. Large numbers of golden toads gather at the shallow pools, with males typically outnumbering females.

Tadpole Survival

Most toads lay very large numbers of small eggs (several thousand in many species) that hatch into tiny tadpoles. The eggs of the golden toad, however, are large, with a sizeable part consisting of yolk, and the average clutch size is only about 300. It is thought that this pattern evolved because the breeding pools used by the golden toad could become very crowded and did not support a sufficient growth of algae to provide food for large numbers of tadpoles. Golden toad tadpoles need the nutrients provided by the yolk if they are to grow quickly and metamorphose (transform into an adult) before their breeding ponds dry out.

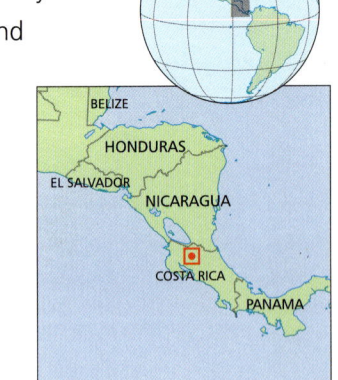

DATA PANEL

Golden toad (sapo dorado)
Bufo periglenes
Family: Bufonidae
World population: Probably 0
Habitat: Montane (mountainous) cloud forest
Distribution: Monteverde Cloud Forest Preserve, Cordillera de Tilaran, Costa Rica
Size: Length: male 1.5–2 in (4.1–4.8 cm); female 1.8–2.3 in (4.7–5.4 cm)
Form: Male bright red or orange; female mottled black, red, and yellow
Diet: Insects and other invertebrates
Breeding: Clutch size of about 300 eggs laid March–June; hatch into tadpoles
Related endangered species: Amatola toad (*Bufo amatolicus*) VU; boreal toad (*B. boreas*) EN; Yosemite toad (*B. canorus*) EN; black toad (*B. exsul*) VU; Houston toad (*B. houstonensis*) EN; Amargosa toad (*B. nelsoni*) EN
Status: IUCN CR; CITES I

The golden toad *appears to have become a victim of climate change, dying out because its habitat has become too dry for breeding.*

See also: Climate Change 1: 53; Toad, Natterjack 9: 74; Toad, Western 9: 76

Most toads lay their eggs in large, permanent ponds that are rich in algae and other nutrients.

Mysterious Decline

The golden toad was first described in 1964, having been observed during the breeding season. In 1987 1,500 animals were counted, but in both 1988 and 1989 only one individual was recorded at Monteverde in Costa Rica. Since then not a single golden toad has been seen. Over the same period about 20 percent of the frog and toad species found at Monteverde declined dramatically in numbers. During this time 25 species disappeared; only five have reappeared since. The species that were affected were those most dependent on standing water for breeding.

The cause of the dramatic population decline is not understood.

Monteverde is a nature reserve and is not subject to habitat destruction of any kind, nor are any herbicides, pesticides, or other chemicals used in the locality.

A detailed analysis of the climate at Monteverde suggests that climate change may be responsible for the demise of the golden toad and other frog and toad species. Since the 1970s the number of days each year when the forest is shrouded in cloud has diminished, affecting the local fauna. Bird and reptile species that once occurred at lower, drier altitudes have moved into higher altitudes. It seems that the golden toads died out when their habitat became too dry for successful breeding.

Toad, Mallorcan Midwife

Alytes muletensis

The Mallorcan midwife toad has an unusual reproductive strategy. Confined to a restricted habitat, it is now being sustained by a captive-breeding and release program.

The tiny Mallorcan midwife toad was known as a fossil long before it was discovered alive; it was found alive and named as recently as 1977. Now confined to about 10 isolated localities in the Sierra de Tramuntana, a mountainous region in western Mallorca, it once lived throughout the island. Its natural habitat is now fully protected, and a captive-breeding program is producing a steady supply of young animals that are released annually into suitable new sites.

Smaller than the three species of midwife toads that live on the European mainland, the Mallorcan midwife toad became isolated about 7 million years ago, when a rise in sea level separated Mallorca from Spain. Living in streams, pools, and wells throughout the island, its survival came under threat in Roman times, when nonnative animals were introduced to the island. The viperine snake is a predator of midwife toads, while the Spanish green frog is a competitor, its tadpoles feeding on the same kind of food. Both species thrive at low altitudes, but have not been able to colonize Mallorca's impressive mountainous regions. As a result, the Mallorcan midwife toad is confined to a few remote limestone ravines.

Call of the Wild

Following winter rains, which briefly turn their habitat into a raging torrent, Mallorcan midwife toads begin to call. The call is a soft, simple "peep" and, unusually, is produced by both sexes. It enables individuals to find each other in deep, rocky fissures. Mating, which takes place on land, is complex and protracted, and involves an elaborate series of leg movements by which a string of ten to 20 large, yolk-filled eggs becomes tightly wrapped around the male's hindlegs. The male then carries them around for several weeks until they are ready to hatch.

The brooding period lasts for three to 10 weeks and averages four weeks; it is longer in cold weather and can be costly for males. While carrying eggs, males are not able to pursue prey actively and so tend to lose weight. In addition, the egg string sometimes becomes so tightly wrapped around a leg that its blood supply is cut off and the leg is lost.

When the eggs are fully developed, the male briefly enters a pool and deposits them; soon afterward they hatch into tadpoles. Tadpole development and growth can take more than a year, and the tadpoles grow to a considerable size. Indeed, growth in the tadpole stage represents a greater proportion of total lifetime growth than in any other frog.

DATA PANEL

Mallorcan midwife toad (ferreret)
Alytes muletensis
Family: Discoglossidae
World population: Unknown
Distribution: Mallorca
Habitat: Around pools in deep ravines at high altitude
Size: Length: 1.2–1.8 in (3–4 cm)
Form: Pale yellow or ocher with numerous dark-brown, black, or dark-green spots
Diet: Small invertebrates
Breeding: Spring and summer (March–July). Male carries eggs wrapped around hindlegs for several weeks; tadpole development lasts about 1 year
Related endangered species: Betic midwife toad (*Alytes dickhilleni*) VU
Status: IUCN CR; not listed by CITES

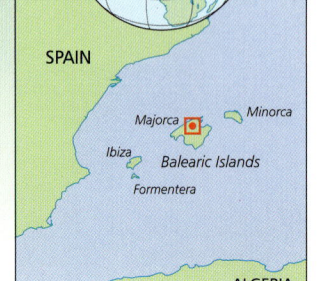

See also: Introductions 1: 54; Captive Breeding 1: 87; Reintroduction 1: 92; Toad, Golden 9: 70

Having passed a string of eggs to a male, the female, liberated from parental duties, develops a new batch of eggs; by the time they are mature, after about three weeks, there are males available who have gotten rid of their first batch of eggs. The breeding season lasts several months, and during it a female can lay up to three or four batches of eggs. Because females can generally produce eggs faster than males can brood them (an effect that is especially marked in cool weather), females commonly have to fight one another to mate with a willing male.

On the Brink of Extinction

When zoologists discovered the Mallorcan midwife toad alive, they realized that it was not only extremely rare, but also in danger of extinction. Its restricted habitat was a major cause for concern. It was immediately protected, and in 1985 a captive-breeding program was established involving a number of zoos and universities across Europe. The Mallorcan midwife toad thrives and breeds readily in captivity, and by 1989 large numbers of tadpoles and young adults were being shipped back to Mallorca to be released into the wild. Releases were made at localities with a suitable habitat where there were no wild toads. The species is now established at 12 new sites, in addition to the 13 natural ones. The range over which the species occurs has been doubled, and it is estimated that about 25 percent of the total population was bred in captivity.

The Mallorcan midwife toad illustrates the potential of captive-breeding programs in the conservation of endangered animals. It is a particularly suitable technique for amphibians because they have a high reproductive potential that is only rarely realized under natural conditions. Amphibians typically produce a large number of eggs. However, most die, either as eggs or tadpoles, through a variety of natural causes in the wild. In captivity eggs and tadpoles can be protected from such hazards so that the reproductive potential of a species can be exploited in its conservation.

The Mallorcan midwife toad *now provides a focal point for an environmental education program that involves other threatened species in Mallorca.*

Toad, Natterjack

Bufo calamita

A species with habitat requirements that are different from other frogs and toads, the natterjack has disappeared from much of its range as a result of degradation and loss of its habitat.

The natterjack toad runs rather than hops across the ground; unlike most toads, it has small hindlimbs that are too weak for hopping or jumping. It has a horny tubercle on each of its hind feet, and it uses them to dig, at remarkable speed, into the soft, sandy soils it inhabits. It lives in its burrow by day, digging deep enough to reach damp soil. As a result, natterjacks are able to thrive in habitats that are very dry at the surface. It also uses its burrow when hibernating during the winter. Individuals show attachment to their burrows, returning to the same site each day.

As with most toads, the natterjack has dry, warty skin, and in some individuals the warts are marked by red spots. Its most characteristic feature is the thin, pale-yellow stripe that runs down the middle of its back, the function of which is not known. The skin on its belly is granular (grainy looking) and able to take up water from damp spots in the ground. In contrast to common toads, in which the females are considerably larger than the males, male and female natterjacks are similar in size. One difference between the sexes is the swollen pad that male natterjacks develop on their thumbs during the breeding season; the pads enable the male to clasp the female firmly during mating and thereby to resist the attempts of rival males to displace him.

Prolonged Breeding Season

Natterjacks emerge to breed later in the spring than other European frogs and toads—as late as April in Britain. Breeding activity may continue, somewhat sporadically, until August in years when breeding ponds do not dry out in the summer. Tadpoles may metamorphose into adults at any time between June and September. Some individuals of both sexes may breed more than once during extended breeding seasons. In some years, however, ponds evaporate before the tadpoles have completed their development, in which case no young natterjacks are produced. Adults can live for up to 17 years, so that individuals are likely to

---

DATA PANEL

Natterjack toad (running toad)

Bufo calamita

Family: Bufonidae

World population: Unknown

Distribution: Western and northern Europe

Habitat: Open landscapes with light, sandy soil, including heathland and sand dunes

Size: Length: 2–4 in (5–10 cm)

Form: Gray or green above with narrow yellow stripe down middle of back; pale on belly. Warty skin; prominent parotid glands on head. Eye has green iris with horizontal pupil. Hard tubercles on hind feet

Diet: Beetles and other small invertebrates

Breeding: Spring and summer; males call to attract females; eggs laid in long strings

Related endangered species: Amargosa toad *(Bufo nelsoni)* EN; Amatola toad *(B. amatolicus)* VU; black toad *(B. exsul)* VU; Houston toad *(B. houstonensis)* EN; western toad *(B. boreas)** EN; Yosemite toad *(B. canorus)* EN

Status: Not listed by IUCN; not listed by CITES

See also: Habitat Loss 1: 38; Pesticides 1: 51; Frog, Harlequin 5: 8; Toad, Golden 9: 70; Toad, Western 9: 76

experience some good and some bad breeding seasons during their lives.

Males have a loud, churring call that humans can hear from as far away as 0.6 miles (1 km). While calling, the male inflates a large vocal sac under his chin. Females approach, and amplexus (the mating embrace) is followed by egg laying, in which two long strings of eggs are deposited among water plants. Natterjack egg strings differ from those of common toads in having a single rather than a double row of eggs. One female lays between 2,800 and 4,000 eggs at a time. Natterjack eggs, tadpoles, and adults are distasteful to potential predators and so are protected.

Competition Among Males

Males vary in their ability to sustain the energetic level of calling that is necessary to attract females. In larger breeding populations some males do not call at all but instead show "satellite" behavior, sitting silently by the side of a calling male and trying to intercept females that approach. In very large populations, such as those found in some parts of Spain, calling males can attract so many satellites that no females are able to reach them. In this situation all males abandon calling as a means of obtaining females, and mating becomes a competitive scramble like that seen in common toads.

Specific Habitat Requirements

Natterjacks prefer open habitats such as heathland and coastal sand dunes that are too dry for common frogs and toads. They suffer if they happen to breed in the same ponds as other frogs and toads because their tadpoles, hatching out several weeks later, cannot compete with the larger tadpoles of their rivals.

Natterjacks have disappeared from many parts of their range, mainly because their habitat has been degraded or destroyed. Where heathland has been replaced by woodland, common frogs and toads have moved in. In some areas natterjacks have been badly affected by pollution from pesticides and fertilizers used on farmland. The species is particularly endangered at the extremes of its range, in Britain, Scandinavia, and the former Soviet Union.

The natterjack toad has dry, warty skin, sometimes marked with red spots. It can take up moisture from the ground through the granular skin on its belly.

Toad, Western

Bufo boreas

Once common throughout the western United States and Canada, the western toad has vanished from many parts of its range over the last 30 years. Although its decline is well documented, the causes of its depleted numbers are not known.

The huge geographical range of the western toad, stretching from the Baja California region of Mexico in the south to Alaska in the north; from sea level to altitudes of over 11,800 feet (3,600 m), suggests that it is a very adaptable species. It is found in a wide variety of habitats, including desert streams, grassland, woodland, and mountain meadows—its main requirement is only some kind of temporary or permanent water body nearby where it can breed. The western toad's remarkable ability to live in such a diversity of habitats has not, however, prevented it from declining and, in some areas, probably becoming extinct.

Gray or green in color with dark blotches, the western toad has a distinctive white or cream stripe running down the middle of its back. Its skin is warty, the warts mostly positioned within the dark blotches, some of which may be a rusty red color. Compared to many toads, it has rather small hind legs, and it typically runs over the ground, rather than hops. The male is, on average, slightly smaller than the female and somewhat less warty.

Two subspecies are recognized. The boreal toad occupies the northern part of the range, whereas the California toad is found farther south in California, western Nevada, and Baja California in Mexico.

Explosive Breeding

The western toad spends much of its life underground, either digging into soft soil or using the burrows of other animals, such as ground squirrels. It is described as an "explosive breeder," meaning that it has a very short and frenetic breeding season. Early in the spring—which can be any time from late January to July, depending on latitude, altitude, and local climatic conditions—large numbers of toads suddenly emerge from their winter hiding places and move toward ponds, lakes, and streams. Males do not call to attract females, but simply move around a breeding pond looking for females. At lower altitudes western toads are generally active only during the night, but at higher altitudes where it is cold at night, they are active by day. In the water the more numerous males grapple over females. Once a pair is firmly clasped

DATA PANEL

Western toad (boreal toad)

Bufo boreas

Family: Bufonidae

World population: Unknown

Distribution: Western U.S. and Canada

Habitat: Varied: includes desert streams and springs, grassland, woodland, and mountain meadows; in or near ponds, lakes, reservoirs, rivers, and streams

Size: Length: 2.5–5 in (6.2–12.5 cm)

Form: Brown, gray, or greenish with large, dark blotches; often also some rusty-red blotches; white or cream stripe down the middle of the back; warty skin

Diet: Small invertebrates

Breeding: Spring and summer (January–July, depending on latitude, altitude, and local conditions); explosive breeder; female produces thousands of eggs in long strings

Related endangered species: Amargosa toad *(Bufo nelsoni)* EN; Amatola toad *(B. amatolicus)* VU; black toad *(B. exsul)* VU; Houston toad *(B. houstonensis)* EN; Yosemite toad *(B. canorus)* EN

Status: IUCN EN; not listed by CITES

See also: Disease 1: 55; Research 1: 84; Toad, Golden 9: 70; Toad, Natterjack 9: 74

together, the male on the female's back, they make their way to a spawn site, where the female lays two long strings of eggs. Spawning is usually communal, with all the females in a population laying their eggs in one spot. The most likely benefit of such behavior is that the temperature inside a mass of spawn is slightly higher than that of the surrounding water, encouraging more rapid development of the eggs.

Population Decline

A survey carried out in Colorado in 1982 revealed that 11 populations of western toads known to exist in 1971 had vanished. In 1988 surveys in the central Rocky Mountains found western toads in only 10 of the 59 historically recorded sites. In Yosemite National Park in 1992 they were present in only one of many sites where they had been recorded in 1924. The species is now virtually extinct in Utah, and in Wyoming it has declined in the Yellowstone and Grand Teton National Parks.

Over much of its range the western toad has probably been adversely affected by deforestation, which has destroyed and fragmented its habitat. The period over which it has declined has also been a time when several serious droughts have occurred, preventing breeding in some years. Such factors do not explain the decline of the species in protected areas where its habitat has not been destroyed.

At some sites up to 95 percent of eggs have failed to hatch, a rate of mortality that is associated with an infection by the freshwater fungus, *Saprolegnia ferax*. The tendency of the species to breed communally exacerbates the effect of fungal infection. Experimental studies have shown that mortality among the eggs of western toads, as for other species, is increased by exposure to the elevated levels of ultraviolet radiation (especially UV-B) that now frequently occur in areas such as Oregon as a result of thinning of the ozone layer. Disease has also been suggested as a cause of the toad declines. Another possibility is that one or more environmental factors, such as increased UV-B or pollution, has weakened their immune systems so that they have lost their resistance to once-harmless diseases.

The western toad *is an adaptable species inhabiting a huge range throughout the western United States. It is found in a variety of habitats, from mountain meadows to deserts.*

Toadlet, Corroboree

Pseudophryne corroboree

The corroboree toadlet has suffered a widespread and serious decline in numbers during the last 20 years, the causes of which are unknown. However, it is now protected and is the subject of a captive-breeding program.

The corroboree toadlet is one of Australia's most striking and distinctive frogs. Bright yellow or greenish yellow in color, it has a number of long, black stripes. Females are slightly larger, on average, than males, and body size in both sexes tends to be greater at higher altitudes.

The toadlet is a ground-living frog and has a restricted range in the southern Alps of New South Wales, where it is found at altitudes above 3,300 feet (1,000 m). The animals from more northern parts of the species' range tend to be greenish rather than yellow, and the northern form has been designated as a separate species, *Pseudophryne pengilleyi*.

The corroboree toadlet was first found in 1947, but it was not named until 1953. At that time it was quite an abundant species, but it suffered a dramatic population decline throughout its range between 1980 and 1999. By the end of this period the corroboree toadlet had disappeared from 85 percent of the sites where it had previously been recorded. Moreover, in 77 percent of the remaining populations fewer than five reproductively active male toadlets were found.

Now there are only three populations that contain more than 15 males. The causes of this decline are not known, but it is thought that prolonged drought may be partly responsible. Part of the corroboree toadlet's range falls within Kosciusko National Park in New South Wales, and a conservation program for the species was set up there in 1996.

Low Reproductive Potential

In November the males start moving from their terrestrial habitat to flooded bogs, where they make simple, water-filled burrows in the moss. The females arrive between four and eight weeks later, and the males call to them, producing a drawn-out "ark" sound. The female lays between 10 and 38 large, yolk-filled eggs in the male's burrow, and he stays close to them for between two and four weeks. The eggs take between six and eight months to hatch, and the young toadlets take three years to reach sexual maturity. The relatively small clutch size and the slow development of the toadlet means that, unlike many other frogs, the corroboree cannot produce huge numbers of offspring in a breeding season.

DATA PANEL

Corroboree toadlet (corroboree frog)

Pseudophryne corroboree

Family: Myobatrachidae

World population: A few hundred

Distribution: Southern Alps, New South Wales, Australia

Habitat: Woodland and heath at high altitudes: 4,270–5,780 ft (1,300–1,760 m)

Size: Length: (both sexes) 1–3 in (2.5–3 cm)

Form: Yellow or yellow-green, with black stripes; smooth, shiny skin; ridges on back; short, thick legs with no webbing between fingers or toes

Diet: Small invertebrates, especially ants and termites

Breeding: Spring and summer (November–January). Males defend water-filled burrows in moss in which females lay 10–40 eggs; males guard the eggs

Related endangered species: Red-crowned toadlet (*Pseudophryne australis*) LRnt; Bibron's toadlet (*P. bibronii*) LRnt

Status: IUCN EN; not listed by CITES

See also: Captive Breeding 1: 87; Frog, Tinkling 5: 12

The corroboree toadlet *lives in woodland and heathland outside the breeding season, but migrates to marshy areas to breed.*

One of Ten

The corroboree toadlet is one of a group of 10 similar species. Seven of them are found in southeastern Australia, and three in the extreme west. Although secretive in their habits, hiding under logs and rocks during the day, most of them are brightly colored. In all species the males call to attract the females. (Corroboree is, in fact, a native Australian word for a noisy gathering.) However, their ears are poorly developed in comparison with most frogs; they have no outer ear at all, and the inner ear lacks many of the components typical of frogs' ears.

The fact that the calls of the 10 toadlet species are similar, combined with what is probably a poor sense of hearing, may explain why hybrids between the different toadlet species are quite common, especially in areas where their ranges overlap. All the toadlets produce a few large eggs, and in some species the tadpoles have the ability to become dormant during dry periods.

Captive Breeding

In 1997 the situation was so urgent that it was decided that a captive-breeding program should be established. The program involved finding spawn at three sites and dividing each spawn mass into two halves. One half was left where it was found; the other was taken away to a special frog-breeding facility in Melbourne. The survival of both sets of spawn was carefully monitored. For two of the three sites more eggs survived among the captive eggs than among those left in their natural habitat.

It remains to be seen whether captive breeding will ensure the long-term survival of the corroboree toadlet. A major problem is that the species has become so rare, and its remaining populations so small, that it has lost much of its original genetic diversity and is becoming increasingly inbred. Inbreeding increases the chances of harmful genes appearing and also reduces the capacity of a population to adapt to environmental change.

Toothcarp, Valencia

Valencia hispanica

The Valencia toothcarp is rated as one of the 24 most endangered species of vertebrate in the world. Three locations—two of them near Valencia and one near Castellón in Spain—hold the last three remaining populations of this fish.

The Valencia toothcarp is a small, minnowlike fish. It is one of only a few European species of egg-laying killifish, most other species occurring in Africa and the New World. Some species of toothcarp are low in number, and many are threatened in the wild.

Toothcarp Characteristics

Despite the inclusion of "carp" in their name, toothcarps are not related to the carps proper that—with the minnows and their relatives—constitute the family Cyprinidae of the order Cypriniformes. The illusion of relatedness is reinforced by the name of one toothcarp family, the Cyprinodontidae. The Cyprinodontidae, along with their relatives in other toothcarp families (like the Valenciidae to which the Valencia toothcarp belongs), are all members of the order Cyprinodontiformes.

Numerous anatomical and other characteristics separate the order Cypriniformes from the order Cyprinodontiformes. For example, carps and their relatives within the Cypriniformes do not have any jaw teeth, while the toothcarps most certainly do, hence their name. Reproductively, too, there are significant differences. Cypriniformes characteristically produce relatively large numbers of eggs (several hundred thousand per spawning in the case of the larger species). The Cyprinodontiformes, on the other hand, produce few, with numbers sometimes being as low as five or six.

Within the toothcarps there are two subdivisions. One is the livebearing toothcarps, which—as their name suggests—do not lay eggs, but give birth to fully formed young. The other is the egg-laying toothcarps, which lay eggs. A few egg-laying carp species employ internal fertilization, just as the livebearing toothcarps do. The Valencia toothcarp belongs to the egg-laying toothcarps.

DATA PANEL

Valencia toothcarp (samaruc)

Valencia hispanica

Family: Valenciidae

World population: Unknown, but restricted to just 3 populations

Distribution: Spain: Peñíscola (in Castellón); Albufera de Valencia (just south of Valencia); Pego-Oliva (between Valencia and Alicante)

Habitat: Clean, clear, slow-flowing or standing waters with dense aquatic vegetation

Size: Female up to 2.8 in (7 cm); male smaller

Form: Elongated, laterally compressed body; large eyes; well-formed, rounded fins. Peñíscola males are uniform bluish-green; those from other localities have brown sheen in anterior half of body. All carry thin, vertical stripes, particularly in posterior half of body. Females drabber (browner) overall

Diet: Small aquatic invertebrates; small aerial insects that may fall into the water

Breeding: Two peaks of activity in spawning season: early spring and end of summer. Males establish territories that are visited by females. Eggs laid among fine-leaved vegetation; hatching takes about 1 week

Related endangered species: Corfu toothcarp (*Valencia letourneuxi*) EN

Status: IUCN EN; not listed by CITES

See also: Tourism 1: 42; The Animal Kingdom 1: 58; Pupfish, Devil's Hole 7: 94

TOOTHCARP, VALENCIA

The Valencia toothcarp *prefers clean, slow-flowing water with plenty of vegetation. Its diet includes small insects such as mosquitoes.*

Survival Pressures

In its natural habitat the Valencia toothcarp tends to occupy clean, clear, slow-flowing or static, well-vegetated bodies of water. It is also known to tolerate high levels of salt, an indication that in former days it occupied brackish (salty) regions along the coast. However, all the current known localities for the species are strictly freshwater ones.

Because of its requirements for clean, clear water the Valencia toothcarp has been unable to adapt to the consequences of an expanding human population in the region. The tourist industry is a major threat to the fish's habitat. The construction of tourist developments, for example, has often led to the destruction of toothcarp habitat and increased levels of water pollution. The channeling of water for irrigation or other water-supply projects is another threat to the fish's survival.

The Valencia toothcarp is not only at risk from human threats. Even where water and other habitat conditions favor the survival of the species, introduced species have put the fish under severe pressure. For example, the mosquitofish—itself a toothcarp (but a livebearing one)—was introduced into Spain in the early 1920s as a biological means of controlling malarial mosquitoes. The mosquitofish competes with the Valencia toothcarp for space and food. In addition, a female mosquitofish can store sperm from a single mating and use it to fertilize a series of egg batches during the breeding season. As a result, she produces far larger numbers of young than the Valencia female. Introduced predators also pose a threat.

Recovery Plans

Saving a species that faces such diverse and intense pressures presents a complex challenge. One obvious measure is captive breeding, and captive-bred stocks now exist in Spain and elsewhere. However, more permanent habitat-based measures are needed if the species is to survive in the wild.

Of prime importance is the protection of at least some of the fish's existing locations, in the hope that such habitats will recover sufficiently to allow their Valencia populations to expand. Another measure is the setting up of reserves in areas that used to be inhabited by Valencia toothcarps. Stocking them from captive-bred or healthy wild populations is envisaged. To ensure the success of the reintroductions, such habitats need to be fully restored.

Tortoise, Desert

Gopherus agassizii

Natural predators have always threatened the desert tortoise, but in the past few decades the greatest threat has come from humans.

The desert tortoise has inhabited arid desert regions in the southwestern United States for over 10,000 years. It has now been adopted as the "state reptile" of California, although it is also found in parts of Utah, Arizona, and Nevada.

The desert tortoise lives in areas with fewer than 5 inches (12 cm) of rainfall per year, summer temperatures of over 140°F (60°C), and below freezing in winter. Moisture from its food, and surface water when available, is stored in its bladder and will sustain the tortoise for many months. Desert tortoises avoid extremes of heat and cold by sheltering in burrows, often up to 30 feet (10 m) long, which they dig using their powerful forelimbs. During their active periods they scoop out shallow scrapes under bushes or rocky overhangs to use as shelter.

The desert tortoise and the related gopher tortoise are described as "keystone species" because many other animals depend on them. Their burrows are used by snakes, lizards, mammals, and various insects. If the tortoises and their habitat go, then these could also disappear. Natural predators such as coyotes, bobcats, foxes, skunks, ravens, and eagles have always preyed on tortoise eggs and young, but the greatest threat is now from collection and habitat destruction.

Tortoises are still popular as pets, but they are sometimes dumped in an unsuitable habitat when they are no longer wanted. The release of sick tortoises into the wild is thought to have caused severe outbreaks of upper respiratory tract disease in some wild populations. Once numbers are declining, simply maintaining a population level becomes difficult since breeding is a slow process. Females do not breed until they are between 15 and 20 years old; they may not breed at all in times of food shortage, and the survival rate of hatchlings is low. Due to harsh conditions and predators, only an estimated 1 to 3 percent survive to adulthood.

Habitat destruction is a major threat. Desert areas that were once of little use are now in increased demand for urban development, mining, waste, landfill, dumping, military training, and other uses. Increased road building and resulting traffic cause many tortoise deaths. Fire kills tortoises and destroys the vegetation that provides cover and food. Burned or otherwise damaged sites tend to be invaded by nonnative (alien) plants that are not the tortoises' preferred food. A similar loss of

DATA PANEL

Desert tortoise

Gopherus agassizii

Family: Testudinidae

World population: Unknown

Distribution: Sonoran and Mojave deserts

Habitat: Hot, arid deserts with firm sand, low growth, and open spaces

Size: Length: up to 15 in (38 cm); males are larger than females and can weigh almost 15 lb (7 kg)

Form: Domed, brownish shell with lighter yellowish area, slightly flattened forelimbs, and sturdy hind limbs. An extended shield at the front of the shell is used to flip other males during combat

Diet: Annual wildflowers, grasses, cacti, and other shrubs

Breeding: Two or 3 clutches of 2–14 eggs per year

Related endangered species: Gopher tortoise (*Gopherus polyphemus*) VU; Bolson tortoise (*G. flavomarginatus*) VU

Status: IUCN VU; CITES I

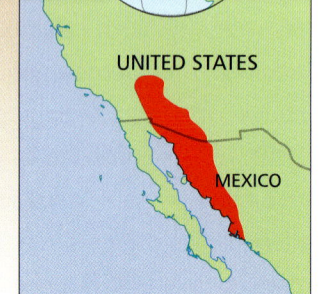

vegetation and invasion by alien plants results from overgrazing by cows, sheep, and feral burros (small donkeys). These grazers also disturb the soil, compacting nests, and possibly trampling emerging or sheltering hatchlings. Off-road vehicles have a similar effect on these fragile desert ecosystems.

Tortoise Protection

In 1974 the Desert Tortoise Preservation Committee was formed to promote the welfare of the desert tortoise. Several reserves have been designated, some of which have fenced roads and culverts under the highway to allow safe passage.

Numerous government agencies at federal, state, and local level are involved in habitat protection. The Federal Bureau of Land Management administers much of the reserved areas. State fish and game departments are also involved, while certain universities assist in ecological and population surveys.

The desert tortoise *has forelimbs specialized for excavation. Their burrows are often used by other animals, which form interdependent communities with the tortoises.*

All desert tortoises are now protected by law; it is an offense to kill them, molest them, or sell or buy them, and permits are needed for captive specimens, which must be tagged. The permit system is organized by the California Turtle and Tortoise Club (CTTC). The only legal way to obtain a desert tortoise is by using the CTTC adoption scheme or by being given a captive-bred specimen.

For several years an argument has been in progress over proposals to dump nuclear waste in Ward Valley, supposedly a protected area. That has been vetoed, and 6 million acres cannot now be altered or destroyed.

Tortoise, Egyptian

Testudo kleinmanni

The Egyptian tortoise is the smallest tortoise species in the Northern Hemisphere and one of the smallest in the world. In 1982 it was classified as Vulnerable; today it is officially Endangered.

The Egyptian tortoise has a relatively small range: mainly the narrow coastal strip along the North African coast from Libya, through Egypt into Israel, extending at the most some 56 miles (90 km) inland. It was discovered in Israel in 1963. The largest population there lives between Beersheba and the Egyptian border; others inhabit scattered areas of the Negev Desert. A field survey in 1994, financed by the Turtle Recovery Program, concluded that it had all but disappeared from its former territory in Egypt, although a few unsurveyed, remote areas may still hold small populations. Its CITES rating was immediately moved from Appendix II to Appendix I, which prohibits trade, but enforcement of the law and CITES regulations is lax in North Africa.

Diminishing Numbers

Uncontrolled collecting has been accompanied by severe habitat destruction. In the recent past house building and tourist development have expanded rapidly along the coast over much of the tortoise's former habitat. Large areas have been reclaimed for agriculture, and programs of road building, irrigation, and sand extraction have been implemented. Many suitable tortoise areas have disappeared forever.

Further degradation of the habitat had been caused by the goats and sheep belonging to the wandering Bedouin herdsmen; the animals eat the same plants as the tortoise. Traditionally the Bedouin moved them around on foot when the sparse grazing was exhausted. However, the animals can now be moved using trucks and are taken to remote areas that might have remained untouched.

All species of small tortoise fetch high prices in Britain, Europe, and the United States. Illegal consignments, sometimes including Egyptian tortoises, are occasionally seized. Commercial collection in Egypt has ended due to the lack of tortoises, but they still come in from Libya. The Libyan authorities occasionally crack down at the border, but at one time they were demanding a tax on tortoises taken across. Israel recently banned the export of all its wildlife, but its tortoise populations are under pressure as a result of building development and agricultural expansion.

Tortoise Care

Steps are being taken in Egypt to save the species. In 1997 Tortoise Care was set up after 200 tortoises were seized by

DATA PANEL

Egyptian tortoise

Testudo kleinmanni

Family: Testudinidae

World population: Unknown

Distribution: North Africa

Habitat: Arid, sandy areas with sparse vegetation

Size: Length: males up to 3.8 in (9.5 cm); females up to 5 in (12.7 cm)

Form: Head, legs, and soft parts light yellow; most specimens bear 2 V-shaped dark marks on the plastron (lower shell)

Diet: Grasses and annual plants

Breeding: Typically 1 egg (occasionally 2) laid at monthly intervals until 4 or 5 have been laid

Related endangered species: Greek tortoise (*Testudo graeca*) VU; Hermann's tortoise (*T. hermanni*) LRnt; western Hermann's tortoise (*T. h. hermanni*) EN; Horsfield's tortoise (*T. horsfieldii*) VU

Status: IUCN EN; CITES I

See also: Organizations 1: 10; tortoise species 9: 82–91

The Egyptian tortoise *is distinguished from other tortoises mainly by its small size, which has made it popular with collectors.*

Egyptian police. They were given medical treatment, and shelters were built—some tortoises even produced eggs, which were successfully hatched. The project has grown, thanks to local and outside assistance from bodies including the Cairo American College, the Tortoise Trust (an American-British organization), the Danish government, the Netherlands government, and the Zoological Society of London.

Captive breeding is under way in Egypt (160 eggs hatched successfully in 1999), and supervised releases using radio-tracking equipment have taken place. The Tortoise Trust and some British zoos are also breeding Egyptian tortoises.

A tortoise sanctuary has been established in a nature reserve at Zaranik on the north Sinai coast, with the help of the Egyptian Environmental Affairs Agency. The sanctuary also includes a visitor center where local Bedouins are employed as guards, and craft items based on the theme of tortoises are sold. Zaranik was formerly part of the Egyptian tortoises' natural range; although it is listed as an internationally important wetland and is also the Egyptian coast's largest green turtle nesting site, the area is still under pressure from proposed development.

Many Egyptian tortoise specimens are owned by collectors in Europe and the United States, and their young are sometimes offered for sale, particularly in the United States. The legality of such sales varies from one country to another.

The Tortoise Care organization in Egypt is pressing the government to give greater protection to the Egyptian tortoise and its habitats. Its members are also planning to set up more reserves in which the diminutive tortoise may live and breed in safety.

Tortoise, Galápagos Giant

Geochelone nigra

Before permanent settlers arrived on the Galápagos Islands in the 1830s, there were huge numbers of giant tortoises. Since then habitat destruction and immigrant predators have taken their toll.

Lying off the coast of Ecuador and almost on the equator, the Galápagos Islands achieved lasting fame after the English naturalist Charles Darwin published his theory of evolution in *The Origin of Species* (1859). The book was written after his visit to the islands in 1835. The area was already well known to whalers and other seamen who, between 1789 and 1860, took tortoises to keep on their ships as sources of fresh meat. The tortoises, with water stored in their bladders, would survive on the ships for several months until they were needed. Whaling declined after 1860, when petroleum started to be used instead of whale oil for lighting. Apart from humans, the tortoises had no predators except some birds, which took hatchlings.

Galápagos tortoises are the largest in the world. One male specimen measured 4.3 feet (1.3 m) and weighed about 425 pounds (200 kg). There is considerable variation in the shape of the shell, depending on which island they inhabit, a phenomenon that was noted by Darwin and helped form his theories. Some tortoises have domed shells; others have "saddleback" shells that allow the head to be raised higher. The length of the neck and size of the head also vary; they were considered to be a single species, but scientific study showed that there were 15 different "races" from the various islands, and each one has a third name to distinguish it from others. Three races are now extinct, and some of the others are very rare.

When settlers came to the islands in the 1830s, they brought pigs, goats, dogs, cattle, and burros (donkeys), some of which escaped and began to breed, causing a further decline in tortoise numbers. Pigs and dogs eat eggs and hatchlings; the other animals destroy the vegetation and trample tortoise nests. Rats and fire ants, both introduced species, also eat large numbers of hatchlings.

DATA PANEL

Galápagos giant tortoise

Geochelone nigra

Family: Testudinidae

World population: About 10,000

Distribution: Galápagos Islands, Pacific Ocean

Habitat: Volcanic islands; hot and dry with rocky outcrops; some forested areas with grassy patches

Size: Length: up to 4 ft (1.2 m). Weight: up to 500 lb (227 kg)

Form: Huge tortoise with gray-brown shell and hard-scaled legs; some have domed shells; others are saddleback (resembling a saddle in shape)

Diet: Almost any green vegetation

Breeding: About 7–20 eggs buried in soil

Related endangered species: All subspecies of *Geochelone nigra* are on the IUCN Red List, including the Abingdon Island tortoise (*Geochelone nigra abingdoni*) EW; Duncan Island tortoise (*G. n. ephippium*) EW; Charles Island tortoise (*G. n. galapagoensis*) EX; Hood Island tortoise (*G. n. hoodersis*) CR. The Brazilian giant tortoise (*G. denticulata*) is VU

Status: IUCN VU; CITES I

See also: Introductions 1: 54; Reintroduction 1: 92; tortoise species 9: 82–91

In 1928 a New York Zoological Society expedition collected 180 tortoises and allocated them to zoos as far away as Australia. Some of them have bred to second generation, and one from San Diego zoo was returned to the islands for a captive-breeding program. Following pressure from scientists, the Charles Darwin Foundation was formed in 1959, followed in 1964 by the Charles Darwin Research Station. The islands became a national park, and laws were passed to prevent the removal of any animals.

Long-Term Plans

It is estimated that some islands may need 100 years to recover their vegetation and tortoise populations.

The recovery program instituted by the research station has included collecting eggs from the wild and incubating them artificially, and removing introduced animals. The first young were released in 1970.

Collecting eggs in the wild for incubation has progressed to breeding some tortoises at the research station. The first hatchlings were released in 1975, and in 1991 the first wild-bred hatchling was found on the island. The highlight of the program was the release, early in 2000, of the thousandth tortoise on Espanola.

The tortoise population of the islands has almost doubled in recent years, and laws have been passed to restrict settlement and protect the coastal waters. Quarantine laws forbid the introduction of nonnative plants and animals.

One problem was that some of the races had been reduced to very low numbers, and their lack of genetic diversity was a cause for concern. Even today it is possible that more tortoises may be found on islands where populations are low. This would seem to be the only hope for a tortoise nicknamed Lonesome George, the sole survivor of a race from Pinta Island. He was discovered in 1971 and moved to the station with two females of another race, but as yet no eggs have been produced, and no Pinta female can be found.

Galápagos giant tortoises *are now rare or extinct on many of the islands because of habitat destruction and the introduction of animals that prey on the young or compete with adults for food.*

Tortoise, Geometric

Psammobates geometricus

The geometric tortoise is found only within the Republic of South Africa in a few small areas of grassland, some of which are now reserves. Threatened by habitat destruction, it is strictly protected and is said to be Africa's rarest reptile.

There are three species of South African tent tortoises: the geometric tortoise, the tent tortoise, and the Kalahari tortoise. The names of the geometric and tent tortoise derive from the domes, or conical scutes on their shells. (The Kalahari tortoise has a smooth shell.) All three species have a geometric pattern of yellow rays and are highly sought after by tortoise keepers. The geometric tortoise is the largest of the three and has the most restricted range.

Shrinking Habitat

The vegetation zone of the southwestern and southern Cape, from Port Elizabeth to Cedarberg, is known as fynbos, a woody scrubland where heathers and proteas are the main plants. The area is subject to fires in the dry season, and plants such as the protea (South Africa's national flower) are "fire-adapted," needing the heat in order to seed. Urban development has taken over some of the area, and extensive sections have come under wheat and vine cultivation. Formerly, the geometric tortoise had a more extensive range along the coast to the north of Cape Town, with two inland populations, which are now extinct.

Predators

Apart from humans, the tortoise's main enemies are small carnivores, secretary birds, and crows. Like many other tortoises, geometric hatchlings have a soft shell and are easy pickings. Habitat destruction, the construction of roads, and the creation of open areas make the tortoises more vulnerable to predators and allow alien plants to become established, further degrading their habitat.

The geometric tortoise would seem to have particular dietary requirements, a factor that might explain why they have not done well in captivity. Substantial numbers were once taken for the pet trade, but relatively few have survived, and captive-breeding successes are rare. The tortoises are also prone to respiratory diseases if kept in humid conditions or at less than optimal temperatures.

Conservation and the Future

In 1993 concern over the tortoise's fate led to the establishment of a conservation strategy. The first task was to train people to conduct field surveys to assess population numbers. The remaining habitat is under constant threat of being plowed since about 80 percent is privately owned. Publicity material has been produced about threatened plants and animals of the lowland veld in order to gather public support. Persuading landowners to cooperate has been vital.

Although some reserves, such as Roomans River Reserve, have been established, more land is needed to prevent further decline. At the Briers-Louw Reserve, controlled burnings to improve the habitat were carried out in 1995, but fire can also be a threat. Early in 1999 wildfire destroyed a substantial area, but fortunately did not cause many tortoise deaths before it was extinguished. The safest population is in the Elandsberg Private Nature Reserve—thanks to the work of a private landowner.

The tortoise's future depends on protection of its habitat. In spite of the small clutch size, populations could increase, given time, since they are thought to live for about 30 years and are mature at eight years.

See also: Natural Disasters **1:** 57; Education **1:** 94; tortoise species **9:** 82–91

TORTOISE, GEOMETRIC

DATA PANEL

Geometric tortoise
Psammobates geometricus

Family: Testudinidae

World population: 2,000–3,000

Distribution: Western Cape, South Africa

Habitat: Low-lying coastal grasslands

Size: Length: male 4 in (10 cm); female 5 in (12.7 cm). Weight: male 7 oz (207 g); female 15 oz (430 g)

Form: High-domed shell: background color black. Scutes have bright yellow center with radiating yellow markings. Plastron (lower shell) yellow with radiating faint black lines. On forelimbs large scales are interspersed with small scales

Diet: Mainly grassland plants; carrion and snails

Breeding: Between 2 and 4 eggs buried in soil. Incubation 5–7 months

Related endangered species: Argentine tortoise *(Geochelone chilensis)* VU; Aldabra giant tortoise *(G. gigantea)* VU; Galápagos giant tortoise *(G. nigra)** VU; radiated tortoise *(G. radiata)* VU; African spurred tortoise *(G. sulcata)* VU; Burmese starred tortoise *(G. platynota)* CR; Plowshare tortoise* *(G. yniphora)* EN

Status: IUCN EN; CITES I

The geometric tortoise *is a herbivore with a particular taste for the plants of the grasslands of the South African veld.*

Tortoise, Plowshare

Geochelone yniphora

The plowshare tortoise, found only in Madagascar, is one of the world's most endangered reptiles. When conservation efforts began, researchers were unable to find many specimens in the wild. However, a captive-breeding project is slowly helping increase numbers.

Madagascar has five land tortoise species, and four are endemic to the island (present only on Madagascar). One, the hingeback tortoise, was introduced to the island from Africa. Like much of Madagascar's wildlife, the plowshare has declined in numbers, although it probably never had a wide distribution. It was certainly plentiful enough to be exported for food in substantial numbers between the 17th and 19th centuries.

Among the Malagasy people the plowshare tortoise, or *angonoka*, as it is known locally, was subject to a *fady* (taboo) and was not eaten. However, people often took them from the wild, believing that keeping them as pets would protect their chickens.

Changing Habitat

When surveys began in the 1970s, researchers realized that the species was restricted to four small areas of dry forest near Baly Bay in the northwest of the island. In two of the sites the existence of tortoises was assumed because droppings were found; no tortoises were actually seen.

The size of the forests has not been greatly reduced in recent years. However, they have been changed as a result of human activity. It is common practice for herdsmen to burn dry undergrowth so that their cattle can graze on the fresh green shoots when they sprout. Burning is also used to clear land in order to cultivate crops such as rice and cassava. When the farmers or herders move on to a fresh site, plants such as bamboo colonize the abandoned areas, so the habitat is no longer suitable for tortoises. Feral (wild) pigs, which are now more common, are also a threat; they dig up tortoise nests to eat the eggs.

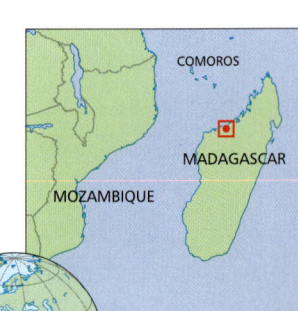

DATA PANEL

Plowshare tortoise (angonoka)

Geochelone yniphora

Family: Testudinidae

World population: Between 100 and 400

Distribution: Northwestern Madagascar

Habitat: Dry, deciduous forests with clearings and grass areas

Size: Length: about 18 in (45 cm); males larger than females. Weight: 21–32 lb (10–15 kg)

Form: High-domed shell, light yellow with dark markings on top extending down the sides in triangles. Plastron (lower shell) in males has distinctive, upwardly curved, beaklike extension at front

Diet: Grass and vegetation

Breeding: Between 3 and 5 eggs laid in soil; 4–5 clutches a year. Incubation period of 6–9.5 months

Related endangered species: Radiated tortoise (*Geochelone radiata*) VU

Status: IUCN EN; CITES I

See also: Exploitation of Live Animals 1: 49; Captive Breeding 1: 87; tortoise species 9: 82–89

The Road to Recovery

At the time of the surveys the Direction des Eaux et Fôrets (DEF), a Malagasy government body, was maintaining seven plowshares, together with 43 radiated tortoises, at its Ivoloina forestry station on the east coast. Although the radiated tortoises were breeding, the high humidity of the east coast did not suit the plowshares, whose natural habitat has a short wet season followed by dry conditions, and they did not reproduce.

After consultation with a number of conservation bodies Project Angonoka, a captive-breeding center, was set up in the DEF forestry station at Ampijora in Mahasangu Province in 1986. Although it is 94 miles (150 km) from existing tortoise habitats, it has a similar dry climate. The tortoises from Ivoloina were transferred there, and further specimens were added. By the end of 1993, 108 young specimens had been produced. Eggs were left where they had been buried by females, but protective mesh fences were placed around the sites.

Highly valued by the pet trade, the plowshares are threatened by unscrupulous collectors, but in 1998 five tortoises between the ages of eight and nine and weighing about 4 pounds (2 kg) were released into the wild. Radio tracking and regular checks showed that the young plowshares survived their first year. The release site was an area in which no tortoises had been seen for 20 years.

Project Angonoka is ongoing, but recovery is a slow process; adults do not breed until they are about 20 years old. Furthermore, not every egg hatches, and not every hatchling survives. Young tortoises also have to mature for several years before they can be released. Protected reserves with fencing to exclude pigs are essential in order to prevent damage to nests. In the meantime, the tortoises are still at risk. The project depends on sufficient funds, the prevention of illegal collecting, and persuading people that the tortoises are worth protecting—a difficult task in an area of great poverty where they can be illegally sold.

The plowshare tortoise *gets its name from the extension of the plastron (shaped like a plow blade, or "share") that protrudes from beneath the neck in males. Rival males use them to try to overturn each other when fighting during the breeding season.*

Totoaba

Totoaba macdonaldi

It seems odd that demand for a particular soup could have been a major factor in bringing the totoaba to the edge of extinction. The soup—made from totoaba swim bladder—is a culinary delight in Southeast Asia, thousands of miles from the totoaba's homeland.

The totoaba was once numerous in the Gulf of California. According to some reports, it could be found from the mouth of the Rio Colorado southward to Mulegé on the western side of the gulf, and Mazatlán on the eastern side. Other reports placed the western range as far down as Bahia Concepción and the eastern one to the Rio El Fuerte around Los Mochis. Today the distribution is much reduced and confined to the northern part of the Gulf of California (Sea of Cortéz).

During the 1920s the totoaba—the largest of the "drums" (bony fish that make a drumming noise)—was fished almost exclusively for its swim bladder. The organ allows fish to control their buoyancy; air can be pumped into or extracted from the swim bladder, allowing the fish to float or sink. The totoaba's swim bladder was dried (it was referred to as "seen kow" when in this state) and then cooked and eaten or used as stock for soup. Totoaba was considered a delicacy by members of the Chinese community in Guaymas, a small town on the mainland coast of the Gulf of California. Swim-bladder soup was already well known to the Chinese inhabitants, so finding a rich source of the delicacy on their doorstep in the form of 3-pound (1.5-kg) swim bladders from the totoaba presented exciting possibilities for commerce.

Bladder Boom...and Collapse

Gradually, the market grew for dried totoaba bladders, especially after experimental shipments to Southeast Asia were undertaken by Mexican entrepreneurs. As news of the lucrative industry spread, further fishing, drying, and exporting interests moved into the area. Trade was so successful that it soon led to the disappearance of the totoaba from local waters. Fishing operations followed the fish north, ending up at the top end of the Gulf, where the Colorado River enters the sea, and where totoaba were particularly abundant.

The industry boomed, and people flocked to the area, to the extent that three new villages were established. Over the next 20 years or so catches increased as more sophisticated fishing technology was implemented. The

DATA PANEL

Totoaba

Totoaba macdonaldi (Cynoscion macdonaldi)

Family: Sciaenidae

World population: Unknown

Distribution: Gulf of California, Mexico; mainly northern parts

Habitat: Deep marine waters; shallow estuarine or marshy, brackish (salty) waters during spawning season

Size: Length: up to 6.6 ft (2 m). Weight: up to 300 lb (135 kg)

Form: Perchlike fish; dull-colored on top, fading to lighter tones below; 2 dorsal (back) fins (1 with a deep notch); posterior edge of first just touches anterior edge of second; large head and mouth; lateral line organ (pressure-sensitive organ) on side from head back into tail

Diet: Fish; shrimp and other crustacea

Breeding: Migrates in spring to shallow estuarine or marshy brackish areas in delta of Rio Colorado for spawning. After spawning, adults migrate south, into deeper water. Juveniles thought to stay in northern Gulf for about 2 years

Related endangered species: None

Status: IUCN CR; CITES I

See also: Luxury Products 1: 46; Cod, Trout 3: 56

The totoaba's *large mouth is characteristic of its predatory habits. It feeds on other fish and crustacea.*

totoaba fishery eventually became the second largest fish industry in Mexico, after shrimp.

However, eventually catches began to decline, reaching their lowest in 1958. A combination of factors brought about the collapse of the industry, the sheer numbers of fish collected being only one of them. In addition, large numbers of juveniles were being caught by shrimp trawlers, thus affecting replenishment of stocks. The overriding factor, however, was the fact that the area around the mouth of the Colorado was where the totoaba migrated to spawn. Mature specimens collected during the breeding season in spring meant a significant decrease in the reproductive capacity of the species as a whole, which, in turn, meant that the juveniles being caught in shrimp nets could not be replaced.

Immediate Action

Swift action was needed. A 45-day fishing ban was implemented during the breeding season, and a sanctuary was created. Despite positive results, new threats had come into play. Shrinking of the marshy spawning grounds as a result of dam-building on the Colorado River posed a serious problem. In addition, the reduction of freshwater flow into the Gulf as a result of the dams led to an increase in salinity in the remaining spawning grounds, exerting yet another negative effect on the totoaba.

By 1979, although commercial fishing had been banned four years earlier, the totoaba was declared an endangered species; some scientists predicted that the species would be extinct by 2000. The establishment of a biosphere reserve in the Upper Gulf in 1993 has been beneficial, and captive breeding may also help protect the totoaba in years to come. However, there is concern in some quarters about the management of the Colorado River. Although it is not yet extinct, there are fears for the fate of the totoaba.

Tragopan, Temminck's

Tragopan temminckii

The fantastic adornments and bizarre courtship dance of the male Temminck's tragopan make it one of the most astonishing of all the pheasants. It is one of the few that seems to be in no immediate danger, although it suffers the effects of hunting, habitat destruction, and sheer ignorance.

It is a paradox that some of the most glamorous, extravagantly plumed, and ornamented of all birds—the pheasants—should also be among the most mysterious and elusive. A few species, such as the blue peacock, the ring-necked pheasant, and the red jungle fowl have been domesticated and carried all over the world, but most of their wild relatives are so rarely seen and little studied that until quite recently some of the more exotic Chinese species were dismissed as figments of the oriental imagination.

Of the 48 pheasant species all but one are confined to Asia. There they live mainly in the dense rain forests of the tropics or in the mountain forests of the Himalayas and southern China. They are furtive birds; the females are cryptically colored, and the males usually keep their most spectacular features for their courtship displays. Most males are still intensely colorful, however, which may explain why they keep to shadowy undergrowth where they are well hidden.

Feathered Glory

Most pheasants feed on the ground, but the five species of tragopan are unusual in being just as at home in the trees. This allows them to enjoy a wider variety of food, from mosses and bamboo shoots to the flowers and fruit of trees. In the fall Temminck's tragopan, the most widely distributed of the family, spends time eating the berries of trees such as rowan and viburnum found on the mountain slopes. In winter it moves downhill and switches to grasses and ferns, often digging them out from beneath the snow.

Uniquely for pheasants, tragopans also nest in the trees. Mated females make nests (from twigs, leaves, and feathers) up to 26 feet (8 m) from the forest floor. Newly hatched chicks must jump or clamber to the ground to find food. Within two or three days they are able to fly back up to perches where they roost nightly beneath their mother's wings.

The male takes no part in these domestic arrangements. He is, in any case, too conspicuous to be welcome. A mature male Temminck's tragopan is a magnificent sight, with silver-spotted crimson plumage and overlapping silver

DATA PANEL

Temminck's tragopan

Tragopan temminckii

Family: Phasianidae

World population: About 100,000 birds

Distribution: Eastern Himalayas, from Bhutan, northeastern Myanmar (Burma), and northern Vietnam to central China

Habitat: Dense evergreen or mixed forest with rhododendron or bamboo thickets

Size: Length: male 25 in (64 cm); female 23 in (58 cm). Weight: male 3 lb (1.4 kg); female 2.2 lb (1 kg)

Form: Plump gamebird with short, rounded wings, strong legs, and a moderate-length, rounded tail. Male deep red with pearly gray spots below; has inflatable blue-and-red lappet (flap) and erectile horns. Female gray-brown above, mottled black; pale brown with black patches and pale spots below

Diet: Mainly leaves, grasses, ferns, bamboo shoots, flowers, berries, and seeds; occasionally insects

Breeding: Male often polygamous (has many sexual partners); female nests alone in trees in May–June, incubating 3–5 eggs for 3.5–4 weeks. Chicks fledge within about 14 days

Related endangered species: Blyth's tragopan (*Tragopan blythii*) VU; Cabot's tragopan (*T. caboti*) VU; western tragopan (*T. melanocephalus*) VU; satyr tragopan (*T. satyra*) LRnt

Status: Not listed by IUCN; not listed by CITES

See also: Pasture 1: 38; Hunting 1: 42; Research 1: 84; Guan, Horned 5: 44

disks on his breast that gleam in the forest gloom like newly minted coins. Yet even this is inadequate to win the favors of a female tragopan.

On seeing an eligible female, he slips behind a rock and then rises to peer over the top. As he does so, a lappet on his neck expands and unfurls into a flap of scarlet-patterned, electric-blue skin, while a pair of blue horns rise on his head. After few seconds he fans his tail and beats his wings, then starts making weird clicking and gasping sounds as he crouches behind his rock again. Then comes the climax, as he suddenly rears up on tiptoe with his wings outspread downward, hissing and inflating his lappet to its fullest extent. Stunned by this vision, the female may then allow him to mate.

Losing Ground

Few people have seen this astonishing display because the tragopan is so secretive. It is becoming a rarer sight as the bird's habitat is steadily eroded by logging and the removal of the forest understory. Small timber is cut for firewood or to provide fodder for livestock; it is denuded by browsing goats or cleared altogether for farmland. The tragopans themselves are also hunted for food— an occupational hazard for a big, plump pheasant.

Temminck's tragopan may survive all this, for although its numbers are dwindling, it has a wide range. Other tragopans are more vulnerable because they are far more restricted. Many other pheasants— over two-thirds of all species—are considered at risk.

Effective conservation is vital for the survival of these glorious birds, but it is hampered by a lack of data. The birds live in some of the least-known regions in the world, and in many cases their populations and even details of their lives are virtually unknown. Since 1993 the World Pheasant Association has been trying to gather as much information as possible in an effort to find out just which species are in danger, why, and what can be done about it.

A Temminck's tragopan *male (below) shows spectacular plumage, while the female is less brightly colored. The birds are only rarely seen by humans.*

Glossary

Words in SMALL CAPITALS refer to other entries in the glossary.

Adaptation features of an animal that adjust it to its environment; may be produced by evolution—e.g., camouflage coloration
Adaptive radiation where a group of closely related animals (e.g., members of a FAMILY) have evolved differences from each other so that they can survive in different NICHES
Adhesive disks flattened disks on the tips of the fingers or toes of certain climbing AMPHIBIANS that enable them to cling to smooth, vertical surfaces
Adult a fully grown sexually mature animal; a bird in its final PLUMAGE
Algae primitive plants ranging from microscopic, single-celled forms to large forms, such as seaweeds, but lacking proper roots or leaves
Alpine living in mountainous areas, usually over 5,000 feet (1,500 m)
Ambient describing the conditions around an animal, e.g., the water temperature for a fish or the air temperature for a land animal
Amphibian any cold-blooded VERTEBRATE of the CLASS Amphibia, typically living on land but breathing in the water; e.g., frogs, toads, newts, salamanders
Amphibious able to live on both land and in water
Amphipod a type of CRUSTACEAN found on land and in both fresh and seawater
Anadromous fish that spend most of their life at sea but MIGRATE into fresh water for breeding, e.g., salmon
Annelid of the PHYLUM Annelida in which the body is made up of similar segments, e.g., earthworms, lugworms, leeches
Anterior the front part of an animal
Arachnid one of a group of ARTHROPODS of the CLASS Arachnida, characterized by simple eyes and four pairs of legs. Includes spiders and scorpions
Arboreal living in trees
Aristotle's lantern complex chewing apparatus of sea-urchins that includes five teeth
Arthropod the largest PHYLUM in the animal kingdom in terms of the number of SPECIES in it. Characterized by a hard, jointed EXOSKELETON and paired jointed legs. Includes INSECTS, spiders, crabs, etc.
Baleen horny substance commonly known as whalebone and growing as plates in the mouth of certain whales; used as a fringelike sieve for extracting plankton from seawater
Bill often called the beak: the jaws of a bird, consisting of two bony MANDIBLES, upper and lower, and their horny sheaths
Biodiversity the variety of SPECIES and the variation within them
Biome a major world landscape characterized by having similar plants and animals living in it, e.g., DESERT, jungle, forest
Biped any animal that walks on two legs. See QUADRUPED
Blowhole the nostril opening on the head of a whale through which it breathes
Breeding season the entire cycle of reproductive activity, from courtship, pair formation (and often establishment of territory) through nesting to independence of young
Bristle in birds a modified feather, with a bare or partly bare shaft, like a stiff hair; functions include protection, as with eyelashes of ostriches and hornbills, and touch sensors to help catch INSECTS, as with flycatchers
Brood the young hatching from a single CLUTCH of eggs
Browsing feeding on leaves of trees and shrubs

Cage bird A bird kept in captivity; in this set it usually refers to birds taken from the wild
Canine tooth a sharp stabbing tooth usually longer than the rest
Canopy continuous (closed) or broken (open) layer in forests produced by the intermingling of branches of trees
Carapace the upper part of a shell in a CHELONIAN
Carnivore meat-eating animal
Carrion rotting flesh of dead animals
Casque the raised portion on the head of certain REPTILES and birds
Catadromous fish that spend most of their life in fresh water but MIGRATE to the sea for SPAWNING, e.g., eels
Caudal fin the tail fin in fish
Cephalothorax a body region of CRUSTACEANS formed by the union of the head and THORAX. See PROSOMA
Chelicerae the first pair of appendages ("limbs") on the PROSOMA of spiders, scorpions, etc. Often equipped to inject venom
Chelonian any REPTILE of the ORDER Chelonia, including the tortoises and turtles, in which most of the body is enclosed in a bony capsule
Chrysalis the PUPA in moths and butterflies
Class a large TAXONOMIC group of related animals. MAMMALS, INSECTS, and REPTILES are all CLASSES of animals
Cloaca cavity in the pelvic region into which the alimentary canal, genital, and urinary ducts open
Cloud forest moist, high-altitude forest characterized by a dense UNDERSTORY and an abundance of ferns, mosses, and other plants growing on the trunks and branches of trees
Clutch a set of eggs laid by a female bird in a single breeding attempt
Cocoon the protective coat of many insect LARVAE before they develop into PUPAE or the silken covering secreted to protect the eggs
Colonial living together in a colony
Coniferous forest evergreen forests found in northern regions and mountainous areas, dominated by pines, spruce, and cedars
Costal riblike
Costal grooves grooves running around the body of some TERRESTRIAL salamanders; they conduct water from the ground to the upper parts of the body
Coverts small feathers covering the bases of a bird's main flight feathers on the wings and tail, providing a smooth, streamlined surface for flight
Crustacean member of a CLASS within the PHYLUM Arthropoda typified by five pairs of legs, two pairs of antennae, a joined head and THORAX, and calcerous deposits in the EXOSKELETON; e.g., crabs, shrimps, etc.

Deciduous forest dominated by trees that lose their leaves in winter (or in the dry season)
Deforestation the process of cutting down and removing trees for timber or to create open space for growing crops, grazing animals, etc.
Desert area of low rainfall typically with sparse scrub or grassland vegetation or lacking it altogether
Diatoms microscopic single-celled ALGAE
Dispersal the scattering of young animals going to live away from where they were born and brought up
Diurnal active during the day
DNA (deoxyribonucleic acid) the substance that makes up the main part of the chromosomes of all living things; contains the genetic code that is handed down from generation to generation
Domestication process of taming and breeding animals to provide help and useful products for humans
Dormancy a state in which—as a result of hormone action—growth is suspended and METABOLIC activity is reduced to a minimum
Dorsal relating to the back or spinal part of the body; usually the upper surface
Down soft, fluffy, insulating feathers with few or no shafts found after hatching on young birds and in ADULTS beneath the main feathers

Echolocation the process of perception based on reaction to the pattern of reflected sound waves (echos); occurs in bats
Ecology the study of plants and animals in relation to one another and to their surroundings
Ecosystem a whole system in which plants, animals, and their environment interact
Ectotherm animal that relies on external heat sources to raise body temperature; also known as "cold-blooded"
Edentate toothless; also any animals of the order Edentata, which includes anteaters, sloths, and armadillos
Endemic found only in one geographical area, nowhere else
Epitoke a form of marine ANNELID having particularly well developed swimming appendages
Estivation inactivity or greatly decreased activity during hot weather
Eutrophication an increase in the nutrient chemicals (nitrate, phosphate, etc.) in water, sometimes occurring naturally and sometimes caused by human activities, e.g., by the release of sewage or agricultural fertilizers
Exoskeleton a skeleton covering the outside of the body or situated in the skin, as found in some INVERTEBRATES
Explosive breeding in some AMPHIBIANS when breeding is completed over one or a very few days and nights
Extinction process of dying out at the end of which the very last individual dies, and the SPECIES is lost forever

Family a group of closely related SPECIES that often also look quite

GLOSSARY

similar. Zoological FAMILY names always end in -idae. Also used to describe a social group within a SPECIES comprising parents and their offspring
Feral domestic animals that have gone wild and live independently of people
Flagship species A high-profile SPECIES, which (if present) is likely to be accompanied by many others that are typical of the habitat. (If a naval flagship is present, so is the rest of the fleet of warships and support vessels)
Fledging period the period between a young bird hatching and acquiring its first full set of feathers and being able to fly
Fledgling young bird that is capable of flight; in perching birds and some others it corresponds with the time of leaving the nest
Fluke either of the two lobes of the tail of a whale or related animal; also a type of flatworm, usually parasitic

Gamebird birds in the ORDER Galliformes (megapodes, cracids, grouse, partridges, quail, pheasants, and relatives); also used for any birds that may be legally hunted by humans
Gene the basic unit of heredity, enabling one generation to pass on characteristics to its offspring
Genus (**genera**, pl.) a group of closely related SPECIES
Gestation the period of pregnancy in MAMMALS, between fertilization of the egg and birth of the baby
Gill Respiratory organ that absorbs oxygen from the water. External gills occur in tadpoles. Internal gills occur in most fish

Harem a group of females living in the same territory and consorting with a single male
Hen any female bird
Herbivore an animal that eats plants (grazers and BROWSERS are herbivores)
Hermaphrodite an animal having both male and female reproductive organs
Herpetologist ZOOLOGIST who studies REPTILES and AMPHIBIANS
Hibernation becoming inactive in winter, with lowered body temperature to save energy. Hibernation takes place in a special nest or den called a hibernaculum
Homeotherm an animal that can maintain a high and constant body temperature by means of internal processes; also called "warm-blooded"
Home range the area that an animal uses in the course of its normal activity
Hybrid offspring of two closely related SPECIES that can breed; it is sterile and so cannot produce offspring

Ichthyologist ZOOLOGIST specializing in the study of fish
Inbreeding breeding among closely related animals (e.g., cousins), leading to weakened genetic composition and reduced survival rates
Incubation the act of keeping the egg or eggs warm or the period from the laying of eggs to hatching
Indwellers ORGANISMS that live inside others, e.g., the California Bay pea crab, which lives in the tubes of some marine ANNELID worms, but do not act as PARASITES
Indigenous living naturally in a region; native (i.e., not an introduced SPECIES)
Insect any air-breathing ARTHROPOD of the CLASS Insecta, having a body divided into head, THORAX, and abdomen, three pairs of legs, and sometimes two pairs of wings
Insectivore animal that feeds on INSECTS. Also used as a group name for hedgehogs, shrews, moles, etc.
Interbreeding breeding between animals of different SPECIES, varieties, etc. within a single FAMILY or strain; Interbreeding can cause dilution of the GENE pool
Interspecific between SPECIES
Intraspecific between individuals of the same SPECIES
Invertebrates animals that have no backbone (or other bones) inside their body, e.g., mollusks, INSECTS, jellyfish, crabs
Iridescent displaying glossy colors produced (e.g., in bird PLUMAGE) not as a result of pigments but by the splitting of sunlight into light of different wavelengths; rainbows are made in the same way

Joey a young kangaroo living in its mother's pouch
Juvenile a young animal that has not yet reached breeding age

Keel a ridge along the CARAPACE of certain turtles or a ridge on the scales of some REPTILES
Keratin tough, fibrous material that forms hair, feathers, nails, and protective plates on the skin of VERTEBRATE animals
Keystone species a SPECIES on which many other SPECIES are wholly or partially dependent
Krill PLANKTONIC shrimps

Labyrinth specialized auxiliary (extra) breathing organ found in some fish
Larva an immature form of an animal that develops into an ADULT form through METAMORPHOSIS
Lateral line system a system of pores running along a fish's body. These pores lead to nerve endings that allow a fish to sense vibrations in the water and help it locate prey, detect PREDATORS, avoid obstacles, and so on. Also found in AMPHIBIANS
Lek communal display area where male birds of some SPECIES gather to attract and mate with females
Livebearer animal that gives birth to fully developed young (usually refers to REPTILES or fish)

Mammal any animal of the CLASS Mammalia—warm-blooded VERTEBRATE having mammary glands in the female that produce milk with which it nurses its young. The class includes bats, primates, rodents, and whales
Mandible upper or lower part of a bird's beak or BILL; also the jawbone in VERTEBRATES; in INSECTS and other ARTHROPODS mandibles are mouth parts mostly used for biting and chewing
Mantle cavity a space in the body of mollusks that contains the breathing organs
Marine living in the sea
Matriarch senior female member of a social group
Metabolic rate the rate at which chemical activities occur within animals, including the exchange of gasses in respiration and the liberation of energy from food
Metamorphosis the transformation of a LARVA into an ADULT
Migration movement from one place to another and back again; usually seasonal
Molt the process in which a bird sheds its feathers and replaces them with new ones; some MAMMALS, REPTILES, and ARTHROPODS regularly molt, shedding hair, skin, or outer layers
Monotreme egg-laying MAMMAL, e.g., platypus
Montane in a mountain environment
Natural selection the process whereby individuals with the most appropriate ADAPTATIONS are more successful than other individuals and therefore survive to produce more offspring. Natural selection is the main process driving evolution in which animals and plants are challenged by natural effects (such as predation and bad weather), resulting in survival of the fittest
Nematocyst the stinging part of animals such as jellyfish, usually found on the tentacles
Nestling a young bird still in the nest and dependent on its parents
New World the Americas
Niche part of a habitat occupied by an ORGANISM, defined in terms of all aspects of its lifestyle
Nocturnal active at night
Nomadic animals that have no fixed home, but wander continuously
Noseleaf fleshy structures around the face of bats; helps focus ULTRASOUNDS used for ECHOLOCATION

Ocelli markings on an animal's body that resemble eyes. Also, the tiny, simple eyes of some INSECTS, spiders, CRUSTACEANS, mollusks, etc.
Old World non-American continents
Olfaction sense of smell
Operculum a cover consisting of bony plates that covers the GILLS of fish
Omnivore an animal that eats a wide range of both animal and vegetable food
Order a subdivision of a CLASS of animals, consisting of a series of animal FAMILIES
Organism any member of the animal or plant kingdom; a body that has life
Ornithologist ZOOLOGIST specializing in the study of birds
Osteoderms bony plates beneath the scales of some REPTILES, particularly crocodilians
Oviparous producing eggs that hatch outside the body of the mother (in fish, REPTILES, birds, and MONOTREMES)

Parasite an animal or plant that lives on or within the body of another (the host) from which it obtains nourishment. The host is often harmed by the association
Passerine any bird of the ORDER Passeriformes; includes SONGBIRDS
Pedipalps small, paired leglike appendages immediately in front of the first pair of walking legs of spiders

and other ARACHNIDS. Used by males for transferring sperm to the females
Pelagic living in the upper waters of the open sea or large lakes
Pheromone scent produced by animals to enable others to find and recognize them
Photosynthesis the production of food in green plants using sunlight as an energy source and water plus carbon dioxide as raw materials
Phylum zoological term for a major grouping of animal CLASSES. The whole animal kingdom is divided into about 30 PHYLA, of which the VERTEBRATES form part of just one
Placenta the structure that links an embryo to its mother during pregnancy, allowing exchange of chemicals between them
Plankton animals and plants drifting in open water; many are minute
Plastron the lower shell of CHELONIANS
Plumage the covering of feathers on a bird's body
Plume a long feather used for display, as in a bird of paradise
Polygamous where an individual has more than one mate in one BREEDING SEASON. Monogamous animals have only a single mate
Polygynous where a male mates with several females in one BREEDING SEASON
Polyp individual ORGANISM that lives as part of a COLONY—e.g., a coral—with a saclike body opening only by the mouth that is usually surrounded by a ring of tentacles
Population a distinct group of animals of the same SPECIES or all the animals of that SPECIES
Posterior the hind end or behind another structure
Predator an animal that kills live prey
Prehensile capable of grasping
Primary forest forest that has always been forest and has not been cut down and regrown at some time
Primates a group of MAMMALS that includes monkeys, apes, and ourselves
Prosoma the joined head and THORAX of a spider, scorpion, or horseshoe crab
Pupa an INSECT in the stage of METAMORPHOSIS between a caterpillar (LARVA) and an ADULT (imago)

Quadruped any animal that walks on four legs

Range the total geographical area over which a SPECIES is distributed

Raptor bird with hooked beak and strong feet with sharp claws (talons) for seizing, killing, and dealing with prey; also known as birds of prey. The term usually refers to daytime birds of prey (eagles, hawks, falcons, and relatives) but sometimes also includes NOCTURNAL owls
Regurgitate (of a bird) to vomit partly digested food either to feed NESTLINGS or to rid itself of bones, fur, or other indigestible parts, or (in some seabirds) to scare off PREDATORS
Reptile any member of the cold-blooded CLASS Reptilia, such as crocodiles, lizards, snakes, tortoises, turtles, and tuataras; characterized by an external covering of scales or horny plates. Most are egg-layers, but some give birth to fully developed young
Roost place that a bird or bat regularly uses for sleeping
Ruminant animals that eat vegetation and later bring it back from the stomach to chew again ("chewing the cud") to assist its digestion by microbes in the stomach

Savanna open grasslands with scattered trees and low rainfall, usually in warm areas
Scapulars the feathers of a bird above its shoulders
Scent chemicals produced by animals to leave smell messages for others to find and interpret
Scrub vegetation dominated by shrubs—woody plants usually with more than one stem
Scute horny plate covering live body tissue underneath
Secondary forest trees that have been planted or grown up on cleared ground
Sedge grasslike plant
Shorebird Plovers, sandpipers, and relatives (known as waders in Britain, Australia, and some other areas)
Slash-and-burn agriculture method of farming in which the unwanted vegetation is cleared by cutting down and burning
Social behavior interactions between individuals within the same SPECIES, e.g., courtship
Songbird member of major bird group of PASSERINES
Spawning the laying and fertilizing of eggs by fish and AMPHIBIANS and some mollusks
Speciation the origin of SPECIES; the diverging of two similar ORGANISMS through reproduction down through the generations into different forms resulting in a new SPECIES
Species a group of animals that look similar and can breed with each other to produce fertile offspring
Steppe open grassland in parts of the world where the climate is too harsh for trees to grow
Subspecies a subpopulation of a single SPECIES whose members are similar to each other but differ from the typical form for that SPECIES; often called a race
Substrate a medium to which fixed animals are attached under water, such as rocks onto which barnacles and mussels are attached, or plants are anchored in, e.g., gravel, mud, or sand in which AQUATIC plants have their roots embedded
Substratum see SUBSTRATE
Swim bladder a gas or air-filled bladder in fish; by taking in or exhaling air, the fish can alter its buoyancy
Symbiosis a close relationship between members of two SPECIES from which both partners benefit

Taxonomy the branch of biology concerned with classifying ORGANISMS into groups according to similarities in their structure, origins, or behavior. The categories, in order of increasing broadness, are: SPECIES, GENUS, FAMILY, ORDER, CLASS, PHYLUM
Terrestrial living on land
Territory defended space
Test an external covering or "shell" of an INVERTEBRATE such as a sea-urchin; it is in fact an internal skeleton just below the skin
Thorax (**thoracic**, adj.) in an INSECT the middle region of the body between the head and the abdomen. It bears the wings and three pairs of walking legs
Torpor deep sleep accompanied by lowered body temperature and reduced METABOLIC RATE
Translocation transferring members of a SPECIES from one location to another
Tundra open grassy or shrub-covered lands of the far north

Underfur fine hairs forming a dense, woolly mass close to the skin and underneath the outer coat of stiff hairs in MAMMALS
Understory the layer of shrubs, herbs, and small trees found beneath the forest CANOPY
Ungulate one of a large group of hoofed animals such as pigs, deer, cattle, and horses; mostly HERBIVORES
Uterus womb in which embryos of MAMMALS develop
Ultrasounds sounds that are too high-pitched for humans to hear
UV-B radiation component of ultraviolet radiation from the sun that is harmful to living ORGANISMS because it breaks up DNA

Vane the bladelike main part of a typical bird feather extending from either side of its shaft (midrib)
Ventral of or relating to the front part or belly of an animal (see DORSAL)
Vertebrate animal with a backbone (e.g., fish, MAMMAL, REPTILE), usually with skeleton made of bones, but sometimes softer cartilage
Vestigial a characteristic with little or no use, but derived from one that was well developed in an ancestral form; e.g., the "parson's nose" (the fatty end portion of the tail when a fowl is cooked) is the compressed bones from the long tail of the reptilian ancestor of birds
Viviparous (of most MAMMALS and a few other VERTEBRATES) giving birth to active young rather than laying eggs

Waterfowl members of the bird FAMILY Anatidae, the swans, geese, and ducks; sometimes used to include other groups of wild AQUATIC birds
Wattle fleshy protuberance, usually near the base of a bird's BILL
Wingbar line of contrasting feathers on a bird's wing
Wing case one of the protective structures formed from the first pair of nonfunctional wings, which are used to protect the second pair of functional wings in INSECTS such as beetles
Wintering ground the area where a migrant spends time outside the BREEDING SEASON

Yolk part of the egg that contains nourishment for a growing embryo

Zooid individual animal in a colony; usually applied to corals or bryozoa (sea-mats)
Zoologist person who studies animals
Zoology the study of animals

Further Reading

Mammals

Macdonald, David, *The Encyclopedia of Mammals*, Barnes & Noble, New York, U.S., 2001

Payne, Roger, *Among Whales*, Bantam Press, U.S., 1996

Reeves, R. R., and Leatherwood, S., *The Sierra Club Handbook of Whales and Dolphins of the World*, Sierra Club, U.S., 1983

Sherrow, Victoria, and Cohen, Sandee, *Endangered Mammals of North America*, Twenty-First Century Books, U.S., 1995

Whitaker, J. O., *Audubon Society Field Guide to North American Mammals*, Alfred A. Knopf, New York, U.S., 1996

Birds

Attenborough, David, *The Life of Birds*, BBC Books, London, U.K., 1998

BirdLife International, *Threatened Birds of the World*, Lynx Edicions, Barcelona, Spain and BirdLife International, Cambridge, U.K., 2000

del Hoyo, J., Elliott, A., and Sargatal, J., eds., *Handbook of Birds of the World* Vols 1 to 6, Lynx Edicions, Barcelona, Spain, 1992–2001

Sayre, April Pulley, *Endangered Birds of North America*, Scientific American Sourcebooks, Twenty-First Century Books, U.S., 1977

Scott, Shirley L., ed., *A Field Guide to the Birds of North America*, National Geographic, U.S., 1999

Stattersfield, A., Crosby, M., Long, A., and Wege, D., eds., *Endemic Bird Areas of the World: Priorities for Biodiversity Conservation*, BirdLife International, Cambridge, U.K., 1998

Thomas, Peggy, *Bird Alert: Science of Saving*, Twenty-First Century Books, U.S., 2000

Fish

Bannister, Keith, and Campbell, Andrew, *The Encyclopedia of Aquatic Life*, Facts On File, New York, U.S., 1997

Buttfield, Helen, *The Secret Lives of Fishes*, Abrams, U.S., 2000

Reptiles and Amphibians

Corbett, Keith, *Conservation of European Reptiles and Amphibians*, Christopher Helm, London, U.K., 1989

Corton, Misty, *Leopard and Other South African Tortoises*, Carapace Press, London, U.K., 2000

Hofrichter, Robert, *Amphibians: The World of Frogs, Toads, Salamanders, and Newts*, Firefly Books, Canada, 2000

Stafford, Peter, *Snakes*, Natural History Museum, London, U.K., 2000

Insects

Borror, Donald J., and White, Richard E., *A Field Guide to Insects: America, North of Mexico*, Houghton Mifflin, New York, U.S., 1970

Pyle, Robert Michael, *National Audubon Society Field Guide to North American Butterflies*, Alfred A. Knopf, New York, U.S., 1995

General

Adams, Douglas, and Carwardine, Mark, *Last Chance to See*, Random House, London, U.K., 1992

Allaby, Michael, *The Concise Oxford Dictionary of Ecology*, Oxford University Press, Oxford, U.K., 1998

Douglas, Dougal, and others, *Atlas of Life on Earth*, Barnes & Noble, New York, U.S., 2001

National Wildlife Federation, *Endangered Species: Wild and Rare*, McGraw-Hill, U.S., 1996

Websites

http://www.abcbirds.org/ American Bird Conservancy. Articles, information about campaigns and bird conservation in the Americas

http://elib.cs.berkeley.edu/aw/ AmphibiaWeb information about amphibians and their conservation

http://animaldiversity.ummz.umich.edu/ University of Michigan Museum of Zoology animal diversity web. Search for pictures and information about animals by class, family, and common name. Includes glossary

www.beachside.org sea turtle preservation society

http://www.birdlife.net BirdLife International, an alliance of conservation organizations working in more than 100 countries to save birds and their habitats

http://www.surfbirds.com Articles, mystery photographs, news, book reviews, birding polls, and more

http://www.birds.cornell.edu/ Cornell University. Courses, news, nest-box cam

http://www.cites.org/ CITES and IUCN listings. Search for animals by scientific name of order, family, genus, species, or common name. Location by country and explanation of reasons for listings

www.ufl.edu/natsci/herpetology/crocs.htm crocodile site, including a chat room

www.darwinfoundation.org/ Charles Darwin Research Center

http://www.open.cc.uk/daptf DAPTF–Decllining Amphibian Population Task Force. Providing information and data about amphibian declines. (International Director, Professor Tim Halliday, is co-author of this set)

http://www.ucmp.berkeley.edu/echinodermata the echinoderm phylum—starfish, sea-urchins, etc.

http://endangered.fws.gov information about endangered animals and plants from the U.S. Fish and Wildlife Service, the organization in charge of 94 million acres of wildlife refuges

http://forests.org/ includes forest conservation answers to queries

www.traffic.org/turtles freshwater turtles

www.iucn.org details of species, IUCN listings and IUCN publications

http://www.pbs.org/journeytoamazonia the Amazonian rain forest and its unrivaled biodiversity

http://www.audubon.org National Audubon Society, named after the ornithologist and wildlife artist John James Audubon (1785–1851). Sections on education, local Audubon societies, and bird identification

www.nccnsw.org.au site for threatened Australian species

http://cmc-ocean.org facts, figures, and quizzes about marine life

http://wwwl.nature.nps.gov/wv/ The U.S. National Park Service wildlife and plants site. Factsheets on all kinds of animals found in the parks

www.ewt.org.za endangered South African wildlife

http://www.panda.org World Wide Fund for Nature (WWF). Newsroom, press releases, government reports, campaigns. Themed photogallery

http://www.greenchannel.com/wwt/ Wildfowl and Wetlands Trust (U.K.). Founded by artist and naturalist Sir Peter Scott, the trust aims to preserve wetlands for rare waterbirds. Includes information on places to visit and threatened waterbird species

http://wdcs.org/ Whale and Dolphin Conservation Society site. News, projects, and campaigns. Sightings database

List of Animals by Group

Listed below are the common names of the animals featured in the A–Z part of this set grouped by their class, i.e., Mammals, Birds, Fish, Reptiles, Amphibians, and Insects and Invertebrates.

Bold numbers indicate the volume number and are followed by the first page number of the two-page illustrated main entry in the set.

Mammals
addax **2**:4
anoa, mountain **2**:20
anteater, giant **2**:24
antelope, Tibetan **2**:26
armadillo, giant **2**:30
ass
  African wild **2**:34
  Asiatic wild **2**:36
aye-aye **2**:42
babirusa **2**:44
baboon, gelada **2**:46
bandicoot, western barred **2**:48
banteng **2**:50
bat
  ghost **2**:56
  gray **2**:58
  greater horseshoe **2**:60
  greater mouse-eared **2**:62
  Kitti's hog-nosed **2**:64
  Morris's **2**:66
bear
  grizzly **2**:68
  polar **2**:70
  sloth **2**:72
  spectacled **2**:74
beaver, Eurasian **2**:76
bison
  American **2**:86
  European **2**:88
blackbuck **2**:94
camel, wild bactrian **3**:24
cat, Iriomote **3**:30
cheetah **3**:40
chimpanzee **3**:42
  pygmy **3**:44
chinchilla, short-tailed **3**:46
cow, Steller's sea **3**:70
cuscus, black-spotted **3**:86
deer
  Chinese water **4**:6
  Kuhl's **4**:8
  Père David's **4**:10
  Siberian musk **4**:12
desman, Russian **4**:14
dhole **4**:16
dog
  African wild **4**:22
  bush **4**:24
dolphin
  Amazon river **4**:26
  Yangtze river **4**:28
dormouse
  common **4**:30
  garden **4**:32
  Japanese **4**:34
drill **4**:40
dugong **4**:46
duiker, Jentink's **4**:48
dunnart, Kangaroo Island **4**:50
echidna, long-beaked **4**:60
elephant
  African **4**:64
  Asian **4**:66
elephant-shrew, golden-rumped **4**:68
ferret, black-footed **4**:72
flying fox
  Rodrigues (Rodriguez) **4**:84
  Ryukyu **4**:86
fossa **4**:90
fox, swift **4**:92
gaur **5**:18
gazelle, dama **5**:20
gibbon, black **5**:26
giraffe, reticulated **5**:30
glider, mahogany **5**:32
gorilla
  mountain **5**:38
  western lowland **5**:40
gymnure, Hainan **5**:48
hare, hispid **5**:50
hippopotamus, pygmy **5**:52
horse, Przewalski's wild **5**:58
hutia, Jamaican **5**:64
hyena
  brown **5**:66
  spotted **5**:68
ibex, Nubian **5**:70
indri **5**:84
jaguar **5**:86
koala **6**:10
kouprey **6**:14
kudu, greater **6**:16
lemur
  hairy-eared dwarf **6**:22
  Philippine flying **6**:24
  ruffed **6**:26
leopard **6**:28
  clouded **6**:30
  snow **6**:32
lion, Asiatic **6**:34
loris, slender **6**:46
lynx, Iberian **6**:52
macaque
  barbary **6**:54
  Japanese **6**:56
manatee, Florida **6**:68
markhor **6**:72
marten, pine **6**:74
mink, European **6**:78
mole, marsupial **6**:80
mole-rat
  Balkans **6**:82
  giant **6**:84
monkey
  douc **6**:86
  Goeldi's **6**:88
  proboscis **6**:90
mouse, St. Kilda **6**:92
mulgara **6**:94
numbat **7**:14
nyala, mountain **7**:18
ocelot, Texas **7**:20
okapi **7**:22
orang-utan **7**:26
oryx
  Arabian **7**:28
  scimitar-horned **7**:30
otter
  European **7**:32
  giant **7**:34
  sea **7**:36
ox, Vu Quang **7**:44
panda
  giant **7**:48
  lesser **7**:50
pangolin, long-tailed **7**:52
panther, Florida **7**:54
pig, Visayan warty **7**:68
pika, steppe **7**:74
platypus **7**:82
porpoise, harbor **7**:86
possum, Leadbeater's **7**:88
potoroo, long-footed **7**:90
prairie dog, black-tailed **7**:92
pygmy-possum, mountain **8**:4
quagga **8**:8
rabbit
  Amami **8**:12
  volcano **8**:14
rat, black **8**:24
rhinoceros
  black **8**:26
  great Indian **8**:28
  Javan **8**:30
  Sumatran **8**:32
  white **8**:34
rock-wallaby, Prosperine **8**:36
saiga **8**:42
sea lion, Steller's **8**:62
seal
  Baikal **8**:70
  gray **8**:72
  Hawaiian monk **8**:74
  Mediterranean monk **8**:76
  northern fur **8**:78
sheep, barbary **8**:88
shrew, giant otter **8**:90
sifaka, golden-crowned **8**:92
sloth, maned **9**:6
solenodon, Cuban **9**:16
souslik, European **9**:18
squirrel, Eurasian red **9**:28
tahr, Nilgiri **9**:46
takin **9**:50
tamarin, golden lion **9**:52
tapir
  Central American **9**:56
  Malayan **9**:58
tenrec, aquatic **9**:64
thylacine **9**:66
tiger **9**:68
tree-kangaroo, Goodfellow's **10**:4
vicuña **10**:28
whale
  blue **10**:40
  fin **10**:42
  gray **10**:44
  humpback **10**:46
  killer **10**:48
  minke **10**:50
  northern right **10**:52
  sei **10**:54
  sperm **10**:56
  white **10**:58
wildcat **10**:62
wolf
  Ethiopian **10**:64
  Falkland Island **10**:66
  gray **10**:68
  maned **10**:70
  red **10**:72
wolverine **10**:74
wombat, northern hairy-nosed **10**:76
yak, wild **10**:90
zebra
  Grevy's **10**:92
  mountain **10**:94

Birds
akiapolaau **2**:6
albatross, wandering **2**:8
amazon, St. Vincent **2**:14
asity, yellow-bellied **2**:32
auk, great **2**:38
barbet, toucan **2**:54
bellbird, three-wattled **2**:82
bird of paradise, blue **2**:84
bittern, Eurasian **2**:90
blackbird, saffron-cowled **2**:92
bowerbird, Archbold's **3**:8
bustard, great **3**:10
cassowary, southern **3**:28
cockatoo, salmon-crested **3**:52
condor, California **3**:60
coot, horned **3**:62
cormorant, Galápagos **3**:64
corncrake **3**:66
courser, Jerdon's **3**:68
crane, whooping **3**:76
crow, Hawaiian **3**:82
curlew, Eskimo **3**:84
dipper, rufous-throated **4**:18

LIST OF ANIMALS BY GROUP

dodo **4**:20
duck
  Labrador **4**:42
  white-headed **4**:44
eagle
  harpy **4**:52
  Philippine **4**:54
  Spanish imperial **4**:56
finch
  Gouldian **4**:74
  mangrove **4**:76
firecrown, Juan Fernández **4**:78
flamingo, Andean **4**:80
flycatcher, Pacific royal **4**:82
fody, Mauritius **4**:88
grebe, Atitlán **5**:42
guan, horned **5**:44
gull, lava **5**:46
honeyeater, regent **5**:54
hornbill, writhed **5**:56
huia **5**:60
hummingbird, bee **5**:62
ibis, northern bald **5**:72
kagu **5**:88
kakapo **5**:90
kea **5**:92
kestrel
  lesser **5**:94
  Mauritius **6**:4
kite, red **6**:6
kiwi, brown **6**:8
lark, Raso **6**:18
lovebird, black-cheeked **6**:48
macaw
  hyacinth **6**:58
  Spix's **6**:60
magpie-robin, Seychelles **6**:62
malleefowl **6**:64
manakin, black-capped **6**:66
mesite, white-breasted **6**:76
murrelet, Japanese **7**:4
nene **7**:10
nuthatch, Algerian **7**:16
owl
  Blakiston's eagle **7**:38
  Madagascar red **7**:40
  spotted **7**:42
parrot, night **7**:58
peafowl, Congo **7**:60
pelican, Dalmatian **7**:62
penguin, Galápagos **7**:64
petrel, Bermuda **7**:66
pigeon
  pink **7**:70
  Victoria crowned **7**:72
pitta, Gurney's **7**:78
plover, piping **7**:84
quetzal, resplendent **8**:10
rail, Guam **8**:18
rockfowl, white-necked **8**:38
sandpiper, spoon-billed **8**:54

scrub-bird, noisy **8**:56
sea-eagle, Steller's **8**:64
siskin, red **8**:94
spatuletail, marvelous **9**:20
spoonbill, black-faced **9**:26
starling, Bali **9**:30
stilt, black **9**:32
stork, greater adjutant **9**:34
swallow, blue **9**:42
swan, trumpeter **9**:44
takahe **9**:48
tanager, seven-colored **9**:54
teal, Baikal **9**:62
tragopan, Temminck's **9**:94
turaco, Bannerman's **10**:10
vanga, helmet **10**:26
vireo, black-capped **10**:32
vulture, Cape griffon **10**:34
warbler
  aquatic **10**:36
  Kirtland's **10**:38
woodpecker
  ivory-billed **10**:78
  red-cockaded **10**:80
wren, Zapata **10**:86

Fish
anchovy, freshwater **2**:16
angelfish, masked **2**:18
archerfish, western **2**:28
barb, bandula **2**:52
caracolera, mojarra **3**:26
catfish, giant **3**:32
cavefish, Alabama **3**:34
characin, blind cave **3**:38
cichlids, Lake Victoria haplochromine **3**:48
cod
  Atlantic **3**:54
  trout **3**:56
coelacanth **3**:58
dace, mountain blackside **3**:90
danio, barred **3**:94
darter, watercress **4**:4
dragon fish **4**:36
eel, lesser spiny **4**:62
galaxias, swan **5**:16
goby, dwarf pygmy **5**:34
goodeid, gold sawfin **5**:36
ikan temoleh **5**:82
lungfish, Australian **6**:50
paddlefish **7**:46
paradisefish, ornate **7**:56
pirarucu **7**:76
platy, Cuatro Ciénegas **7**:80
pupfish, Devil's Hole **7**:94
rainbowfish, Lake Wanam **8**:20
rasbora, vateria flower **8**:22
rocky, eastern province **8**:40
salmon, Danube **8**:52
seahorse, Knysna **8**:68
shark
  basking **8**:80

  great white **8**:82
  silver **8**:84
  whale **8**:86
sturgeon, common **9**:36
sucker, razorback **9**:38
sunfish, spring pygmy **9**:40
toothcarp, Valencia **9**:80
totoaba **9**:92
tuna, northern bluefin **10**:8
xenopoecilus **10**:88

Reptiles
alligator
  American **2**:10
  Chinese **2**:12
boa
  Jamaican **3**:4
  Madagascar **3**:6
chameleon, south central lesser **3**:36
crocodile, American **3**:80
dragon, southeastern lined earless **4**:38
gecko, Round Island day **5**:22
gharial **5**:24
Gila monster **5**:28
iguana
  Fijian crested **5**:74
  Galápagos land **5**:76
  Galápagos marine **5**:78
  Grand Cayman blue rock **5**:80
Komodo dragon **6**:12
lizard
  blunt-nosed leopard **6**:36
  flat-tailed horned **6**:38
  Ibiza wall **6**:40
  sand **6**:42
python, woma **8**:6
racer, Antiguan **8**:16
skink, pygmy blue-tongued **9**:4
snake
  eastern indigo **9**:10
  leopard **9**:12
  San Francisco garter **9**:14
tortoise **9**:82
  Egyptian **9**:84
  Desert **9**:82
  Galápagos giant **9**:86
  geometric **9**:88
  plowshare **9**:90
tuatara **10**:6
turtle
  Alabama red-bellied **10**:12
  bog **10**:14
  Chinese three-striped box **10**:16
  hawksbill **10**:18
  pig-nosed **10**:20
  western swamp **10**:22
  yellow-blotched sawback map **10**:24
viper, Milos **10**:30
whiptail, St. Lucia **10**:60

Amphibians
axolotl **2**:40
frog
  gastric-brooding **4**:94
  green and golden bell **5**:4
  Hamilton's **5**:6
  harlequin **5**:8
  red-legged **5**:10
  tinkling **5**:12
  tomato **5**:14
mantella, golden **6**:70
newt, great crested **7**:12
olm **7**:24
salamander
  California tiger **8**:44
  Japanese giant **8**:46
  Ouachita red-backed **8**:48
  Santa Cruz long-toed **8**:50
toad
  golden **9**:70
  Mallorcan midwife **9**:72
  natterjack **9**:74
  western **9**:76
toadlet, corroboree **9**:78

Insects and Invertebrates
ant, European red wood **2**:22
beetle
  blue ground **2**:78
  hermit **2**:80
butterfly
  Apollo **3**:12
  Avalon hairstreak **3**:14
  birdwing **3**:16
  Hermes copper **3**:18
  large blue **3**:20
  large copper **3**:22
clam, giant **3**:50
crab
  California Bay pea **3**:72
  horseshoe **3**:74
crayfish, noble **3**:78
cushion star **3**:88
damselfly, southern **3**:92
earthworm, giant gippsland **4**:58
emerald, orange-spotted **4**:70
leech, medicinal **6**:20
longicorn, cerambyx **6**:44
mussel, freshwater **7**:6
nemertine, Rodrigues **7**:8
sea anemone, starlet **8**:58
sea fan, broad **8**:60
sea-urchin, edible **8**:66
snail, *Partula* **9**:8
spider
  great raft **9**:22
  Kauai cave wolf **9**:24
tarantula, red-kneed **9**:60
worm
  palolo **10**:82
  velvet **10**:84

Set Index

A **bold** number indicates the volume number and is followed by the relevant page number or numbers (e.g., **1**:52, 74).

Animals that are main entries in the A–Z part of the set are listed under their common names, alternative common names, and scientific names. Animals that appear in the data panels as Related endangered species are also listed under their common and scientific names.

Common names in **bold** (e.g., **addax**) indicate that the animal is a main entry in the set. Underlined page numbers (e.g., **2**:<u>12</u>) indicate the first page of the two-page main entry on that animal.

Italic volume and page references (e.g., *1:57*) indicate illustrations of animals in other parts of the set.

References to animals that are listed by the IUCN as Extinct (EX), Extinct in the Wild (EW), or Critically Endangered (CR) are found under those headings.

spp. means species.

A

Aceros spp. **5**:56
  A. leucocephalus **5**:<u>5</u>
Acestrura bombus **4**:78
Acinonyx jubatus **3**:<u>40</u>
Acipenser
  A. nudiventris **9**:36
  A. sturio **9**:<u>36</u>
Acrantophis madagascariensis **3**:<u>6</u>
Acrocephalus spp. **10**:36
  A. paludicola **10**:<u>36</u>
adaptation, reproductive strategies **1**:25
addax 2:<u>4</u>
Addax nasomaculatus **2**:<u>4</u>
Adelocosa anops **9**:<u>24</u>
Adranichthyis kruyti **10**:88
Aegialia concinna **2**:80
Aegypius monachus **10**:34
Aepypodius bruijnii **6**:<u>64</u>
Afropavo congensis **7**:<u>60</u>
Agapornis
  A. fischeri **6**:48
  A. nigrigenis **6**:<u>48</u>
Agelaius xanthomus **2**:92
Aglaeactis aliciae **4**:78
agricultural land use **1**:38, 61
agricultural practices **1**:52, 74; **2**:60, 63, 73, 92; **3**:10, 13, 67, 85; **4**:19, 24, 75; **5**:50, 94; **6**:6, 36, 38, 48, 82, 95; **7**:12, 19; **8**:95; **9**:4, 18; **10**:14, 34
Ailuroedus dentirostris **3**:8
Ailuropoda melanoleuca **7**:<u>48</u>
Ailurus fulgens **7**:<u>50</u>
akiapolaau 2:<u>6</u>
ala Balik **8**:52
Alabama **3**:34
alala **3**:<u>82</u>
Alauda razae **6**:<u>18</u>

albatross
  various **2**:9
  wandering 2:<u>8</u>
Algeria **7**:16
alien species **1**:71; **2**:7, 56, 77; **3**:27, 65, 83; **4**:15, 20, 50, 76, 78, 79, 88; **5**:6, 11, 17, 22, 36, 43, 46, 50, 61, 64, 74, 76, 88, 92; **6**:8, 19, 62, 65, 78, 80, 94; **7**:5, 9, 10, 14, 59, 66, 70, 82, 90; **8**:12, 19, 20, 40, 16; **9**:9, 16, 28, 32, 38, 48, 72, 81, 88; **10**:60, 87, 88
Alligator
  A. mississippiensis **2**:<u>10</u>
  A. sinensis **2**:<u>12</u>
alligator
  American 2:<u>10</u>
  Chinese 2:<u>12</u>
Allocebus trichotis **6**:<u>22</u>
Allotoca maculata **5**:36
Alsophis spp. **8**:16
  A. antiguae **8**:<u>16</u>
Alytes muletensis **9**:<u>72</u>
Amandava formosa **4**:74
amarillo **5**:36
amazon
  St. Vincent 2:<u>14</u>
  various **2**:14
Amazona spp. **2**:14
  A. guildingii **2**:<u>14</u>
Amblyopsis
  A. rosae **3**:34
  A. spelaea **3**:34
Amblyornis flavifrons **3**:8
Amblyrhynchus cristatus **5**:<u>78</u>
Ambystoma
  A. macrodactylum croceum **8**:51
  A. mexicanum **2**:<u>40</u>
Amdystoma spp. **8**:44
  A. californiense **8**:<u>44</u>
Ameca splendens **5**:36

Ammotragus lervia **8**:<u>88</u>
amphibians **1**:76
  diversity **1**:76
  risks **1**:78
  strategies **1**:76
  see also List of Animals by Group, page 100
Anas spp. **9**:62
  A. formosa **9**:<u>62</u>
  A. laysanensis **7**:10
  A. wyvilliana **7**:10
anchovy, freshwater 2:<u>16</u>
Andes **2**:74; **3**:46; **4**:80; **10**:28
Andrias
  A. davidianus **8**:46
  A. japonicus **8**:<u>46</u>
anemone *see* sea anemone
angelfish
  masked 2:<u>18</u>
  resplendent pygmy **2**:19
Angola **10**:94
angonoka **9**:<u>90</u>
animal products **1**:46; **3**:28, 75; **10**:42, 58
anoa
  lowland **2**:20; **6**:14
  mountain 2:<u>20</u>
Anoa mindorensis **2**:20
Anodorhynchus spp. **6**:60
  A. hyacinthus **6**:58
Anser erythropus **7**:10
ant, European red wood 2:<u>22</u>
anteater
  banded **7**:<u>14</u>
  fairy **2**:25
  giant 2:<u>24</u>
  marsupial **7**:<u>14</u>
  scaly **7**:<u>52</u>
antelope 2:4, <u>26</u>; 94; **4**:48; **5**:20; **6**:16; **7**: 18, 28, 30; **8**:42
Anthornis melanocephala **5**:54
Anthracoceros
  A. marchei **5**:56
  A. montani **5**:56
Antigua **8**:16
Antilope cervicapra **2**:<u>94</u>
Antilophia bokermanni **6**:66
aoudad **8**:<u>88</u>
ape, barbary **6**:<u>54</u>
Aplonis spp. **9**:30
Apodemus sylvaticus hirtensis **6**:<u>92</u>
Apteryx spp. **6**:9
  A. mantelli **6**:<u>8</u>
aquaculture **8**:55
aquarium trade **1**:49; **4**:36; **8**:23, 69, 84
Aquila spp. **4**:56
  A. adalberti **4**:<u>56</u>
Aramidopsis palteni **3**:66
arapaima **7**:<u>76</u>
Arapaima gigas **7**:<u>76</u>
archerfish
  few-scaled **2**:<u>28</u>
  large-scaled **2**:<u>28</u>

  western **2**:<u>28</u>
Archiboldia papuensis **3**:<u>8</u>
archipelagos **1**:32
  see also islands
Arctic **2**:70
Arctic Ocean **10**:58
Arctocephalus spp. **8**:62, 78
Ardeotis nigriceps **3**:10
Argentina **3**:46; 62; **4**:18
Arizona **3**:60
armadillo
  giant 2:<u>30</u>
  various **2**:30
arowana, Asian **4**:<u>36</u>
artificial fertilization **1**:88
Asia **3**:10, 66; **6**:20
asity
  Schlegel's **2**:32
  yellow-bellied 2:<u>32</u>
Aspidites ramsayi **8**:<u>6</u>
ass
  African wild 2:<u>34</u>; **8**:8
  Asiatic wild 2:<u>36</u>; **8**:8
  half- **2**:36
  Syrian wild *1:37*
Astacus astacus **3**:<u>78</u>
Asterina phylactica **3**:88
Astyanax mexicanus **3**:38
Atelopus varius **5**:<u>8</u>
Atlantic Ocean **3**:54, 88; **8**:72, 76, 80; **9**:36; **10**:8, 40, 43
Atlantisia rogersi **3**:66
Atlapetes flaviceps **4**:76
Atrichornis
  A. clamosus **8**:<u>56</u>
  A. rufescens **8**:56
auk, great 2:<u>38</u>
aurochs *1:37*
Australia **2**:16, 28, 48, 56; **3**:16; **4**:38, 46, 50, 58, 74, 94; **5**:12, 32, 54; **6**:10, 51, 64, 80, 94; **7**:14, 58, 82, 88, 90; **8**:4, 6, 36, 56; **9**:4, 66, 78; **10**:20, 22, 77
Austroglanis barnardi **3**:32
avadavat, green **4**:74
avahi **5**:84; **8**:93
Avahi occidentalis **5**:84; **8**:93
Axis kuhlii **4**:<u>8</u>
axolotl 2:<u>40</u>; **8**:44
aye-aye 2:<u>42</u>

B

babirusa 2:<u>44</u>
baboon, gelada 2:<u>46</u>
Babyrousa babyrussa **2**:<u>44</u>
baiji **4**:<u>28</u>
Balaenoptera
  B. acutorostrata **10**:<u>50</u>
  B. borealis **10**:<u>54</u>
  B. musculus **10**:<u>40</u>
  B. physalus **10**:<u>42</u>
Balantiocheilos melanopterus **8**:<u>84</u>
Balantiopteryx infusca **2**:64
Balearic Islands **6**:40; **9**:72

Bali **9**:30, 68
Baltic **8**:72; **9**:36
bandicoot
  eastern barred **2**:48
  golden **2**:48
  greater rabbit-eared *1:36*
  little barred **2**:<u>48</u>
  Shark Bay striped **2**:<u>48</u>
  western barred 2:<u>48</u>
Bangladesh **2**:72
banteng 2:<u>50</u>
barb
  bandula 2:<u>52</u>
  seven-striped **5**:<u>82</u>
  various **2**:52
barbet
  toucan 2:<u>54</u>
  various **2**:54
Barbus (Puntius) spp. **2**:52
  B. (P.) bandula **2**:<u>52</u>
bat
  Australian false vampire **2**:56
  ghost 2:<u>56</u>
  gray 2:<u>58</u>
  greater horseshoe 2:<u>60</u>
  greater mouse-eared 2:<u>62</u>
  Guatemalan **2**:62
  Indiana **2**:62
  Kitti's hog-nosed 2:<u>64</u>
  Morris's 2:<u>66</u>
  mouse-tailed **2**:<u>64</u>
  myotis, various **2**:66
  sheath-tailed **2**:<u>64</u>
  see also flying fox
Bawean Island **4**:8
bear
  Asian black **2**:68
  Asiatic black **2**:74
  brown **2**:68
  grizzly 2:<u>68</u>
  Mexican grizzly *1:37*; **2**:68
  polar 2:<u>70</u>
  sloth 2:<u>72</u>
  spectacled 2:<u>74</u>
beaver, Eurasian 2:<u>76</u>
beetle
  blue ground 2:<u>78</u>
  Ciervo scarab **2**:80
  delta green ground **2**:78
  Giuliani's dune scarab **2**:80
  hermit 2:<u>80</u>
  longhorn **6**:<u>44</u>
  scarab **2**:80
behavior studies **1**:85
bellbird
  bare-throated **2**:82
  Chatham Island **5**:54
  three-wattled 2:<u>82</u>
Belontia signata **7**:56
beloribitsa **8**:52
beluga **10**:58
Bering Sea **8**:62
Bermuda **7**:66
bettong, northern **7**:90
Bettongia tropica **7**:90
Bhutan **8**:28; **9**:50
big-game hunting **1**:47; **9**:68

SET INDEX

bilby **2**:48
bioaccumulation, toxins **1**:50, 51–52
biodiversity **1**:19
biogeographical areas **1**:19
Bioko Island **4**:40
biomes **1**:18–20
biosphere **1**:22
bird, elephant *1*:37
bird of paradise
  blue 2:84
  McGregor's **2**:84
  Raggiana *1*:46
BirdLife International (BI) **1**:12, 67
birds **1**:64–67
  conservation organizations for **1**:12–13, 67, 88
  diversity **1**:64
  flightless **1**:28, 64
  history **1**:64–65
  risks **1**:64–67
  see also List of Animals by Group, page 100
Bison
  B. bison **2**:86
  B. bonasus **2**:88
bison
  American *1*:15; **2**:86
  European 2:88
  wood *1*:37
bittern 2:90
  Australasian **2**:90
  Eurasian 2:90
  great **2**:90
Black Sea **8**:80; **9**:36
blackbird
  Jamaican **2**:92
  saffron-cowled 2:92
  yellow-shouldered **2**:92
blackbuck 2:94
bluebuck *1*:37
boa
  Cuban tree **3**:4
  Dumeril's **3**:6
  emerald tree *1*:74
  Jamaican 3:4
  Madagascar 3:6
  Madagascar tree **3**:6
  Mona Island **3**:4
  Puerto Rican **3**:4
  Virgin Islands **3**:4
Bolivia **2**:74; **3**:46, 62; **4**:18
bonobo **3**:44
bonytongue **4**:36
boom and bust **1**:21
Borneo **6**:30, 90; **7**:26; **8**:84
Bos
  B. frontalis **5**:18
  B. grunniens **10**:90
  B. javanicus **2**:50
  B. sauveli **6**:14
Bostrychia bocagei **5**:72
Botaurus
  B. poiciloptilus **2**:90
  B. stellaris **2**:90
Botswana **10**:34

bowerbird
  Archbold's 3:8
  various **3**:8
Brachylophus
  B. fasciatus **5**:74
  B. vitiensis **5**:74
Brachyramphus marmoratus **7**:4
Bradypus torquatus **9**:6
Branta
  B. ruficollis **7**:10
  B. sandvicensis **7**:10
Brazil **6**:58, 60, 66; **7**:76; **9**:6, 52, 54
British Columbia **5**:10
brush-turkey, Bruijin's **6**:64
Bubalus
  B. bubalis **2**:20
  B. depressicornis **2**:20; **6**:14
  B. quarlesi **2**:20
Bubo blakistoni **7**:38
Budorcas taxicolor **9**:50
buffalo **2**:87
  Indian water **2**:20
  see also bison
Bufo spp. **9**:70, 74, 76
  B. boreas **9**:76
  B. calamita **9**:74
  B. periglenes **9**:70
Bunolagus monticularis **8**:12, **8**:13
buntingi, various **10**:88
Burma *see* Myanmar
Burramys parvus **8**:4
bushdog **4**:93
bushmeat trade **1**:44
bustard
  great 3:10
  various **3**:10
Butan **7**:50
butterfly *1*:83
  Apollo 3:12
  Avalon hairstreak 3:14
  birdwing 3:16
  Hermes copper 3:18
  large blue 3:20
  large copper 3:22
  obi birdwing **3**:16
  Queen Alexandra's birdwing **3**:16
  Richmond birdwing **3**:16
  Rothschild's birdwing **3**:16
  swallowtail, various **3**:12

C

Cacatua spp. **3**:52
  C. moluccensis **3**:52
cachalot **10**:56
Cachorrito, various **7**:94
cage-bird trade **1**:49; **2**:14, 55; **3**:52; **4**:55, 74; **5**:44; **6**:48, 58; **7**:72, 78; **8**:94; **9**:30, 54
cahow **7**:66
Caimen, black **2**:10, 12
Calicalicus rufocarpalis **10**:27
California **3**:14, 18, 60; **9**:14

Callaeas cinerea **5**:60
catbird, tooth-billed **3**:8
callimico **6**:88
Callimico goeldii **6**:88
Callithrix
  C. flaviceps **6**:88
  C. nigriceps **6**:88
Callorhinus ursinus **8**:78
Calotes liocephalus **4**:38
Camarhynchus heliobates **4**:76
Cambodia **2**:50; **5**:26, 82; **6**:14, 86; **9**:34
camel, wild bactrian 3:24
Camelus
  C. bactrianus **3**:24
  C. dromedarius **3**:25
Cameroon **4**:40; **10**:10
Campephilus
  C. imperialis **10**:78
  C. principalis **10**:78
Camptorhynchus labradorius **4**:42
Canada **2**:70, 86; **3**:74, 76, 84; **4**:42; **5**:10; **7**:36, 42, 84; **9**:44, 76; **10**:74
canine distemper **1**:56
Canis
  C. lupus **10**:68
  C. rufus **10**:72
  C. simensis **10**:64
Cape Verde Islands **6**:18
Capito spp. **2**:54
Capra
  C. falconeri **6**:72
  C. nubiana **5**:70
  C. walia **5**:71; **6**:73
Caprolagus
  C. hispidus **5**:50
Capromys brownii **5**:64
captive breeding **1**:22, 57, 87; **2**:12, 15, 19, 34, 43, 53, 86, 88, 94; **3**:4, 7, 13, 27, 33, 42, 47, 49, 53, 56, 60, 77, 81, 83, 95; **4**:6, 10, 12, 24, 28, 31, 36, 45, 53, 55, 60, 66, 85, 88, 92; **5**:5, 15, 22, 24, 28, 37, 38, 41, 52, 58, 64, 75, 77, 80, 82, 88, 93; **6**:5, 12, 26; **7**:11, 28, 46, 56, 70, 77, 81, 90; **8**:6, 14, 16, 19, 23, 53, 69, 85, 88, 95; **9**:9, 10, 15, 30, 33, 37, 41, 49, 52, 58, 68, 72, 79, 81, 85, 87, 91; **10**:7, 9, 14, 17, 21, 23, 25, 60, 70, 72, 88
captivity **10**:49
Carabus
  C. intricatus **2**:78
  C. olympiae **2**:78
caracolera, mojarra 3:26
Carcharhinus spp. **8**:86
Carcharias spp. **8**:86
Carcharodon carcharias **8**:82
Carcinoscorpius rotundicoruda **3**:74

Carduelis spp. **8**:94
  C. cucullata **8**:94
Carettochelys insculpta **10**:20
Caribbean **5**:80; **7**:84; **8**:16, 80; **10**:60
carp *1*:52
carpione del Garda **8**:52
Carpodectes antoniae **2**:82
cassowary
  Australian **3**:28
  common **3**:28
  double-wattled **3**:28
  dwarf **3**:28
  northern **3**:28
  southern 3:28
  two-wattled **3**:28
Castor fiber **2**:76
Casuarius
  C. bennetti **3**:28
  C. casuarius **3**:28
  C. unappendiculatus **3**:28
cat
  African wild **3**:31
  Asiatic golden **3**:32
  bay **3**:30
  black-footed **3**:31
  European wild **3**:31
  fishing **3**:32
  flat-headed **3**:30
  Iriomote **3**:30
  jungle **3**:32
  leopard **3**:32
  margay **3**:31
  sand **3**:32
  tiger **3**:31
catfish
  Barnard's rock **3**:32
  giant 3:32
  Mekong **3**:32
  Thailand giant **3**:32
Catopuma badia **3**:30
cavefish
  Alabama **3**:34
  various **3**:34
Centropyge resplendens **2**:19
Cephalophus
  C. adersi **4**:49
  C. jentinki **4**:48–49
  C. nigrifrons **4**:49
Cephalopterus glabricollis **2**:82
Cephalorhynchus hectori **10**:48
Cerambyx cerdo **6**:44
Ceratophora tennentii **4**:38
Ceratotherium simum **8**:34
Cercartetus macrurus **8**:4
cetaceans *see* dolphin; porpoise; whale
Cetorhinus maximus **8**:80
Chad **7**:30
Chaetophractus retusus **2**:30
chameleon
  Labord's **3**:36
  Madagascar forest **3**:36
  Senegal *1*:72
  south central lesser 3:36
chamois cattle **9**:50

characin
  blind cave 3:38
  naked **3**:38
characodon, black prince **5**:36
Characodon spp. **5**:36
Charadrius spp. **7**:84
  C. melodus **7**:84
cheetah *1*:57; **3**:40
Chile **3**:46, 62; **4**:78
chimpanzee 3:42
  common **3**:42
  dwarf 3:44
  pygmy 3:44
China **2**:12, 26, 36; **3**:12, 24, 32; **4**:6, 10, 12, 16, 28; **5**:26, 58, 94; **6**:30, 32; **7**:32, 38, 48, 50; **9**:50, 62, 94; **10**:16, 90
chinchilla
  long-tailed **3**:46
  short-tailed 3:46
Chinchilla breviacaudata **3**:46
chiru **2**:26
Chlamydogobius squamigenus **5**:34
Chlamydotis undulata **3**:10
Chlamyphorus truncatus **2**:30
Chlorochrysa nitidissima **4**:76
Chloropipo flavicapilla **6**:66
Chocó Endemic Bird Area **2**:54
Choeropsis liberiensis **5**:52
Choloepus
  C. didactylus **9**:6
  C. hoffmanni **9**:6
Chondrohierax wilsonii **6**:7
Chrysocyon brachyurus **10**:70
Cichlasoma spp. **3**:26
  C. bartoni **3**:26
cichlid
  Barton's **3**:26
  Lake Victoria haplochromine 3:48
  Steindachner's **3**:26
Ciconia
  C. boyciana **9**:34
  C. stormi **9**:34
Cinclus schulzi **4**:18
Cistothorus apolinari **10**:86
CITES *see* Convention on International Trade in Endangered Species of Wild Fauna and Flora
clam, giant 3:50
class, taxonomic group **1**:58–59
classification
  animal kingdom **1**:58
  species **1**:26
  taxonomic **1**:58–59
Clemmys spp. **10**:14
  C. muhlebergii **10**:14
climate change **1**:8, 53, 78; **2**:56; **3**:13; **6**:48; **7**:30, 48, 66, 88; **8**:36; **9**:70
cloning **5**:19
Cnemidophorus
  C. hyperythrus **10**:61

103

C. vanzoi **10**:60
cochin **6**:86
cockatoo
 salmon-crested 3:52
 various **3**:52
cod
 Atlantic 3:54
 blue-nosed **3**:56
 Clarence River **3**:56
 Mary River **3**:56
 northern **3**:54
 rock **3**:56
 trout 3:56
coelacanth 3:58
 Sulawesi **3**:58
Coelingena prunellei **9**:20
Coenagrion
 C. hylas freyi **3**:92
 C. mercuriale **3**:92
Coleura seychellensis **2**:64
collecting **2**:80; **3**:13, 63, 82;
 6:21; **7**:24; **8**:23; **10**:78
Colombia **2**:54
colugo **6**:24–25
 Malayan **6**:22
Columba spp. **7**:71
 C. mayeri **7**:70
Columbia **2**:74
combtail **7**:56
Commander Islands **8**:78
commensalism **3**:34
communities **1**:22
Comoro Islands **3**:58
competition **2**:7, 34, 48, 55,
 56, 77; **3**:13, 24, 27, 29, 31,
 44; **4**:15, 19, 24, 32, 45, 79,
 89; **5**:6, 11, 19, 31, 36, 43,
 66, 74, 76, 92; **6**:62, 72, 78,
 84; **7**:30, 59, 65, 66, 88;
 8:21, 25, 34, 36, 63, 88; **9**:9,
 28, 49, 66, 72, 86; **10**:55,
 72, 77, 90, 95
computer modeling **1**:8
condor
 Andean **3**:60
 California 1:86; **3**:60
coney **5**:64
Congo **7**:60
Conolophus
 C. pallidus **5**:76
 C. subcristatus **5**:76
conservation **1**:10–13, 67,
 84–95
Conservation Dependent *see*
 Lower Risk, Conservation
 Dependent
Conservation International (CI)
 1:12
conservation research **1**:84–86
Convention on International
 Trade in Endangered Species
 of Wild Fauna and Flora
 (CITES) **1**:11, 16–17
coot
 Caribbean **3**:62
 Hawaiian **3**:62
 horned 3:62
 Mascarene **3**:62
cooter, Rio Grande **10**:12

Copsychus
 C. cebuensis **6**:62
 C. sechellarum **6**:62
coral
 red **3**:51
 reef **1**:82
 see also sea fan
Corallium rubrum **3**:51; **8**:60, 61
cormorant
 Galápagos 3:64
 Pallas's *1*:36
 various **3**:64
corncrake 3:66
Corvus spp. **3**:82
 C. hawaiiensis **3**:82
Costa Rica **8**:10; **9**:70
costs, conservation **1**:87–89
cotinga
 turquoise **2**:82
 yellow-billed **2**:82
Cotinga ridgwayi **2**:82
courser, Jerdon's 3:68
cow
 golden fleeced **9**:50
 sea **4**:46
 Steller's sea *1*:36; **3**:70
crab
 California Bay pea 3:72
 California fiddler **3**:73
 horseshoe 3:74
 king **3**:74
crane
 various **3**:76
 whooping 3:76
Craseonycteris thonglongyai
 2:64
crawfish, noble **3**:78
crayfish
 noble 3:78
 Tennessee cave **3**:78
creeper, Hawaii **2**:6
Crex crex **3**:66
crimson-wing, Shelley's **4**:74
Critically Endangered (CR),
 IUCN category, definition,
 1:14; **2**:4, 12, 34, 52, 80;
 3:34, 46, 58, 60, 68, 82, 84,
 94; **4**:10, 28, 54, 76, 78, 84,
 88, 94; **5**:12, 16, 34, 71, 72,
 74, 80; **6**:14, 18, 34, 60, 62;
 7:6, 54, 58, 68, 78; **8**:20, 26,
 30, 32, 76, 92; **9**:30, 32, 36,
 52, 70, 72, 92; **10**:16, 18,
 22, 30, 64, 72, 76, 78
crocodile 1:75
 American 3:80
 various **3**:80
Crocodile Specialist Group
 (CSG) **3**:81
Crocodylus spp. **3**:80
 C. acutus **3**:80
Crocuta crocuta **5**:68
crossbreeding **1**:26
 see also interbreeding
crow
 Hawaiian 3:82
 various **3**:82
Cryptoprocta ferox **4**:90
Cryptospiza shelleyi **4**:74

Ctenophorus yinnietharra **4**:38
Cuba **5**:62; **10**:78, 86
culling **8**:72; 79
Cuon alpinus **4**:16
Cuora spp. **10**:16
 C. trifasciata **10**:16
curlew
 Eskimo 3:84
 slender-billed **8**:54
 various **3**:84
cuscus
 black-spotted 3:86
 various **3**:86
cushion star 3:88
Cyanopsitta spixii **6**:60
Cyanoramphus unicolor **5**:92
Cyclades Islands **10**:30
cyclones **7**:70
Cyclopes spp. **2**:25
Cyclura
 C. colleo **5**:80
 C. nubila lewisi **5**:80
 C. n. spp. **5**:80
Cygnus buccinator **9**:44
Cynocephalus
 C. varigatus **6**:22
 C. volans **6**:22
Cynomys spp. **7**:92
 C. ludovicianus **7**:92
Cynoscion macdonaldi **9**:92
Cyprinodon spp. **7**:94
 C. diabolis **7**:94
cypriniformes **9**:80
cyprinodontiformes **9**:80

D

dace
 mountain blackside 3:90
 Tennessee **3**:90
Dactilopsila tatei **5**:32; **7**:88
Dalatias licha **8**:86
dam building **1**:40; **2**:92; **4**:19,
 26, 29; **5**:83; **7**:82; **8**:47, 53;
 9:37; **10**:37
damselfly
 Frey's **3**:92
 southern 3:92
danio, barred 3:94
Danio pathirana **3**:94
darter
 Maryland **4**:4
 watercress 4:4
Darwin, Charles **1**:28; **5**:76
Dasycercus cristicauda **6**:94
Data Deficient (DD), IUCN
 category, definition **1**:16
Daubentonia madagascariensis
 2:42
DDT **1**:50, 51–52
deer
 Bawean **4**:8
 black musk **4**:12
 Chinese water 4:6
 forest musk **4**:12
 Kuhl's 4:8
 Père David's 4:10
 Schomburgk's *1*:36
 Siberian musk 4:12

deforestation **1**:38, 41, 73; **2**:7,
 22, 31, 42, 44, 65, 72, 75,
 83, 85; **3**:8, 29, 44, 87; **4**:34,
 40, 48, 52, 55, 60, 61, 66,
 84, 86, 88, 91; **5**:26, 38, 40,
 44, 45, 49, 52, 57, 63, 83,
 84, 86, 88; **6**:4, 8, 14, 22,
 24, 26, 31, 46, 58, 63, 66,
 70, 76, 86, 88, 91; **7**:26, 35,
 38, 41, 51, 68, 70, 78, 89;
 8:11, 12, 23, 32, 38, 41, 47,
 49, 65, 91; **9**:7, 31, 34, 52,
 54, 76; **10**:4, 21, 24, 26, 72,
 78, 85
Delphinapterus leucas **10**:58
Democratic Republic of Congo
 3:42; **5**:38, 40; **7**:22; **8**:34
Dendrocopus dorae **10**:80
Dendroica spp. **10**:38
 D. kirtlandii **10**:38
Dendrolagus spp. **10**:4
 D. goodfellowi **10**:4
desertification **1**:38–40; **5**:20
desman
 Pyrenean **4**:14
 Russian 4:14
Desmana moschata **4**:14
developing countries,
 conservation **1**:89, 95
devilfish **10**:44
dhole 4:16
Dicerorhinus sumatrensis **8**:32
Diceros bicornis **8**:26
dinosaurs **1**:34–35
Diomedea spp. **2**:9
 D. amsterdamensis **2**:9
 D. antipodensis **2**:9
 D. dabbenena **2**:9
 D. exulans **2**:8
dipper, rufous-throated 4:18
disease **1**:40, 55–56, 65, 79;
 2:7, 50, 89; **3**:29, 42, 57, 78,
 83; **4**:5, 22, 26, 57, 94; **5**:12,
 38; **6**:10, 14, 46, 48, 56;
 8:28, 36; **9**:56, 66, 76, 82;
 10:64, 72
dispersal corridors *see* habitat
 corridors
dodo 1:28–29, *31*, 37; **4**:20
dog
 African wild 4:22
 Asian wild **4**:16
 bush 4:24
 red **4**:16
Dolomedes plantarius **9**:22
dolphin
 Amazon river 4:26
 boto **4**:26–27
 Chinese river **4**:28
 Ganges river **4**:26, 28
 Hector's **4**:48
 Indus river **4**:26, 28
 pantropical spotted **10**:48
 pink **4**:26
 striped **10**:48
 whitefin **4**:28
 Yangtze river **4**:28
 see also porpoise
domestic animals **1**:38–40, 56

 see also alien species; grazing
dormouse
 common **4**:30
 garden **4**:32
 hazel *1*:53; **4**:30
 Japanese **4**:34
 various **4**:30, 32, 34
dotterel, New Zealand **7**:84
dragon
 southeastern lined earless
  4:38
 Yinnietharra rock **4**:38
 see also Komodo dragon
dragon fish 4:36
dragonfly
 orange-spotted emerald **4**:70
 various **4**:70
drainage *see* wetland drainage
drift nets *see* fishing nets
drill 4:40
Driloleirus americanus **4**:58;
 10:82
Driloleirus macelfreshi **4**:58
drought **1**:52; **3**:38; **8**:51
Drymarchon corais couperi
 9:10
Dryomys nitedula **4**:30
Dryomys sichuanensis **4**:32, 34
duck
 Labrador 4:42
 pink-headed **4**:44
 various **7**:10
 white-headed 4:44
dugong 4:46; **6**:69
Dugong dugon **4**:46
duiker
 Ader's **4**:49
 Jentink's 4:48
 Ruwenzori black-fronted **4**:49
 squirrel **4**:48
dunnart
 Kangaroo Island **1**:24, 50
 sooty **4**:50
 various **4**:50
Durrell Wildlife Conservation
 Trust (DWCT) **1**:12
Dusicyon australis **10**:66
Dyscophus antongilii **5**:14

E

eagle
 Adalbert's **4**:56
 bald *1*:94
 greater spotted **4**:56
 harpy 4:52
 Imperial **4**:56
 monkey-eating 4:54
 New Guinea harpy **4**:53, 54
 Philippine 4:54
 Spanish imperial **4**:56
 white-tailed sea *1*:94; **8**:64
earthworm
 giant gippsland 4:58
 Oregon giant **4**:58
 Washington giant **4**:58;
  10:82
echidna
 long-beaked 4:60

short-beaked **4**:60
Echinus esculentus **8**:66
ecology **1**:18–37
ecosystems **1**:22–24
ecotourism **1**:90–92; **5**:38; **6**:27; **10**:39
Ecuador **2**:54, 74; **4**:82
education **1**:94
Edwardsia ivelli **8**:58
eel, lesser spiny **4**:62
egg collectors **2**:38, 91
El Niño **3**:64; **5**:79; **7**:65; **8**:10
Elaphe situla **9**:12
Elaphrus
　E. viridis **2**:78
　E. davidianus **4**:10
Elassoma
　E. alabamae **9**:40
　E. boehlkei **9**:40
　E. okatie **9**:40
elephant
　African **4**:64
　Asian *1*:95; **4**:66
　Indian **4**:66
elephant-shrew
　golden-rumped 4:68
　various **4**:68
Elephantulus revoili **4**:68
Elephas maximus **4**:66
Eliomys
　E. elanurus **4**:30, 32
　E. quercinus **4**:32
Elusor macrurus **10**:22
Emballonura semicaudata **2**:64
emerald, orange-spotted 4:70
emperor fish **4**:36
Endangered (EN), IUCN category, definition **1**:15
endemic species, definition **1**:30
energy flow **1**:23–24
Enhydra lutris **7**:36
Ephippiorhynchus asiaticus **9**:34
Epicrates
　E. angulifer **3**:4
　E. inornatus **3**:4
　E. monensis grati **3**:4
　E. monensis monensis **3**:4
　E. subflavus **3**:4
Epimachus fastuosus **2**:84
Equus
　E. africanus **2**:34; **8**:8
　E. grevyi **10**:92
　E. hemionus **2**:36
　E. przewalskii **5**:58
　E. quagga **8**:8
　E. zebra **10**:94
　E. z. hartmannii **10**:94
　E. z. zebra **10**:94
Eretmochelys imbricata **10**:18
Eriocnemis mirabilis **4**:78
　E. nigrivestis **9**:20
Erythrura
　E. gouldiae **4**:74
　E. viridifacies **4**:74
Eschrichtius robustus **10**:44
Estrilda poliopareia **4**:74
Etheostoma

E. nuchale **4**:4
E. sellore **4**:4
ethics, conservation **1**:88, 94–95
Ethiopia **2**:34, 46, 66; **6**:84; **7**:18; **10**:64, 92
Euathlus smithi **9**:60
Eubalaena
　E. australis **10**:52
　E. glacialis **10**:52
Eudyptes
　E. pachyrhynchus **7**:64
　E. robustus **7**:64
Eulidia yarrellii **4**:78
Eumetopias jubatus **8**:62
Eunice viridis **10**:82
Eunicella verrucosa **8**:60
Eupleres goudotii **4**:91
European Habitats Directive **6**:52
Euryceros prevostii **10**:26
Eurynorhynchus pygmeus **8**:54
evolution, speciation **1**:26–28
exploitation **1**:49, 62, 75
Extinct (EX), IUCN category, definition **1**:14; **2**:38; **3**:70; **4**:20, 42; **5**:42, 60; **8**:8; **9**:66; **10**:66
Extinct in the Wild (EW), IUCN category, definition, **1**:14; **4**:72; **5**:36, 58; **7**:30; **8**:19
extinction **1**:34, 36
　see also natural extinction

F

falanoka **4**:91
falanouc **4**:91
Falco spp. **5**:95
　F. araea **6**:5
　F. naumanni **5**:94
　F. punctatus **6**:4
falcon, various **5**:95
Falkland Island **10**:66
family, taxonomic group **1**:58–59
Fauna & Flora International (FFI) **1**:12, 88
feather products **1**:46; **2**:85; **5**:50
Federal Bureau of Land Management **9**:83
Felis
　F. iriomotensis **3**:30
　F. pardinis **7**:20
　F. silvestris **10**:62
Ferminia cerverai **10**:86
ferreret **9**:72
ferret, black-footed 4:72
field studies **1**:84
Fiji **5**:74; **10**:82
finback **10**:42
finch
　Cochabamba **4**:76
　Galápagos *1*:28
　Gouldian 4:74
　Hawaiian *1*:27
　mangrove 4:76
　olive-headed brush **4**:76

painted **4**:74
purple-breasted **4**:74
rainbow **4**:74
finner **10**:42
Japan **10**:54
firecrown, Juan Fernández 4:78
fires **1**:57, 73; **2**:25, 33, 59, 62, 92; **3**:19, 83; **4**:24, 68, 75; **5**:50; **6**:10, 42, 46, 65, 76, 81, 86; **7**:14, 17, 55, 88; **8**:14, 56; **9**:82, 89, 90; **10**:32, 38, 86
fish **1**:68–71
　definition **1**:68–69
　diversity **1**:68
　history **1**:69–70
　risks **1**:70–71
　see also List of Animals by Group, page 100
fish-eagle, various **8**:64
fishing **1**:45; **3**:33, 55, 65; **4**:26, 28, 44; **7**:38; **8**:53, 62, 72, 75, 76, 79, 80, 82, 85; **10**:9, 45, 48, 52
　see also overfishing; sports fishing
fishing controls **3**:55
fishing nets **4**:15; **5**:42; **6**:68; **7**:5, 86; **10**:46
fishing techniques **2**:8
fishing-owl, rufous **7**:42
flagship species *1*:9
flamingo
　Andean **4**:80
　various **4**:81
flightless birds **1**:28, 64
flooding **1**:40; **6**:38; **7**:66; **9**:56
florican
　Bengal **3**:10
　lesser **3**:10
flycatcher
　Atlantic royal **4**:82
　Pacific royal 4:82
　royal **4**:82
　tyrant **4**:82
flying fox
　Rodrigues (Rodriguez) **4**:84
　Ryukyu 4:86
fody
　Mauritius 4:88
　Rodrigues **4**:88
　Seychelles **4**:88
food chains/webs **1**:23–24
food shortage **4**:75; **7**:65
forest management **4**:30
Formica
　F. aquilonia **2**:22
　F. lugubris **2**:22
　F. polyctena **2**:22
fossa 4:90
Fossa fossa **4**:91
Foudia
　F. flavicans **4**:88
　F. rubra **4**:88
　F. seychellarum **4**:88
fox
　Simien **10**:64
　South American **10**:66

swift **4**:92
fragmented distribution **1**:8
　see also habitat fragmentation
French Polynesia **9**:8
friarbird, dusty **5**:54
Friends of the Earth **1**:13
frog
　Archey's **5**:6
　corroboree **9**:78
　gastric-brooding 4:94
　golden mantella 6:70
　green and golden bell 5:4
　green and golden swamp **5**:4
　Hamilton's 5:6
　harlequin 5:8
　Maud Island **5**:6
　New England swamp **5**:4, 5
　northern timber **5**:12
　northern tinker **5**:12
　Palestinian painted *1*:37
　platypus **4**:94
　red-legged 5:10
　sharp-snouted day **5**:12
　tinkling 5:12
　tomato 5:14
　various **5**:10
fruit bat see flying fox
Fulica spp. **3**:62
　F. cornuta **3**:62
fund raising, conservation **1**:90
fur trade **1**:46; **2**:46, 74, 76; **3**:46; **4**:14, 92; **5**:86; **6**:28, 31, 33, 75; **7**:20, 34, 36, 82; **8**:70, 72, 78, 90; **10**:28, 74
Furcifer
　F. campani **3**:36
　F. labordi **3**:36
　F. minor **3**:36

G

Gadus morhua **3**:54
Galápagos Islands **3**:64; **4**:76; **5**:46, 76, 78; **7**:64; **9**:80, 86
galaxias
　swan **5**:16
　various **5**:16
Galaxias spp. **5**:16
　F. fontanus **5**:16
Galemys pyrenaicus **4**:14
Gallinula
　G. pacifica **9**:48
　G. sylvestris **9**:48
Gallirallus spp. **8**:18
　G. owstoni **8**:18
Gambelia silus **6**:36
gamekeeping **6**:74
garefowl **2**:38
gaur 5:18
gavial **5**:24
Gavialis gangeticus **5**:24
Gazella
　G. arabica **5**:20
　G. cuvieri **5**:20
　G. dama **5**:20
　G. leptoceros **5**:20

gazelle
　Arabian **5**:20
　Cuvier's **5**:20
　dama 5:20
　sand **5**:20
gecko
　fat-tailed *1*:74
　Namaqua day **5**:22
　Rodrigues day **5**:22
　Round Island day 5:22
　Standing's day **5**:22
genera, taxonomic **1**:58
generalist species **1**:29
genetics **1**:56
Genicanthus personatus **2**:18
Geocapromys
　G. brownii **5**:64
　G. ingrahami **5**:64
Geochelone spp. **9**:86, 89
　F. radiata **9**:90
　G. nigra **9**:86
　G. yniphora **9**:90
Geonemertes rodericana **7**:8
Geopsittacus occidentalis **7**:58
Geronticus
　G. calvus **5**:72
　G. eremita **5**:72
Ghana **8**:38
gharial 5:24
gibbon
　black 5:26
　concolor **5**:26
　crested 5:26
　silvery **5**:26
Gibraltar **6**:54
Gila monster 5:28
Giraffa camelopardalis reticulata **5**:30
giraffe, reticulated 5:30
Girardinichthys spp. **5**:36
Glareola nordmanni **3**:68
glider, mahogany 5:32
Glirulus japonicus **4**:32, 34
Glis glis **4**:30
Globicephala macrorhynchus **10**:48
Glossolepis spp. **8**:20
　G. wanamensis **8**:20
glutton **10**:74
Glyphis gangeticus **8**:86
gnu-goat **9**:50
goat **9**:46
goby
　dwarf pygmy 5:34
　Edgbaston **5**:34
Goodea spp. **5**:36
goodeid
　gold sawfin 5:36
　various **5**:36
goose
　Hawaiian *1*:87; **7**:10
　various **7**:10
Gopherus
　G. agassizii **9**:82
　G. flavomarginatus **9**:82
　G. polyphemus **9**:82
Gorilla
　G. gorilla beringei **5**:38
　G. g. gorilla **5**:40

G. g. graveri **5:**39, 40
gorilla *1:45*
   eastern lowland **5:**39, 40
   mountain *1:91;* **5:**38
   western lowland 5:40
Goura
   G. cristata **7:**72
   G. scheepmaker **7:**72
   G. victoria **7:**72
Grantiella picta **5:**54
Graphiurus ocularis **4:**34
Graptemys spp. **10:**24
   G. flavimaculata **10:**24
grassland destruction **2:**92
grayling, New Zealand *1:*36
grazing animals **1:**38–40; **7:**17
grebe
   Atitlán 5:42
   giant pied-billed **5:**42
   various **5:**42
Greece **9:**12; **10:**30
greenhouse gases **1:**53
Greenland **2:**70
Greenpeace **1:**13
greenshank, spotted **8:**54
griffon, Cape 10:34
ground squirrel
   European **9:**18
   various **9:**18
Grus spp. **3:**76
   G. americana **3:**76
Guam **8:**18
guan
   horned 5:44
   various **5:**44
guanaco **3:**25; **10:**28
Guatemala **5:**42; 44; **8:**10
Guinea **8:**38
gull
   black-billed **5:**46
   lava 5:46
   Olrog's **5:**46
   relict **5:**46
   Saunder's **5:**46
Gulo gulo **10:**74
Guyana, pirarucu **7:**76
Gymnobelideus leadbeateri **7:**88
Gymnocharacinus bergii **3:**38
Gymnogyps californianus **3:**60
Gymnomyza aubryana **5:**54
gymnure
   Hainan 5:48
   various **5:**48
Gyps spp. **10:**34
   G. coprotheres **10:**34

H

habitat conservation **1:**10, 88–92
habitat corridors **4:**67; **6:**36, 65; **7:**55; **10:**23
habitat creation **3:**13; **9:**53; **10:**38
habitat fragmentation **2:**69; **3:**18, 22, 29, 42; **4:**31, 34; **5:**32, 55; **6:**10, 42, 66, 82; **7:**48, 78; **8:**10, 12, 45; **9:**54; **10:**15, 26
habitat management **3:**61, 67; **4:**19; **8:**69
habitat restoration **3:**13, 93; **4:**79; **6:**65; **9:**15; **10:**23
Habroptila wallacii **9:**48
haddock **3:**54
Hainan Island **4:**10; **5:**26, 48
Haliaeetus spp. **8:**64
   H. pelagicus **8:**64
Halichoerus grypus **8:**70, 72
Hapalemur
   H. aureus **6:**26
   H. simus **6:**26
Haplochromis spp. **3:**48
hare
   Amami **8:**12
   bristly **5:**50
   bushman **8:**12, *8:13*
   harsh-furred **5:**50
   hispid 5:50, *8:13*
   mouse **7:**74
   Sumatran **8:**12, *8:13*
Harpia harpyja **4:**52
Harpyopsis novaeguineae **4:**53, 54
harvesting **10:**83
Hawaiian Islands **1:**36; **2:**6, 18; **3:**82; **7:**10; **8:**74; **9:**24
heat pollution **1:**52
Heliangelus spp. **9:**20
   H. zusii **4:**78
Heloderma
   H. horridum **5:**28
   H. suspectum **5:**28
Hemignathus munroi **2:**6
Hemitragus
   H. hylocrius **9:**46
   H. jayakari **9:**46
   H. jemlahicus **9:**46
Herichthys spp. **3:**26
   H. bartoni **3:**26
Heteralocha acutirostris **5:**60
Heteromirafra ruddi **6:**18
Hexanchus griseus **8:**86
Hexaprotodon liberiensis **5:**52
hibernation **1:**53
hide trade *see* fur trade; skin trade
Himalayas **5:**50; **6:**32, 73; **7:**50; **9:**94
Himantopus novaezelandiae **9:**32
Hippocampus capensis **8:**68
hippopotamus
   common **5:**53
   pygmy 5:52
Hippopotamus amphibius tschadensis **5:**53
Hirudo medicinalis **6:**20
Hirundo
   H. atrocaerulea **9:**42
   H. megaensis **9:**42
hog
   pygmy **2:**45
   see also pig
Honduras **8:**10
honeycreeper, Hawaiian **2:**6

honeyeater
   crow **5:**54
   painted **5:**54
   regent 5:54
hornbill
   Mindanao wrinkled **5:**56
   various **5:**56
   writhed 5:56
horns **6:**16, 72; **8:**26, 28, 32, 34
horse, Przewalski's wild 5:58
Houbaropsis bengalensis **3:**10
Hubbsina turneri **5:**36
Hucho hucho **8:**52
huia 5:60
human competition **1:**61–62
human disturbance **2:**4, 59, 63; **3:**41, 75; **4:**28, 56; **5:**43; **6:**42, 84; **7:**63, 84; **8:**38, 74, 76; **10:**34, 46
hummingbird
   bee 5:62
   sapphire-bellied **4:**78
hunting **1:**42–49
   see also big-game hunting; fur trade; persecution; skin trade; traditional medicine
hutia
   Bahamian **5:**64
   Jamaican 5:64
Hyaena brunnea **5:**66
Hydrodamalis gigas **3:**70
Hydropotes inermis **4:**6
hyena
   brown 5:66, 69
   laughing 5:68
   spotted 5:68
   striped **5:**69
Hylobates
   H. concolor **5:**26
   H. moloch **5:**26
Hylomys
   H. hainanensis **5:**48
   H. parvus **5:**48

I

ibex
   Nubian 5:70
   Portuguese *1:*37
   walia **5:**71; **6:**73
ibis
   crested **9:**26
   northern bald 5:72
   scarlet *1:*21
   various **5:**72
Iceland **8:**72
Ichthyophaga
   I. humilis **8:**64
   I. ichthyaetus **8:**64
iguana
   Barrington Island **5:**76
   Cuban ground **5:**80
   Fijian banded **5:**74
   Fijian crested 5:74
   Galápagos land 5:76
   Galápagos marine *1:*28; **5:**78
   Grand Cayman blue rock 5:80

   Jamaican **5:**80
   Little Cayman **5:**80
ikan temoleh 5:82
inbreeding **1:**56, 87; **2:**75, 89; **3:**41, 42, 89; **4:**26, 34, 72; **5:**6, 19, 37, 58, 74; **6:**46, 92; **7:**28; **8:**88; **9:**68, 79; **10:**77
inca, black **9:**20
India **2:**72, 94; **3:**68; **4:**16, 44, 62; **5:**18, 24; **6:**30, 34, 46; **8:**28; **9:**34, 46, 50, 68; **10:**90
Indian Ocean **3:**58; **4:**47; **8:**80
Indian Ocean islands **4:**84
Indochina **5:**18; **6:**86
Indonesia **2:**16, 20, 28, 44, 50; **3:**8, 28, 52; **4:**8, 36, 67; **5:**34; **6:**12, 30; **7:**26, 72; **8:**30, 32, 84; **9:**30, 58; **10:**88
indri 5:84
Indri indri **5:**84
industrial development **1:**40; **5:**11; **8:**55, 65; **9:**27; **10:**22, 31
   see also mining; quarrying
Inia geoffrensis **4:**26
insects *see* invertebrates
interbreeding **1:**26, 40, 57; **2:**50, 88; **3:**27, 38; **4:**45; **5:**37, 58; **6:**79; **7:**69; **9:**33, 38, 79; **10:**62, 64, 68, 72, 90
International Union for the Conservation of Nature (IUCN) **1:**11, 88–89
   categories **1:**14
internet trade **2:**80
introductions **1:**54–55
   see also alien species
invertebrates
   diversity **1:**80
   history **1:**81–83
   risks **1:**83
   see also List of Animals by Group, page 100
Iran **2:**36
Irian Jaya **10:**20
irrigation **1:**40; **2:**36; **3:**11; **4:**19, 26; **7:**55, 81; **8:**53; **9:**84
islands **1:**20
islands *see* individual island names
isolation **1:**26–28; **6:**92; **10:**94
Isoodon auratus **2:**48
IUCN *see* International Union for the Conservation of Nature
ivory *1:*16; **4:**64, 67
Ivory Coast **4:**48; **8:**38

J

jackal, Simien **10:**64
jaguar 5:86
jaguarundi *3:*31
Jamaica **3:**4; **5:**64; **10:**85
Japan **3:**30; **4:**34, 86; **6:**56; **7:**4, 38; **8:**12, 46, 64
Java **4:**16; **6:**30; **9:**68

Jersey Zoo **1:**86
Juan Fernández archipelago **4:**78
junco, Guadalupe **4:**76
Junco insularis **4:**76

K

"K" reproductive strategy **1:**25
kagu 5:88
kaka **5:**51, 92
kakapo 5:90
Kalmykia, saiga **8:**42
Kazakhstan **2:**36; **8:**42
kea 5:92
Kenya **4:**68; **10:**92
kestrel
   lesser 5:94
   Mauritius 6:4
   Seychelles **5:**95; **6:**5
kite
   Cuban **6:**7
   red 1:56; **6:**6
   white-collared **6:**7
kittiwake, red-legged **5:**46
kiwi
   brown *1:66;* **6:**8
   various **6:**9
koala 6:10
kokako **5:**60
Komodo dragon 6:12
Korea **4:**6, 12
kouprey 6:14
kudu, greater 6:16

L

Labrador **8:**72
Lacerta spp. **6:**42
   L. agilis **6:**42
Lake Wanam rainbowfish 8:20
Lama
   L. guanaco **10:**28
   L. guanicöe **3:**25
Lamma nasus **8:**86
land recamation *see* wetland drainage
langur, douc **6:**86
Laos **5:**82; **6:**86; **7:**44; **10:**16
lark
   Raso **6:**18
   Razo **6:**18
   various **6:**18
Larus spp. **5:**46
   L. fuliginosus **5:**46
Lasiorhinus krefftii **10:**77
Lathamus discolor **7:**58
Latimeria
   L. chalumnae **3:**58
   L. menadoensis **3:**58
Latin names **1:**59
Least Concern *see* Lower Risk, Least Concern (LRlc)
leech, medicinal 6:20
Leeward Islands **8:**74
Leiopelma
   L. archeyi **5:**6

L. hamiltoni **5**:6
L. pakeka **5**:6
Leipoa ocellata **6**:64
lemming **1**:21
lemur
  broad-nosed gentle **6**:26
  Coquerel's mouse **6**:22
  golden bamboo **6**:26
  hairy-eared dwarf 6:22
  Philippine flying 6:24
  red-fronted *1*:33
  ruffed 6:26
  variegated **6**:26
  see also indri; sifaka
Leontopithecus spp. **9**:52
  L. chrysopygus **6**:88
  L. rosalia **9**:52
leopard 6:28
  clouded 6:30
  snow 6:32
Leopardus pardalis albescens **7**:20
Lepidopyga lilliae **4**:78
Leptodon forbesi **6**:7
Leptoptilos
  L. dubius **9**:34
  L. javanicus **9**:34
Lesotho **10**:34
Leucopsar rothschildi **9**:30
Liberia **4**:48; **8**:38
life strategies **1**:24–26
light pollution **1**:43, 53
Limnogale mergulus **9**:64
Limulus polyphemus **3**:74
Linnaeus **1**:58
linnet, Warsangli **8**:94
lion *1*:23; **9**:69
  Asiatic 6:34
  Barbary *1*:37
Lipotes vexillifer **4**:28
Litoria
  L. aurea **5**:4
  L. castanea **5**:4
live animal trade **1**:49; **3**:58; **7**:46
  see also aquarium trade; cage-bird trade; medical research; pet trade; scientific research; zoos
lizard
  blunt-nosed leopard 6:36
  flat-tailed horned 6:38
  Gila monster 5:28
  Ibiza wall 6:40
  Komodo dragon 6:12
  Lilford's wall **6**:40
  Mexican beaded **5**:28
  Miles wall **6**:40
  ocellated green *1*:74
  sand 6:42
  Schreiber's green **6**:42
  Soutpansberg rock **6**:42
  spineless forest **4**:38
  Tennent's leaf-nosed **4**:38
locust, desert *1*:81
Loddigesia mirabilis **9**:20
longicorn
  cerambyx 6:44
  rosalia **6**:44

loris
  pygmy **6**:46
  slender 6:46
Loris tardigradus **6**:46
lovebird
  black-cheeked 6:48–49
  Fischer's **6**:48
Lower Risk (LR) IUCN category, definition **1**:16
Lower Risk, Conservation Dependent (LRcd), IUCN category, definition **1**:16
Lower Risk, Least Concern (LRlc), IUCN category, definition **1**:16
Lower Risk, Near Threatened (LRnt), IUCN category, definition **1**:16
Laxities bailout **2**:6
Loxodonta africana **4**:64
lungfish, Australian 6:50
Lutra spp. **7**:35
  L. lutra **7**:32
luxury products **1**:46; **7**:53; **8**:81
Lycaena
  L. dispar **3**:22
  L. hermes **3**:18
Lycaon pictus **4**:22
Lycosa ericeticola **9**:24
lynx, Iberian 6:52
Lynx pardinus **6**:52

M

Macaca spp. **6**:54, 57
  L. fuscata **6**:56
  L. sylvanus **6**:54
macaque
  barbary 6:54
  Japanese 6:56
  various **6**:54, 56
macaw
  black **6**:58
  blue **6**:58
  hyacinth 6:58
  hyacinthine **6**:58
  Jamaican green and yellow *1*:37
  little blue **6**:60
  Spix's 6:60
  various **6**:60
Maccullochella spp. **3**:56
  M. macquariensis **3**:56
Macgregoria pulchra **2**:84
mackerel, Spanish **10**:8
Macrocephalon maleo **6**:64
Macroderma gigas **2**:56
Macrognathus aral **4**:62
Macrotis lagotis **2**:48
Macrovipera schweizeri **10**:30
Macruromys elegans **6**:92
Maculinea arion **3**:20
Madagascar **1**:33; **2**:32, 42; **3**:6, 36; **4**:90; **5**:14, 84; **6**:22, 26, 70, 76; **7**:40; **8**:92; **9**:64, 90; **10**:26
magpie-robin, Seychelles 6:62

Malaysia **2**:50; **4**:16, 36; **5**:18, 82; **6**:30; **7**:26; **8**:32, 84; **9**:58
maleo **6**:64
malleefowl 6:64
Malpulutta kretseri **7**:56
mammals **1**:60–63
  definition **1**:60
  diversity **1**:60
  history **1**:60–61
  risks **1**:61–63
  see also List of Animals by Group, page 100
manakin
  black-capped 6:66
  various **6**:66
manatee
  African **3**:70
  Amazon **3**:70
  American **3**:70
  Florida 1:42; **6**:68
  various **4**:47; **6**:69
Manchuria **4**:12
mandrill **4**:40
Mandrillus
  M. leucophaeus **4**:40
  M. sphinx **4**:40
Manis spp. **7**:52
  M. tetradactyla **7**:52
Manorina melanotis **5**:54
mantella, golden 6:70
Mantella aurantiaca **6**:70
Margaritifera spp. **7**:6
  M. auricularia **7**:6
  M. margaritifera **7**:6, 7
Mariana Islands **8**:18
markhor 6:72
marl **2**:48
Marmaronetta augustirostris **9**:62
marmoset
  black-headed **6**:88
  Goeldi's 6:88
  golden-white tassel-ear **6**:88
marten, pine 6:74
Martes martes **6**:74
mass extinctions **1**:34
Mauritania **8**:76
Mauritius **1**:30–31; **4**:20, 88; **5**:22; **6**:4; **7**:8, 70
maxclapique **5**:36
Mayailurus iriomotensis **3**:30
medical research **2**:31, 41; **3**:42, 44; **6**:56
medical use, medicinal leech **6**:21
medicinal products **2**:12, 73, 75; **3**:42, 54; **4**:6, 12, 46, 80; **5**:24, 26; **6**:31, 46, 72; **7**:53; **8**:12, 26, 28, 30, 32, 42, 69, 81; **9**:21, 68; **10**:16, 21
Mediterranean **3**:88; **4**:44; **8**:76, 80; **9**:36
Megapodius spp. **6**:64
Megaptera novaeangliae **10**:46
Megascolides australis **4**:58
Melanogrammus aeglefinus **3**:54
Melanosuchus niger **2**:10, 12
melidectes, long-bearded **5**:54

Melidectes princeps **5**:54
Mellisuga helenae **5**:62
Melursus ursinus **2**:72
mesite
  brown **6**:77
  subdesert **6**:77
  white-breasted 6:76
Mesitornis
  M. unicolor **6**:77
  M. variegata **6**:76
Metallura
  M. baroni **4**:78
  M. iracunda **4**:78
metaltail
  Perijá **4**:78
  violet-throated **4**:78
metamorphosis **1**:76
Mexico **2**:40; **3**:26, 38, 74; **4**:53; **5**:10, 36, 44; **7**:42, 80, 84; **8**:10, 14; **9**:56, 60, 82, 92; **10**:32
Microgale spp. **9**:64
Micronesia **9**:8
Micropotamogale spp. **9**:64
  M. lamottei **8**:90
  M. ruwenzorii **8**:90
millerbird **10**:36
Milvus milvus **6**:6
Minimum Viable Population (MVP) **1**:21
mining **1**:40; **2**:56; **3**:25, 91; **4**:52, 55, 81; **7**:43, 61; **10**:4, **10**:21
mink
  American *1*:54, 55
  European 4:72; **6**:78
minnow, Sarasin's **10**:88
minor, black-eared **5**:54
Mirafra ashi **6**:18
Mirza coquereli **6**:22
moa, giant **1**:36, *1*:36
mole
  marsupial 6:80
  northern marsupial **6**:80
  southern marsupial **6**:80
mole-rat
  Balkans 6:82
  giant 6:84
  various **6**:84
Monachus
  M. monachus **8**:76
  M. schauinslandi **8**:74
  M. tropicalis **8**:74, 76
Mongolia **2**:36; **3**:12, 24; **5**:58, 94; **8**:42
Monias benschi **6**:77
monkey
  China **6**:86
  douc 6:86
  Goeldi's 6:88
  grizzled leaf **6**:86
  Guizhou snub-nosed **6**:86
  pig-tailed snub-nosed **6**:86
  proboscis 1:40; **6**:90
Monodon monoceros **10**:58
montane biotype **1**:20
moonrat
  dinagat **5**:48
  Hainan **5**:48

moorhen
  Makira **9**:48
  Samoan **9**:48
Morocco **5**:72
Moschus
  M. berezovskii **4**:12
  M. chrysogaster **4**:12
  M. fuscus **4**:12
  M. moschiferus **4**:12
mountains, ecology **1**:20
mouse
  crest-tailed marsupial **6**:94
  Florida **6**:92
  St. Kilda 6:92
Mozambique **10**:34
mulgara 6:94
murrelet
  Japanese 7:4
  various **7**:4
Muscardinus avellanarius **4**:30
mussel
  freshwater 7:6
  freshwater pearl **7**:6
  Spengler's freshwater **7**:6
Mustela spp. **4**:72
  M. lutreola **6**:78
  M. nigripens **4**:72
MVP *see* Minimum Viable Population
Myanmar **4**:36; **6**:30; **7**:50; **8**:32; **9**:50, 94
Mycteria
  M. cinerea **9**:34
  M. leucocephala **9**:34
myna
  Bali **9**:30
  helmeted **9**:30
  Rothschild's **9**:30
Myomimus spp. **4**:34
Myotis spp. **2**:62
  M. cobanensis **2**:66
  M. grisescens **2**:58
  M. morrisi **2**:66
  M. myotis **2**:62
Myrmecobius fasciatus **7**:14
Myrmecophaga tridactyla **2**:24
myxomitosis **1**:55
myzomela, white-chinned **5**:54
Myzomela albigula **5**:54

N

Namibia **10**:94
Nandopsis
  N. bartoni **3**:26
  N. labridens **3**:26, 27
  N. steindachneri **3**:26
Nannoperca oxleyana **3**:56
narwhal **10**:58
Nasalis larvatus **6**:90
National Association of Audubon Societies for the Protection of Wild Birds and Animals **1**:12–13, 88
national parks **1**:13, 92; **2**:24, 46, 64, 69, 83, 89; **3**:4, 16, 25, 69, 76; **4**:16, 19, 24, 40, 48, 55, 60, 67, 68, 79; **5**:41, 46, 66, 69, 72, 77; **6**:30, 34,

47, 52, 94; **7:**17, 19, 26, 41, 61; **8:**14, 28, 31; **9:**7, 53, 64, 78, 87; **10:**21, 28, 64, 77, 87
national wildlife refuges **2:**7; **7:**94; **8:**75; **9:**15, 45
natural disasters **1:**57; **2:**15; **3:**63, 76; **4:**46, 55, 85; **5:**22, 35, 42, 46, 79; **6:**19; **7:**65, 75; **8:**77; **9:**88; **10:**94
natural extinction **4:**32; **7:**88
Natural Resources Conservation Service **9:**10
nature reserves *see* reserves
Near Threatened *see* Lower Risk, Near Threatened (LRnt)
Nematostella vectensis **8:**58
nemertine
  Rodrigues (Rodriguez) **7:**8
nene *1:*87; **7:**10
Neoceratodus forsteri **6:**50
Neodrepanis hypoxanthus **2:**32
Neofelis nebulosa **6:**30
Neopelma aurifrons **6:**66
Neophema chrysogaster **7:**58
Neotoma anthonyi **6:**92
Nepal **2:**72, 94; **5:**24; **6:**30; **7:**50; **8:**28
Nesolagus netscheri **8:**12, *8:13*
Nestor
  N. meridionalis **5:**51, 92
  N. notabilis **5:**92
New Caladonia **5:**88
New Guinea **3:**28, 86; **4:**60; **10:**20
New Mexico **3:**76
New Zealand *1:*89; **5:**6, 50, 60, 92; **6:**8; **9:**32, 48; **10:**6
newt
  Danube **7:**12
  great crested 7:12
  warty **7:**12
Nicaragua **8:**10
Nigeria **4:**40
Nipponia nippon **5:**72; **9:**26
noise pollution **1:**52
Norway **2:**70
Nosy Mangabe **2:**43; **6:**26
Not Evaluated (NE), IUCN category, definition **1:**16
Notiomystis cincta **5:**54
notornis **9:**48
Nova Scotia **8:**72
numbat 7:14
Numenius spp. **3:**84
  N. borealis **3:**84
  N. tenuirostris **8:**54
nuthatch
  Algerian 7:16
  various **7:**16
nyala, mountain 7:18
Nycticebus pygmaeus **6:**46

O

ocelot *3:31*
  Texas 7:20
Ochotona
  O. helanshanenesis **7:**74
  O. kolsowi **7:**74
  O. pusilla **7:**74
off-road vehicles **5:**29; **6:**38; **7:**84; **10:**12, 18
oil products **3:**33; **4:**27, 46; **8:**70, 81; **10:**56
oil spills **7:**5
okapi 7:22
Okapia johnstoni **7:**22
olm 7:24
Oncorhynchus ishikawai **8:**52
Onychorhynchus
  O. occidentalis **4:**82
  O. swainsoni **4:**82
oo, Kauai *1:*36
orang-utan 7:26
orca **10:**48
Orcinus orca **10:**48
Orconectes incomtus **3:**78
orders, taxonomic **1:**58
Oreomystis mana **2:**6
Oreophasis derbianus **5:**44
organizations **1:**11–13, 88
Oriolia bernieri **10:**27
Ornithoptera
  O. aesacus **3:**16
  O. alexandrae **3:**16
  O. richmondia **3:**16
  O. rothschildi **3:**16
Ornithorhynchus anatinus **7:**82
oryx, Arabian 7:28
Oryx
  O. dammah **7:**30
  O. leucoryx **7:**28
oryx
  scimitar-horned 7:30
  white **7:**28
Osmoderma eremita **2:**80
Other (O), category, definition **1:**16
Otis tarda **3:**10
otter
  European *1:*50; **7:**32
  giant 7:34
  sea *1:*24; **7:**36
  various **7:**35
otter shrew, various **9:**64
Otus
  O. hartlaubi **7:**42
  O. ireneae **7:**42
ou **2:**6
overfishing **1:**71; **3:**55, 56; **7:**46, 63; **8:**63, 65, 79; **9:**37, 93; **10:**41, 43
owl
  Blakiston's eagle 7:38
  Blakiston's fish **7:**38
  Madagascar grass **7:**40
  Madagascar red 7:40
  Rodrigues little *1:*37
  rufous fishing- **7:**42
  São Tomé scops- **7:**42
  Sokoke scops- **7:**42
  spotted *1:*85; **7:**42
  various **7:**40
owlet, long-whiskered **7:**42
ox
  Cambodian forest **6:**14
  Vu Quang 7:44
Oxygastra curtisii **4:**70
Oxyura leucocephala **4:**44
ozone layer depletion **1:**53–54, 79; **8:**51

P

Pacific islands **2:**6; **5:**76, 88; **8:**78
Pacific Ocean **3:**50; **4:**47; **8:**62, 78, 80; **9:**8, 86; **10:**40, 43, 44, 82
paddlefish *1:*88; **7:**46
  Chinese **7:**46
paiche **7:**76
Pakistan **2:**94
palila **2:**6
Pan
  P. paniscus **3:**44
  P. troglodytes **3:**42
Panama **8:**10
panda
  giant *1:*9; **7:**48
  lesser 7:50
  red **7:**50
Pandaka pygmaea **5:**34
Pangasianodon gigas **3:**32
pangolin
  long-tailed 7:52
  various **7:**52
panther
  eastern **7:**54
  Florida 7:54
Panthera
  P. leo **9:**69
  P. l. persica **6:**34
  P. onca **5:**86
  P. pardus **6:**28
  P. tigris **9:**68
Pantholops hodgsoni **2:**26
Papilio
  P. jordani **3:**12
  P. leucotaenia **3:**12
Papua New Guinea **2:**16, 28, 84; **3:**8, 16; **7:**72; **8:**20; **10:**4
Paracentrotus lividus **8:**66
Paradisaea rudolphi **2:**84
paradisefish, ornate 7:56
parakeet
  Antipodes **5:**92
  Carolina *1:*37
  Guadeloupe *1:*37
Parapinnixa affinis **3:**72
parasites **3:**13; **4:**75, 94; **10:**33, 38, 72
Pardosa diuturna **9:**24
Parnassius
  P. apollo **3:**12
  P. autocrator **3:**12
parrot
  broad-billed *1:*31
  ground **5:**51
  night 7:58
  owl **5:**50
  St. Vincent **2:**14
  various **7:**58
  see also lovebird
parrotfinch, greenfaced **4:**74
Partula spp. **9:**8
Pavo muticus **7:**60
peacock, Congo **7:**60
peafowl
  Congo 7:60
  green **7:**60
pearl trade **7:**6
pearlshell
  Alabama **7:**6
  Louisiana **7:**6
peat extraction **10:**37
pedomorphism **2:**40; **8:**46
pelican
  Dalmatian **7:**62
  spot-billed **7:**62
Pelicanus
  P. crispus **7:**62
  P. philippensis **7:**62
Penelope spp. **5:**44
Penelopides
  P. mindorensis **5:**56
  P. panini **5:**56
penguin
  Galápagos 7:64
  various **7:**64
Pentalagus furnessi **8:**12
Perameles
  P. bourgainville **2:**48
  P. gunnii **2:**48
perch, oxleyan pygmy **3:**56
perfume **4:**12
perfume trade **10:**56
Peripatus spp. **10:**84
persecution **1:**40, 47; **2:**10, 42, 68, 72, 90; **3:**42; **4:**6, 16, 24, 40, 66; **5:**24, 28, 66, 93; **6:**4, 6, 24, 28, 33, 52, 54, 56, 74, 82; **7:**20, 38, 54, 75; **8:**7, 14, 25, 28, 77, 82; **9:**12, 34, 62, 66; **10:**31, 34, 48, 59, 64, 67, 70, 72, 74, 77
Peru **2:**74; **3:**46; **4:**82; **7:**76; **9:**20
pesticides **1:**50, 51–52; **2:**60; **3:**10, 19, 93; **4:**55; **5:**94; **6:**4, 6, 63; **8:**23, 65; **9:**24; **10:**49
pet trade **2:**22; **3:**42; **5:**15, 28, 38, 41; **6:**24, 26, 38, 70, 87; **7:**26, 53; **9:**14, 52, 60, 82, 84, 88, 91; **10:**12, 14, 16, 21, 24, 31
  see also aquarium trade; cage-bird trade
Petaurus gracilis **5:**32
petrel
  Bermuda *1:*55; **7:**66
  various **7:**66
Petrogale persephone **8:**36
Pezophaps solitaria **4:**20
Pezoporus wallicus **5:**51
Phalacrocorax spp. **3:**64
  P. harrisi **3:**64
Phalanger spp. **3:**86
  P. atrimaculatus **3:**86
  P. maculatus rufoniger **3:**86
Pharomachrus mocinno **8:**10
Phascolarctos cinereus **6:**10
pheasant **9:**94
Phelsuma spp. **5:**22
  P. guentheri **5:**22
Philemon fuscicapillus **5:**54
Philepitta schlegeli **2:**32
Philesturnus carunculatus **5:**60
Philippines **1:**23; **4:**36, 54; **5:**34, 56; **6:**24; **7:**68
Phoca
  P. caspica **8:**70, 72
  P. sibirica **8:**70
Phocarctos hookeri **8:**62
Phocoena
  P. phocoena **7:**86
  P. sinus **7:**86; **10:**56
  P. spinipinnis **7:**86
Phodilus prigoginei **7:**40
Phoeniconparrus
  P. andinus **4:**80
  P. jamesi **4:**81
Phoenicopterus
  P. chilensis **4:**81
  P. minor **4:**81
Phoxinus
  P. cumberlandensis **3:**90
  P. tennesseensis **3:**90
Phrynops
  P. dahli **10:**22
  P. hogei **10:**22
Phrynosoma m'callii **6:**38
phylum **1:**58–59
Physeter macrocephalus **10:**56
Picathartes
  P. gymnocephalus **8:**38
  P. oreas **8:**38
picathartes, white-necked **8:**38
Picoides
  P. borealis **10:**80
  P. ramsayi **10:**80
pig
  Javan warty **2:**45
  Visyan warty 7:68
  see also babirusa; hog
pigeon
  blue *1:*31
  chestnut-tailed **7:**70
  Mauritius pink **7:**70
  passenger *1:*22, 37
  pink 7:70
  southern crowned **7:**72
  various **7:**71
  Victoria crowned 7:72
  western crowned **7:**72
pika
  Helan Shan **7:**74
  Koslov's **7:**74
  steppe 7:74
Pinguinus impennis **2:**38
pintail, Eaton's **9:**62
Pipile spp. **5:**44
Pipra vilasboasi **6:**66
Piprites pileatus **6:**66
pirarucu **7:**76
Pithecophaga jefferyi **4:**54
pitta
  black-breasted **7:**78
  Gurney's 7:78
  various **7:**78
Pitta spp. **7:**78
  P. gurneyi **7:**78
plants, nonnative invasions **9:**40, 42
Platalea minor **9:**26

SET INDEX

Platanista
  P. gangetica **4:**26, 28
  P. minor **4:**26, 28
platy
  Cuatro Ciénegas **7:**80
  Monterrey **7:**80
  Muzquiz **7:**80
  northern **7:**80
  red **5:**36
platypus 7:82
Plethodon spp. **8:**48
  P. serratus **8:**48
plover
  piping 7:84
  various **7:**84
Podarcis
  P. lilfordi **6:**40
  P. milensis **6:**40
  P. pityusensis **6:**40
Podiceps spp. **5:**42
Podilymbus gigas **5:**42
Podogymnura
  P. aureospinula **5:**48
  P. truei **5:**48
Podomys floridanus **6:**92
poisoning **4:**57, 92; **5:**93; **6:**63, 86; **7:**93; **8:**25, 65, 75; **9:**45; **10:**34
Poliocephalus rufopectus **5:**42
pollution **1:**40, 42, 50–53; **2:**10, 22, 40, 52, 77, 91; **3:**13, 35, 38, 49, 65, 76, 89, 95; **4:**5, 15, 19, 27, 29, 44, 70, 80; **5:**11, 15, 35, 43, 79; **6:**68, 78; **7:**24, 32, 35, 36, 46, 55, 63, 66, 77, 81, 82, 84; **8:**23, 41, 53, 55, 59, 62, 65, 69, 70, 75, 85, 91; **9:**14, 27, 34, 37, 38, 41, 45, 65, 75; **10:**12, 15, 21, 25, 41, 43, 45, 49, 52, 59
  see also light pollution; noise pollution; oil spills; pesticides
Polyodon spathula **7:**46
Pongo pygmaeus **7:**26
Poospiza garleppi **4:**76
population modeling **1:**8
populations **1:**20–22
porbeagle **8:**86
Porphyrio mantelli **9:**48
porpoise
  Burmeister's **7:**86
  Gulf of California **7:**86
  harbor 7:86
  vaquita **10:**56
Portugal **6:**52
possum, Leadbeater's 7:88
Potamogale velox **8:**90
potoroo
  Gilbert's **7:**90
  long-footed 7:90
Potorous
  P. gilbertii **7:**90
  P. longipes **7:**90
poverty **1:**89, 95; **3:**7, 37, 45; **8:**29, 34
power cables **4:**57; **7:**63; **10:**34

prairie dog
  black-tailed 7:92
  various **7:**92
pratincole, black-winged **3:**68
Presbytis comata **6:**86
pressure groups **1:**13
Prioailurus planiceps **3:**30
Priodontes maximus **2:**30
Prionailurus iriomotensis **3:**30
Probarbus spp. **5:**82
  P. jullieni **5:**82
Procnias
  P. nudicollis **2:**82
  P. tricarunculata **2:**82
Propithecus
  P. diadema **5:**84; **8:**93
  P. tattersalli **8:**92
  P. verreauxi **5:**84; **8:**93
Prosobonia cancellata **8:**54
Proteus anguinus **7:**24
Psammobates geometricus **9:**88
Psephotus chrysopterygius **7:**58
Psephurus gladius **7:**46
Pseudemydura umbrina **10:**22
Pseudemys
  P. alabamensis **10:**12
  P. gorzugi **10:**12
  P. rubriventris **10:**12
Pseudibis
  P. davisoni **5:**72
  P. gigantea **5:**72
Pseudocotalpa giulianii **2:**80
Pseudophryne spp. **9:**78
  P. corroboree **9:**78
Pseudoryx nghetinhensis **7:**44
Psittirostra psittacez **2:**6
Pterodroma spp. **7:**66
  P. cahow **7:**66
Pteronura brasiliensis **7:**34
Pteropus
  P. dasymallus **4:**86
  P. rodricensis **4:**84
puffleg
  black-breasted **9:**20
  colorful **4:**78
Puma concolor
  P. c. coryi **7:**54
  P. c. cougar **7:**54
pupfish
  Devil's Hole **7:**94
  various **7:**94
Pygathrix nemaeus **6:**86
pygmy-possum
  long-tailed **8:**4
  mountain 8:4
Pygopididae **1:**74
python
  Ramsay's **8:**6
  woma **8:**6

Q

quagga **1:***37*; **8:**8
  Bonte **8:**8
quarrying **1:**40; **2:**58; **3:**69; **6:**42; **10:**30
quetzal, resplendent 8:10

R

"r" reproductive strategy **1:**25
rabbit
  Amami 8:12
  Assam **5:**50
  Ryukyu **8:**12
  volcano *8:*13, 14
racer
  Antiguan 8:16
  various **8:**16
racerunner **10:**60
rail **1:***31*
  Guam 8:18
  invisible **9:**48
  Owston's **8:**18
  various **3:**66; **8:**18
rainbowfish
  Lake Wanam **8:**20
  various **8:**20
Rallus antarcticus **3:**66
Rana spp. **5:**10
  R. aurora **5:**10
Ranthanbore National Park **1:***92*
Raphus cucullatus **4:**20
Rare Animal Relief Effort (RARE) **2:**15
rasbora
  fire **8:**22
  golden **8:**22
  pearly **8:**22
  vateria flower 8:22
Rasbora vaterifloris **8:**22
rat
  Alexandrine **8:**24
  Asian black **1:**55
  black 8:24
  climbing **8:**24
  gray **8:**24
  roof **8:**24
  ship **8:**24
  various **6:**92
  see also mole-rat
rat kangaroo **7:**90
Rattus rattus **8:**24
razorback **10:**42
Red Data Book (IUCN) **1:**10–11, 14
reintroduction **1:**22, 56, 87, 92; **2:**69, 76, 79; **3:**33, 56, 60, 76, 83; **4:**15, 31, 53, 72, 92; **5:**58; **6:**5, 26, 61; **7:**11; **8:**19, 53; **9:**9, 38, 41, 49, 52, 87, 91; **10:**7, 23, 68, 73
relocation *see* translocation
reproductive strategies **1:**25–26
reptiles
  diversity **1:**72
  history **1:**73
  risks **1:**73–75
  see also List of Animals by Group, page 100
research *see* conservation research; medical research; scientific research
reserves **1:**33, 92; **2:**37, 43, 55, 59; **3:**69; **4:**16, 39; **5:**57; **6:**19, 26, 42, 47, 89; **7:**11,

41, 55, 73, 81, 89; **8:**41; **9:**7, 9, 53, 67, 85, 88, 89, 91; **10:**22, 25, 33, 37, 95
  see also national parks; wildlife refuges
reservoir building **2:**31; **7:**43; **9:**41; **10:**34
restricted distribution **1:**8
Rheobatrachus silus **4:**94
Rhincodon typus **8:**86
Rhinoceros
  R. sondaicus **8:**30
  R. unicornis **8:**28
rhinoceros
  black 8:26
  great Indian 8:28
  Javan 8:30
  Sumatran 8:32
  white 8:34
Rhinolophus ferrumequinum **2:**60
Rhinopithecus brelichi **6:**86
Rhinopoma macinnesi **2:**64
Rhinoptilus bitorquatus **3:**68
Rhodonessa caryophyllacea **4:**44
Rhynchocyon
  R. chrysopygus **4:**68
  R. petersi **4:**68
Rhynochetos jubatus **5:**88
Rissa breviostris **5:**46
ritual objects **2:**85; **3:**29; **5:**5
road building **2:**55; **3:**19; **4:**52, 67; **7:**54, 73, 90; **8:**5; **9:**84, 88; **10:**85
road kills **2:**77; **3:**29, 31; **4:**22, 92; **5:**80; **6:**10, 38, 52, 75; **7:**55; **8:**7, 36; **9:**10, 82; **10:**31
roatelo, white-breasted **6:**76
Robinson Crusoe Island **4:**78
rock-wallaby, prosperine 8:36
rockfowl
  bare-headed **8:**38
  gray-necked **8:**38
  white-necked 8:38
rocky, eastern province 8:40
Rodrigues (Rodriguez) Island **7:**8
Romania **6:**82
Romerolagus diazi **8:***13, 14*
rorqual
  common **10:**42
  great northern **10:**40
Rosalia alpina **6:**44
Round Island **5:**22
Royal Society for the Protection of Birds (RSPB) **1:**13, 88
Russia **2:**70; **4:**32; **5:**94; **6:**78; **7:**32, 36, 38, 74; **8:**42, 54, 64; **10:**74
Rwanda **5:**38

S

saddleback **5:**60
Saguinus leucopus **6:**88
Sahara **2:**4
Sahel **5:**20

saiga **8:**42
Saiga tatarica **8:**42
St. Lucia **10:**60
salamander
  California tiger 8:44
  Chinese giant **8:**46
  flatwood **8:**44
  Japanese giant 8:46
  Lake Lerma **8:**44
  Ouachita red-backed **8:**48
  Santa-Cruz long-toed **8:**51
  southern red-backed **8:**48
  various **8:**48
  see also axolotl
Salmo spp. **8:**52
salmon
  Adriatic **8:**52
  Danube 8:52
  European **8:**52
  Satsukimasa **8:**52
  various **1:**68
Salmothymus obtusirostris **8:**52
samaruc **9:**80
Samoa **10:**82
Sandelia bainsii **8:**40
sandpiper
  spoon-billed **8:**54
  Tuamotu **8:**54
Sanzinia madagascariensis **3:**6
sao la **7:**44
Sapheopipo noguchii **10:**78
Sapo Dorado **9:**70
saratoga
  southern **7:**77
  spotted **4:**36
Sarcogyps calvus **10:**34
sardina ciega **3:**38
Scandinavia **3:**12; **8:**72
scientific research **2:**46; **4:**62; **10:**50
Sciurus vulgaris **9:**28
Scleropages
  S. formosus **4:**36
  S. leichardi **7:**77
  S. leichardti **4:**36
Scomberemorus concolor **10:**8
scops-owl **7:**42
Scotopelia ussheri **7:**42
scrub-bird
  noisy 8:56
  rufous **8:**56
  scrubfowl, various **6:**64
sea anemone
  Ivell's **8:**58
  starlet **8:**58
sea cow 4:46
  Steller's **3:**70
sea fan, broad 8:60
sea lion
  Hooker's **8:**62
  northern **8:**62
  Steller's **8:**62
sea-eagle
  Pallas's **8:**64
  Steller's **8:**64
sea-urchin **1:**24
  edible **8:**66
seahorse **1:***69*
  Cape **8:**68

Knysna 8:68
seal
  Baikal 8:70
  Baltic gray 8:70
  Caribbean monk 1:37; 8:74, 76
  Caspian 8:70, 72
  fur, various 8:62
  Galápagos fur 8:78
  gray 8:72
  Guadaloupe fur 8:78
  Hawaiian monk 8:74
  Juan Fernandez fur 8:78
  Mediterranean monk 1:43; 8:76
  northern fur 8:78
seminatural habitats 1:38
Semnornis ramphastinus 2:54
Sephanoides fernandensis 4:78
Sepilok Rehabilitation Center 1:95
Sericulus bakeri 3:8
Seychelles 6:62
shama, black 6:62
shark
  basking 8:80
  great white 8:82
  silver 8:84
  various 8:86
  whale 8:86
shatoosh trade 2:26
sheep, barbary 8:88
shrew
  giant African water 8:90
  giant otter 8:90
  Nimba otter 8:90
  pygmy otter 8:90
Siberia 4:12; 8:54, 70; 9:62, 68; 10:74
sicklebill, black 2:84
Sierra Club 1:13
Sierra Leone 4:48; 8:38
sifaka
  Diadem 5:84; 8:93
  golden-crowned 8:92
  Verreaux's 5:84; 8:93
Simias concolor 6:86
sirenians 3:70; 4:46; 6:68
siskin
  red 8:94
  saffron 8:94
  yellow-faced 8:94
Sites of Special Scientific Interest 6:42
Sitta spp. 7:16
  S. ledanti 7:16
Skiffia francesae 5:36
skin trade 2:11, 36; 3:7, 70, 80; 4:46; 7:53; 8:9, 62, 74, 81, 88; 9:56; 10:58, 94
skink
  pygmy blue-tongued 9:4
  Réunion 1:37
  western 1:74
slash-and-burn agriculture 6:76
sloth
  Hoffmann's two-toed 9:6
  Linné's two-toed 9:6
  maned 9:6

slow reproduction 1:8, 25
Sminthopsis spp. 4:50
  S. aitkeni 4:50
snail, *Partula* 9:8
snake
  Cuban tree boa 3:4
  Cyclades blunt-nosed viper 10:30
  Dumeril's boa 3:6
  eastern indigo 9:10
  emerald tree boa 1:74
  Jamaican boa 3:4
  leopard 9:12
  Madagascar boa 3:6
  Madagascar tree boa 3:6
  Milos viper 10:30
  Mona Island boa 3:4
  Puerto Rican boa 3:4
  racer, Antiguan 8:16
  Ramsay's python 8:6
  San Francisco garter 9:14
  sharp-snouted 1:74
  two-striped garter 9:14
  Virgin Islands boa 3:4
  woma python 8:6
solenodon
  Cuban 9:16
  Haitian 9:16
Solenodon
  S. cubanus 9:16
  S. paradoxus 9:16
solitaire
  Réunion 1:37
  Rodrigues (Rodriguez) 4:20
Solomys poncelleti 6:92
Somalia 2:34
Somatochlora
  S. calverti 4:70
  S. hineana 4:70
Sosippus placidus 9:24
souslik
  European 9:18
  European spotted 9:18
South Africa 3:40; 8:8, 40, 68; 9:89; 10:34, 94
South America 2:24, 30, 54, 74, 92; 3:46, 62, 80, 84; 4:18, 24, 26, 53, 78, 82; 5:86; 6:58, 66, 88; 7:35, 76; 8:94; 9:6, 20, 52, 54; 10:28, 70
Southern Ocean 2:8; 10:40, 43
souvenir trade 2:46; 3:6, 50, 75, 80; 4:67; 5:38, 41; 8:60, 66, 69, 82; 10:18
Spain 1:42–43; 4:56; 6:52; 9:80
Spalax spp. 6:82
  S. graecus 6:82
sparrow
  house 1:64
  Zapata 4:76
spatuletail, marvelous 9:20
specialization 1:28–30
speciation 1:26–28
species
  definition 1:26
  taxonomic groupings 1:58–59

Species Survival Commission (SSC) 1:10
specimen collectors 2:38; 5:60, 72
Speoplatyrhinus poulsoni 3:34
Speothos venaticus 4:24, 93
Spermophilus spp. 9:18
  S. citellus 9:18
Spheniscus
  S. demersus 7:64
  S. humboldti 7:64
  S. mendiculus 7:64
Sphenodon
  S. guntheri 10:6
  S. punctatus 10:6
spider
  great raft 9:22
  Kauai cave wolf 9:24
  red-kneed tarantula 9:60
  wolf, various 9:24
Spilocuscus rufoniger 3:86
Spizocorys fringillaris 6:18
spoonbill
  black-faced 9:26
  lesser 9:26
sport, exploitation of animals for 1:47–48
sports fishing 10:8
squirrel
  Arctic ground 1:24
  Eurasian red 9:28
  European red 9:28
  see also ground squirrel
Sri Lanka 2:52, 72; 3:94; 4:62, 67; 6:46; 7:56; 8:22
starling
  Bali 9:30
  various 9:30
steamerduck, Chubut 4:42
Stenella
  S. attenuata 10:48
  S. coeruleoalba 10:48
Stenodus leucichthys leucichthys 8:52
stilt, black 9:32
stitchbird 5:54
stork
  greater adjutant 9:34
  various 9:34
Strigops habroptilus 5:50
Strix occidentalis 7:42
Strymon avalona 3:14
sturgeon
  Baltic 9:36
  common 9:36
  ship 9:36
Sturnella defilippii 2:92
Sturnus spp. 9:30
sub-Antarctic islands 2:8
sucker
  harelip 9:38
  razorback 9:38
sulphur-bottom 10:40
Sumatra 4:16; 6:30; 7:26
sunangel
  Bogotá 4:78
  various 9:20
sunbeam, purple-backed 4:78

sunfish
  blue-barred pygmy 9:40
  Carolina pygmy 9:40
  oceanic 1:68
  spring pygmy 9:40
  superstition 1:47; 3:86
see also ritual objects; traditional medicine
Sus
  S. cebifrons 7:68
  S. salvanius 2:45
  S. verrucosus 2:45
swallow
  blue 9:42
  white-tailed 9:42
swan, trumpeter 9:44
Synthliboramphus spp. 7:4
  S. wumizusume 7:4
Sypheotides indica 3:10

T
Tachybaptus spp. 5:42
Tachyeres leucocephalus 4:42
Tachyglossus aculeatus multiaculeatus 4:60
Tachyoryctes spp. 6:84
  T. macrocephalus 6:84
Tachypleus
  T. gigas 3:74
  T. tridentatus 3:74
tagging see tracking and tagging
Tahr
  Arabian 9:46
  Himalayan 9:46
  Nilgiri 9:46
  Taiwan 6:30
takahe 9:48
Takin 9:50
tamaraw 2:20
tamarin
  golden lion 9:52
  golden-rumped 6:88
  various 9:52
  white-footed 6:88
Tanagara spp. 9:54
  T. fastuosa 9:54
tanager
  multicolored 4:76
  seven-colored 9:54
  various 9:54
Taphozous troughtoni 2:64
tapir
  Central American 9:56
  Malayan 9:58
  mountain 9:56, 58
Tapirus
  T. bairdii 9:56
  T. pinchaque 9:56, 58
tarantula, red-kneed 9:60
tarictic
  Mindoro 5:56
  Visayan 5:56
tarpan 1:37
Tasmania 5:16; 9:66
Taudactylus
  T. acutirostris 5:12
  T. rheophilus 5:12

Tauraco spp. 10:11
  T. bannermani 10:10
  T. fischeri 10:11
  T. ruspolii 10:11
taxonomic classification 1:26, 58
teal
  Baikal 9:62
  various 9:62
tenrec
  aquatic 9:64
  long-tailed 9:64
  web-footed 9:64
teporingo 8:14
Testudo spp. 9:84
  T. kleinmanni 9:84
tetra, Mexican 3:38
Tetrax tetrax 3:10
Texas 7:20; 10:32
Thailand 2:50, 64; 4:36; 5:82; 6:30; 7:78; 8:32, 84
Thamnophis
  T. gigas 9:14
  T. hammondi 9:14
  T. sirtalis tetrataenia 9:14
Theropithecus gelada 2:46
threat
  IUCN, categories of 1:14–17
threats, general 1: 38–57
Thryothorus nicefori 10:86
thryssa, New Guinea 2:16
Thryssa scratchleyi 2:16
Thunnus spp. 10:8
  T. thynnus 10:8
thylacine 1:36; 9:66
Thylacinus cynocephalus 9:66
Tibet 2:26; 9:50; 10:90
tiger 1:9, 95; 9:68
  Bali 1:36
  Tasmanian 9:66
Tiliqua adelaidensis 9:4
timber treatment chemicals 2:61, 62
toad
  boreal 9:76
  cane 1:54
  golden 9:70
  Mallorcan midwife 1:77; 9:72
  natterjack 9:74
  running 9:74
  Surinam 1:77
  various 9:70, 74, 76
  western 9:76
toadlet
  corroboree 9:78
  various 9:78
tokoeka 6:9
Tolypeutes tricinctus 2:30
toothcarp
  Corfu 9:80
  valencia 9:80
torgos tracheliotus 10:34
Torreornis inexpectata 4:76
tortoise
  Abingdon Island 1:37
  bolson 9:82
  Charles Island 1:37
  desert 9:82

domed *1:31*
Egyptian 9:84
Galápagos giant 9:86
geometric 9:88
gopher **9:**82
Mauritian giant *1:37*
plowshare 9:90
radiated **9:**90
various **9:**84, 86, 89
tortoiseshell trade **10:**18
totoaba 9:92
Totoaba macdonaldi **9:**92
tourism *1:42–43;* **2:***4;* **3:***41, 52, 65;* **5:***38, 88;* **6:***41;* **7:***65;* **8:***5, 14, 69, 76;* **9:***12, 46, 56, 81, 84;* **10:***18, 25, 31*
see also ecotourism
toxins, bioaccumulation **1:**50, 51
Toxotes oligolepis **2:**28
tracking and tagging *1:14–15, 85*
traditional land management **1:**38
traditional medicine **1:**46; **10:**34
Tragelaphus
 T. buxtoni **7:**18
 T. strepsiceros **6:**16
tragopan
 Temminck's 9:94
 various **9:**94
Tragopan spp. **9:**94
 T. temminckii **9:**94
translocation **5:**17; **10:**60
tree-kangaroo
 Goodfellow's 10:4
 various **10:**4
Tremarctos ornatus **2:**74
Trichechus spp. **3:**70; **4:**47; **6:**69
 T. manatus latirostris **6:**68
Tridacna gigas **3:**50
Tringa guttifer **8:**54
triok, Tate's **5:**32; **7:**88
Triturus
 T. cristatus **7:**12
 T. dobrogicus **7:**12
trogon, resplendent **8:**10
trout
 Danube **8:**52
 European river **8:**52
 Ohrid **8:**52
 rainbow *1:71*
tuatara 10:6
 Cook Strait **10:**6
Tubulanus superbus 7.9
tuna
 Atlantic bluefin **10:**8
 northern bluefin 10:8
 various **10:**8
Tunisia **7:**30
turaco
 Bannerman's 10:10
 Fischer's **10:**11
 Prince Ruspoli's 10:11
 various **10:**11
turtle *1:43*
 Alabama red-bellied 10:12
 American red-bellied **10:**12

bog 10:14
box, various **10:**16
Chinese three-striped box 10:16
Fly River **10:**20
green *1:72*
hawksbill 10:18
map, various **10:**24
New Guinea softshell **10:**20
pig-nosed 10:20
various **10:**14, 10:22
western swamp 10:22
yellow-blotched sawback map 10:24
Tympanocryptis lineata pnguicolla **4:**38
Typhlichthys subterraneus **3:**34
Tyto
 T. inexspectata **7:**40
 T. nigrobrunnea **7:**40
 T. soumagnei **7:**40

U
Uganda **5:**38
ultraviolet (UV) radiation damage **8:**51; **9:**76
umbrellabird, bare-necked **2:**82
Uncia uncia **6:**32
United States **2:**10, 58, 68, 70, 86; **3:**14, 15, 18, 34, 60, 72, 74, 76, 80, 90, 84; **4:**4, 42, 72, 93; **5:**10, 28; **6:**36, 38, 68; **7:**20, 36, 42, 46, 54, 84, 92, 94; **8:**45, 48, 51, 58; **9:**10, 14, 38, 40, 44, 60, 76, 82; **10:**12, 14, 24, 32, 38, 72, 74, 80
United States Fish and Wildlife Service **3:**81
urban development **3:**16, 19, 21, 31; **4:**38; **5:**11, 49; **6:**31, 42, 72, 86; **7:**35, 43; **8:**45, 59, 65, 76; **9:**14, 84, 88; **10:**12, 22, 24, 31, 33, 62
Ursus
 U. arctos **2:**68
 U. a. nelsoni **2:**68
 U. maritimus **2:**70
 U. thibetanus **2:**68, 74
UV radiation see ultraviolet radiation

V
Valencia
 V. hispanica **9:**80
 V. letourneuxi **9:**80
vanga
 helmet **10:**26
 various **10:**27
Varanus komodoensis **6:**12
Varecia variegata **6:**26
Venezuela **2:**74; **8:**94
Vicugna vicugna **2:**28
vicuña 10:28
Vietnam **2:**50; **4:**36; **5:**26, 82; **6:**14, 30, 86; **7:**44; **8:**30, 32; **9:**94; **10:**16

viper
 Cyclades blunt-nosed **10:**30
 Milos 10:30
 various **10:**30
 Vipera spp. **10:**30
vireo
 black-capped 10:32
 Chocó **10:**32
 St. Andrew **10:**32
 San Andrès **10:**32
 Vireo
  V. atricapillus **10:**32
  V. caribaeus **10:**32
  V. masteri **10:**32
Viverridae **4:**90
Vulnerable, definition **1:**15–16
Vulpes velox **4:**92
Vultur gryphus **3:**60
vulture
 Cape **10:**34
 Cape griffon 10:34
 various **10:**34

W
wallaby
 prosperine rock 8:36
 Toolache *1:36*
walpurti **7:**14
war *1:47;* **4:***48, 55, 67;* **5:***38, 41, 42, 52;* **6:***16, 86;* **7:***22, 44;* **8:***31, 34*
warbler
 aquatic **10:**36
 Kirtland's 10:38
 Manchurian reed **10:**36
 streaked reed **10:**36
 various **10:**38
Washington Convention see Convention on International Trade in Endangered Species of Wild Fauna and Flora
water balance **1:**40
water buffalo, Indian **2:**20
water extraction **8:**53; **10:**21, 22
water shortages **2:**34, 36; **8:**34; **10:**92
waxbill, Anambra **4:**74
weasel
 black-striped **4:**72
 Colombian **4:**72
 Indonesian mountain **4:**72
weaverbirds **4:**88
West Indies **2:**14
wetland drainage **1:**40, 74; **2:**11, 40, 90; **3:**11, 22, 63, 92; **4:**26, 44, 70; **5:**5, 35; **6:**21, 91; **7:**63; **8:**30, 53, 55, 59; **9:**14, 22, 27, 33, 34, 63; **10:**14, 22, 25, 37, 86
whale
 blue **10:**40
 California gray **10:**44
 coalfish **10:**54
 fin **10:**42
 gray *1:62, 90;* **10:**44
 herring **10:**42
 humpback **10:**46

killer **10:**48
 minke 1:*44;* **10:**50
 northern right 1:*25;* **10:**52
 pollack **10:**54
 right *1:25*
 Rudolphi's **10:**54
 sardine **10:**54
 scrag **10:**44
 sei 10:54
 short-finned pilot **10:**48
 southern right **10:**52
 sperm 10:56
 spermaceti **10:**56
 white 10:58
 whaling **1:**45
whiptail
 Colorado checkered *1:74*
 orange-throated **10:**61
 St. Lucia, *1:86,* **10:**60
white eye, Lord Howe Island *1:36*
wildcat 10:62
wildlife refuge **3:**76; **10:**33, 73
wildlife surveys **1:**84
Williamsonia lintneri **4:**70
Windward Islands **10:**60
wolf **1:**47
 Antarctic **10:**66
 Ethiopian 10:64
 Falkland Island *1:37;* **10:**66
 gray 10:68
 maned **10:**70
 marsupial **9:**66
 red 1:*93;* **10:**72
 Simien **10:**64
 Tasmanian **9:**66
 timber **10:**68
wolverine 10:74
wombat
 northern hairy-nosed 10:77
 Queensland hairy-nosed **10:**76
 soft-furred **10:**76
woodpecker
 Arabian **10:**80
 imperial **10:**78
 ivory-billed 10:78
 Okinawa **10:**78
 red-cockaded 10:80
 Sulu **10:**80
woodstar
 Chilean **4:**78
 little **4:**78
wool trade **2:**26
World Bank **1:**89
World Conservation Union see International Union for the Conservation of Nature
World Parrot Trust **2:**15
World Wide Fund for Nature (WWF) **1:**13
World Wildlife Fund see World Wide Fund for Nature
worm
 Palolo **10:**82
 ribbon **7:**8
 velvet **10:**84
 see also earthworm

wren
 Apolinar's **10:**86
 Fermina **10:**86
 Niceforo's **10:**86
 Stephen Island *1:37*
 Zapata 10:86

X
Xanthomyza phrygia **5:**54
Xanthopsar flavus **2:**92
Xenoglaux loweryi **7:**42
Xenoophorus captivus **5:**36
Xenopirostris damii **10:**27
xenopoecilus 10:88
Xenopoecilus spp. **10:**88
 X. saranisorum **10:**88
Xiphophorus spp.
 X. couchianus **7:**80
 X. gordoni **7:**80
 X. meyeri **7:**80
Xyrauchen texanus **9:**38

Y
yak, wild 10:90
yamane **4:**34
yamion **10:**76
Yellowstone National Park *1:10*
Yugoslavia **7:**24

Z
zacatuche **8:**14
Zaglossus bruijni **4:**60
Zaire see Democratic Republic of Congo
Zambia **6:**48
zebra
 Burchell's **8:**8
 Cape mountain **10:**94
 Grevy's 10:92
 Hartmann's **10:**94
 mountain 10:94
zebu cattle *1:38*
Zimbabwe **4:**22
zoogeographic regions **1:**19, 20
zoos *1:86;* **5:***41;* **8:***38*
 see also captive breeding

Acknowledgments

The authors and publishers would like to thank the following people and organizations:
Aquamarines International Pvt. Ltd., Sri Lanka, especially Ananda Pathirana; Aquarist & Pond keeper Magazine, U.K.; BirdLife International (the global partnership of conservation organizations working together in over 100 countries to save birds and their habitats). Special thanks to David Capper; also to Guy Dutson and Alison Stattersfield; Sylvia Clarke (Threatened Wildlife, South Australia); Mark Cocker (writer and birder); David Curran (aquarist specializing in spiny eels, U.K.); Marydele Donnelly (IUCN sea turtle specialist); Svein Fossa (aquatic consultant, Norway); Richard Gibson (Jersey Wildlife Preservation Trust, Channel Islands); Paul Hoskisson (Liverpool John Moores University); Derek Lambert; Pat Lambert (aquarists specializing in freshwater livebearers); Lumbini Aquaria Wayamba Ltd., Sri Lanka, especially Jayantha Ramasinghe and Vibhu Perera; Isolda McGeorge (Chester Zoological Gardens); Dr. James Peron Ross (IUCN crocodile specialist); Zoological Society of London, especially Michael Palmer, Ann Sylph, and the other library staff.

Picture Credits

Abbreviations
AL   Ardea London
BBC   BBC Natural History Unit
BCC   Bruce Coleman Collection
FLPA   Frank Lane Photographic Agency
NHPA   Natural History Photographic Agency
OSF   Oxford Scientific Films
PEP   Planet Earth Pictures
b = bottom; **c** = center; **t** = top; **l** = left; **r** = right

Jacket
Ibiza wall lizard, illustration by Denys Ovenden from *Collins Field Guide: Reptiles and Amphibians of Britain and Europe*; Grevy's zebra, Stan Osolinski/Oxford Scientific Films; Florida panther, Lynn M. Stone/BBC Natural History Unit; silver shark, Max Gibbs/Photomax; blue whale, Tui de Roy/Oxford Scientific Films

5 Mark Hutchinson; **7** Kevin Schafer/NHPA; **8–9** David Fox/OSF; **10–11** Animals Animals/Zig Leszczynski/OSF; **12–13** Dave Houghton/OSF; **14–15** Frank Schneidermeyer/OSF; **18–19** Hans Dieter Brandl/FLPA; **20–21** C.H. Greenewalt/Vireo; **23** Roger Tidman/NHPA; **25l** William P. Mull; **25r** Hans Pfletschinger/Still Pictures; **27** Masahiro Iijima/AL; **28–29** Survival Anglia/Chris Knights/OSF; **31** C.M. Perrins/OSF; **32–33** Don Hadden/AL; **35** David Tipling/BBC; **37** Hans Reinhard/BCC; **41** Joe Tomelleri; **44–45** Stan Osolinski/OSF; **47** Krupaker Senani/OSF; **48–49** John Cancalosi/BBC; **50–51** Konrad Wothe/OSF; **53** Animals Animals/Shane Moore/OSF; **55** Haroldo Palo Jr./NHPA; **56–57** Animals Animals/Reed/Williams/OSF; **61** Rod Williams/BCC; **63** John Watkins/FLPA; **67** Dave Watts; **69** Anup Shah/BBC; **71** Mike Linley/OSF; **72–73** Chris Mattison/FLPA; **75** Attilio Calegari/OSF; **77** Animals Animals/Zig Leszczynski/OSF; **79** A.N.T./NHPA; **83** Survival Anglia/John Harris/OSF; **85** Animals Animals/Zig Leszczynski/OSF; **86–87** Mark Jones/OSF; **89** & **90–91** David Curl/OSF; **95** Robert Maier/BCC.

Artists

Graham Allen, Norman Arlott, Priscilla Barrett, Trevor Boyer, Ad Cameron, David Dennis, Karen Hiscock, Chloe Talbot Kelly, Mick Loates, Michael Long, Malcolm McGregor, Denys Ovenden, Oxford Illustrators, John Sibbick, Joseph Tomelleri, Dick Twinney, Ian Willis

While every effort has been made to trace the copyright holders of illustrations reproduced in this book, the publishers will be pleased to rectify any omissions or inaccuracies.